PAUL McCARTNEY

DISCLAIMER

All trademarks, illustrations, quotations, company names, registered names, products, characters, logos used or cited in this book are the property of their respective owners and are used in this book for identification purposes only. This book is a publication of Welbeck Non-Fiction Limited and has not been licensed, approved, sponsored, or endorsed by any person or entity and has no connection to Paul McCartney.

Published in 2021 by Welbeck

An Imprint of Welbeck Non-Fiction Limited, part of Welbeck Publishing Group 20 Mortimer Street London W1T 3JW

Text © 2021 Mike Evans

Design © 2021 Welbeck Non-fiction Limited

A CIP catalogue record for this book is available from the British Library

ISBN 978 1 78739 737 8

Printed in Dubai

10 9 8 7 6 5 4 3 2 1

PAUL McCARTNEY

THE STORIES BEHIND THE SONGS

MIKE EVANS

WELBECK

CONTENTS

INTRODUCTION

Paul McCartney's songwriting output as a member of The Beatles, mainly with his co-composer John Lennon, has been exhaustively documented over the years. But since those heady days of the 1960s McCartney has continued as a composer of a wealth of iconic pop songs, as a fearless cutting-edge innovator and, in latter years, as an international musical treasure. In the 50 years since the release of his first post-Beatles' album, *McCartney,* in 1970, to *McCartney III* in 2020, his songwriting has been as varied as his career, from the simplest of pop ditties to epic love ballads and challenging electronic pieces.

Examining in detail over 50 songs from the vast McCartney catalogue, as well as his key studio albums, writing *Paul McCartney: The Stories Behind the Songs* has often been an exercise in deciding what to leave out. Five volumes of classical music are clearly outside the remit of this particular book, as are the boldly instrumental projects under the Fireman name. Other exceptions include two singles featuring Kanye West, neither of which are McCartney compositions, and Paul's participation as part of the 1985 Band Aid release 'Do They Know It's Christmas?'

The final list of inclusions is inevitably subjective and some readers are bound to ask, "Well, what about…?" Such exclusions include 'Give Ireland Back to the Irish' and 'Mary Had a Little Lamb', both singles from 1972, and 'We All Stand Together' (with the Frog Chorus) from the 1984 Rupert Bear animated film *Rupert and the Frog Song.*

Conversely, I have included a few non-original compositions: 'Walking in the Park with Eloise' from 1974, written by Paul's dad Jim McCartney; 'No Other Baby', a UK skiffle record from 1957;

and the old gospel song 'Light from Your Lighthouse', (which is actually credited to McCartney on the recording). Along with his three albums of mainly non-original material – 1988's "Russian" rock 'n' roll release *Choba B CCCP,* the similar *Run Devil Run* collection from 1999, and the 2011 "standards" album *Kisses on the Bottom* – all of these songs reflect the essential influences that informed McCartney's musical taste during his teenage years.

Each featured album includes details of recording and release dates, studio names, full personnel listings, and a summary of every track. Individual songs, which include similar information, are explored in more detail, from their original inspiration and the circumstances of their recording to their final release.

Among invaluable sources (as listed in the Bibliography), special mention should be made of Barry Miles' biography, mainly covering the Beatle years, *Paul McCartney: Many Years From Now,* the essential *Conversations With McCartney* by Paul DuNoyer, and Luca Perasi's *Paul McCartney Recording Sessions (1969–2013),* an exhaustive mine of key data.

At the time of writing, Paul McCartney had released *McCartney III,* his 26th studio album featured in this book, the well-received successor to 1970's *McCartney* and 1980's *McCartney II.* Talking to Jonathan Dean for a major piece in the UK *Sunday Times,* his response to the notion that it might be the final part of a trilogy was characteristically optimistic: "Hang on, what if I do a fourth? I'm not planning on shutting the door just yet."

Mike Evans, April 2021

Above: Paul and Linda McCartney in concert with Wings during their UK tour, 1976.

Opposite: Linda and Paul posing for a portrait, c 1973.

MCCARTNEY

THE LOVELY LINDA
THAT WOULD BE SOMETHING
VALENTINE DAY
EVERY NIGHT
HOT AS SUN/GLASSES
JUNK
MAN WE WAS LONELY
OO YOU
MOMMA MISS AMERICA
TEDDY BOY
SINGALONG JUKE
MAYBE I'M AMAZED
KREEN-AKRORE

(All songs written by Paul McCartney)

Paul McCartney (vocals, guitars, bass guitar, drums, piano,
organ, percussion, Mellotron), Linda McCartney (vocals)

MCCARTNEY

RECORDED: DECEMBER 1, 1969–FEBRUARY 25, 1970 // STUDIOS: HOME STUDIO, LONDON; MORGAN STUDIOS, LONDON; ABBEY ROAD STUDIOS, LONDON // PRODUCER: PAUL MCCARTNEY // RELEASED: APRIL 17, 1970

In late 1969, when The Beatles were nearing the point of disbanding, Paul McCartney embarked on recording his first solo album. And its release in April 1970, immediately prior to the appearance of the band's final collection, *Let It Be* in May, led to more acrimony in a split that was by this time inevitable. The subsequent fall-out from the biggest group in the world breaking up over a variety of issues – mainly business-related, which led to personality clashes – overshadowed the release of *McCartney*, which in retrospect is an album of significance in its own right.

Paul laid down most of the basics for the album at his London home in Cavendish Avenue, St John's Wood, on a simple Studer four-track tape machine, without the technical sophistication afforded by a professional studio. And even though he added overdubs, mixes, and some fresh elements at both Morgan Studios and Abbey Road Studios, the overall feel of the album was certainly one of a DIY collection.

With McCartney playing all the instruments himself, the entire recording was a very deliberate attempt to get away from the sophistication associated with The Beatles' late-1960s albums, the latest of which was *Abbey Road,* released in September 1969. Maintaining secrecy about the project was essential, given the press furore that was already brewing regarding the future of the "Fab Four", and Linda would make the bookings at Morgan and Abbey Road for "Billy Martin". "We decided we didn't want to tell anyone what we were doing," Paul later told *Rolling Stone*. "That way it gets to be like home at the studio. No one knows about it and there is no one in the studio or dropping by." He also said at the time, "I found that I was enjoying working alone as much as I'd enjoyed the early days of The Beatles."

The album opens evocatively with 'The Lovely Linda,' a simple, 45-second love song to his wife, with a Latin-tinged acoustic guitar as sole backing. 'That Would Be Something', the first "full length" number is an atmospheric piece, worthy of perhaps a full band setting, and sung with a bluesy authority. 'Hot as Sun' is one of several instrumental tracks, said to be Polynesian-influenced, segueing into the experimental sound effect of tinkling wine glasses. Other instrumentals, including 'Valentine Day' and 'Momma Miss America' were, according to Paul, more or less improvised on the spot.

There's a nod to the kind of whimsical sing-along favoured on various Beatles tracks with 'Man We Was Lonely' and 'Teddy Boy', the latter having been first written while The Beatles were in India in 1968, and rehearsed by the band in 1969. Likewise, 'Every Night' had also originated as a Beatles' rehearsal track that never saw the light of day. In contrast, there's some tough McCartney rock 'n' roll voicing on 'Oo You', and the nearest to a full-blown production of the classic kind that fans were used to on the most popular track, 'Maybe I'm Amazed'.

The album, in its entirety, was not universally well-received. Many critics (and doubtless many fans) felt it smacked of the kind of ad hoc amateurism not expected from a Beatle. Comparing it to the solo efforts of the other Beatles in 1970, a *Guardian* critic went as far as to call it "boastfully casual". The other ex-Beatles were dismayed when Paul refused to delay its release in favour of the band's *Let It Be*, scheduled to appear just two weeks later, and McCartney himself seemed to confirm the band's break-up as "official" in a self-interview published along with promotional copies of the album. Nevertheless, *McCartney* shot to the top of the US album chart (quickly surrendering its position to *Let It Be*), and peaked at #2 in the UK.

In response to the inevitable backlash that greeted the album's release in some sections of the music press, a tongue-in-cheek letter from McCartney was published in the readers' letters "Mailbag" in the UK's leading music weekly, *Melody Maker*:

Who does Paul McCartney think he is?

We don't see anything of him for a year, and then out he pops from his mysterious hermit-like existence, advertising his new record in a publicity-crazed manner. Does he really think we'll believe he played all the instruments? Let's face it Mailbag, we're not suckers. It's obvious George Martin had a lot to do with it. In fact, if you listen carefully to the end of the third track played backwards, you can almost hear him whistling.

[signed] Paul

"It was an easy album to do, as the things that normally hang a project up, like lack of decision, weren't there... Playing with myself, as they say, was also easy because I knew what I was thinking – the only trouble was that in order to keep time I had to do drums first, on their own – and that was sometimes a bit hard, but fun."

Paul McCartney

MAYBE I'M AMAZED

RECORDED: FEBRUARY 22, 1970
STUDIO: ABBEY ROAD STUDIOS, LONDON
PRODUCER: PAUL MCCARTNEY
COMPOSER: PAUL MCCARTNEY
RELEASED: APRIL 17, 1970

LIVE VERSION
ALBUM: *WINGS OVER AMERICA*
RECORDED: MAY 29, 1976 KEMPER ARENA, KANSAS CITY, USA
PRODUCER: PAUL MCCARTNEY
RELEASED: DECEMBER 10, 1976 (ALBUM) FEBRUARY 4, 1977 (SINGLE)

In the wake of The Beatles' disbanding, if one song heralded Paul McCartney's continuing reputation as a writer of memorable love songs, then 'Maybe I'm Amazed' was that song. Released as the penultimate track on Paul's debut solo album, *McCartney*, it appeared a couple of weeks ahead of The Beatles' final release *Let It Be*, by which time the demise of the "Fab Four" was a fait accompli.

For most of the *McCartney* album, Paul had relied on recordings made at his home studio, but he decided to give 'Maybe I'm Amazed' the full treatment at Abbey Road Studios, Number Two room. As with the deliberately DIY tracks on the rest of the album, he played all the instruments himself – piano, bass, guitar, organ and drums – but with the more technically sophisticated back-up at the studio where The Beatles had made most of their key recordings. To avoid press attention, he booked the session under the assumed name of "Billy Martin". "We had a lot of fun," Paul would tell *Rolling Stone* magazine, "We decided we didn't want to tell anyone what we were doing…".

The composition was immediately applauded as one of McCartney's finest love songs, a passionate paean to his wife Linda, who at the time was frequently blamed by disgruntled Beatles fans – along with John Lennon's wife Yoko Ono – as a contributing factor in the break-up of the group. Whereas several of the songs on *McCartney*, such as 'Teddy Boy' and 'Junk', had been originally written some time earlier for potential use on future Beatles albums, 'Maybe I'm Amazed' was completely new. It reflected a time of traumatic loss caused by the break-up of the band that had shaped his adult life, and the emotional support provided by his wife, who he had only recently married. Seemingly, Linda was a strong influence on his determination to continue writing and recording, a role reflected in the song's lyrics.

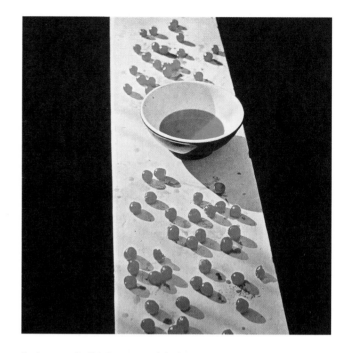

Previous page Paul McCartney outside his home in Cavendish Avenue, St John's Wood, London, in 1967.

Above Designed by Gordon House and Roger Huggett, the front cover for Paul's debut solo album *McCartney*.

Opposite above Paul with Linda and dog Ringo, at their farm near Campbeltown in Scotland, 1971.

Opposite below Back cover to *McCartney*, with a photograph taken by Linda McCartney, of Paul in Scotland with their baby Mary.

And despite the album's mixed reception, most reviews agreed that 'Maybe I'm Amazed' stood out from the rest of the collection, both as a professional-sounding studio production, and a worthy continuation of the McCartney canon. Despite enjoying extensive airplay, the song was never released as a single at the time (except in France and Germany), although an evocative promotional film was made in 1970 by David Putnam featuring a montage of photographs of Paul and his family taken by Linda McCartney.

Nearly seven years later, in February 1977, a single was released of a live version from the 1976 triple album *Wings Over America*, featuring the Wings line-up of Paul and Linda on piano and organ respectively, plus Denny Laine on bass guitar, Jimmy McCulloch on lead guitar, and Joe English on drums. The single reached #10 in the US *Billboard* chart, and #28 in the UK. And over the years, the song has remained a regular highlight of Paul's live shows, delivered with the same passion that characterized the original recording over half a century ago.

"At the time we thought 'Maybe I'm Amazed' was a good track and maybe we should do that as a single, which it probably should have been. But we never did."

Paul McCartney

ANOTHER DAY [SINGLE]

RECORDED: OCTOBER 12, 1970
STUDIO: STUDIO B, COLUMBIA RECORDING, NEW YORK
PRODUCER: PAUL MCCARTNEY
COMPOSERS: PAUL MCCARTNEY, LINDA MCCARTNEY
RELEASED: FEBRUARY 19, 1971 (UK), FEBRUARY 22, 1971 (US)

Originally written and performed during the Beatles' *Let It Be* sessions in 1969, Paul sang 'Another Day' solo at Twickenham Film Studios in early January 1969, accompanying himself on piano. Later that month he performed it at Apple Studios, this time on acoustic guitar. The song continued the McCartney tradition of poetic ballads of isolation and "all the lonely people", perfected on Beatles' tracks such as 'She's Leaving Home' and 'The Fool on the Hill'. Indeed, drummer Denny Seiwell described it as "'Eleanor Rigby' in New York City." Seiwell played on the track, along with guitarist David Spinozza, as part of the *Ram* sessions. However, the track was never used on the album, but appeared as a single three months prior to the LP's release.

The stark narrative describes a simple day in the life of a single working girl who lives alone with her dreams, or more precisely, "the man of her dreams". The banality of her everyday routine at the office is relieved only by brief encounters, which end in rejection.

Paul's descriptive skill hones in on seemingly trivial details – donning stockings and shoes, delving into a raincoat pocket – set against the melancholy background of a mundane life. It's a doomed existence which ends in the girl's emotional breakdown, the drama accentuated by the female presence of Linda on highly effective backing vocals.

'Another Day' was actually the first number to be recorded at the *Ram* sessions, but the decision to release it as a single came at the suggestion of the studio assistant engineer, Dixon Van Winkle, who said, 'We were sitting in Studio A2 one day listening to the takes and Paul asked me to pick the single. I had definite feelings about the record and was in love with 'Another Day'. Paul said, "OK. 'Another Day' it is."'

The song was notoriously name-checked by John Lennon in his acerbic attack on McCartney in 'How Do You Sleep?' on his album *Imagine*, comparing it (implicitly unfavourably) to one of The Beatles' most respected recordings: "The only thing you done was 'Yesterday' / And since you're gone you're just 'Another Day'." But despite his ex-collaborators' barbed remarks, 'Another Day' was a great success as Paul's first single release in a solo capacity, hitting the #5 spot in America and #2 in the UK.

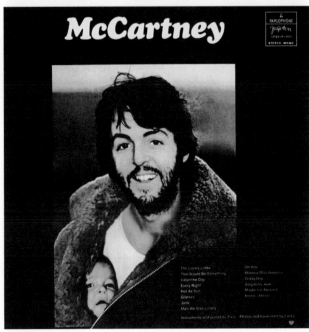

"He'd strap on a guitar or [sit at the] piano and start playing and singing a tune, and we'd learn the tune and start recording... We just did a tune a day."

Denny Seiwell

RAM

TOO MANY PEOPLE

3 LEGS

RAM ON

DEAR BOY
(PAUL AND LINDA MCCARTNEY)

UNCLE ALBERT/ADMIRAL HALSEY
(PAUL AND LINDA MCCARTNEY)

SMILE AWAY

HEART OF THE COUNTRY
(PAUL AND LINDA MCCARTNEY)

MONKBERRY MOON DELIGHT
(PAUL AND LINDA MCCARTNEY)

EAT AT HOME
(PAUL AND LINDA MCCARTNEY)

LONG HAIRED LADY
(PAUL AND LINDA MCCARTNEY)

RAM ON (REPRISE)

THE BACK SEAT OF MY CAR

(All songs written by Paul McCartney, except where indicated)

Paul McCartney (vocals, bass, piano, keyboards, guitars, ukulele), Linda McCartney (vocals),
David Spinozza (guitar), Hugh McCracken (guitar), Denny Seiwell (drums), Heather McCartney
(vocals), Martin Stamm (flugelhorn), New York Philharmonic Orchestra

RAM

RECORDED: OCTOBER 16, 1970–MARCH 1, 1971 // **STUDIOS:** COLUMBIA RECORDING, NEW YORK; A&R RECORDING, NEW YORK; SOUND RECORDING, LOS ANGELES // **PRODUCERS:** PAUL MCCARTNEY, LINDA MCCARTNEY // **RELEASED:** MAY 17, 1971

Paul's second studio excursion as a solo performer was recorded as the split with The Beatles was reaching its most acrimonious point. Its release in May 1971 followed his legal action in the UK High Court to dissolve the group's partnership, making him unpopular with many Beatles fans, and most of the UK and US music press.

In October 1970 Paul and Linda flew to New York with their family to start work on a follow-up to *McCartney*. Rather than the almost solo effort (apart from some vocal assistance from Linda) that had marked the debut album, this time they decided to recruit some additional instrumentalists. Tapping into the session musician circuit, they began holding auditions in an unassuming address in midtown Manhattan, as Paul later recalled: "We went to New York, found a really grotty little basement somewhere and auditioned a bunch of people. We got someone to throw a lot of drummers at us, out of which we picked Denny Seiwell, who's one of the best, and his personality fitted." To deflect unwanted interest, they held the auditions under the pretence of putting together a commercial jingle. Guitarist David Spinozza, who had already been approached by Linda, was recruited at the same time.

The first studio sessions took place at Columbia Recording in New York during October and November 1970, and after the Christmas break, resumed at the A&R Studios from January till the beginning of March 1971. And even before those sessions were completed, McCartney released 'Another Day' in mid-February, recorded at the start of the sessions in October. The song could have provided a great trailer for the album – as Paul's first solo single, it made the charts on both sides of the Atlantic – but three months in advance, was perhaps a little premature for the May release of *Ram*.

The only album to be credited to both Paul and Linda, *Ram* was greeted with inevitable derision in many quarters. After the deliberately home-made sound of *McCartney*, many reviewers felt that for a fully-fledged studio production – with actual session players, no less – *Ram* was an equal let-down. There was a common feeling that the songs were trivial, "inconsequential" (*Rolling Stone*) and not worthy of serious consideration. And, to add fuel to the fire, in the whole "who broke up the Beatles?" saga, Paul was now cast as the villain in chief. As a consequence, while the other ex-Beatles were enjoying plaudits for their own solo projects, *Ram* was cast in something of a pre-ordained negative light.

In the fullness of time, however, opinions have changed. *Ram* has since been assessed as a full-on, solid collection, with the myriad mix of influences that permeated the early-1970s rock landscape. Nearest to Paul's rock 'n' roll roots, the 12-bar-based '3 Legs' was seen, particularly by George Harrison and Ringo Starr, as a comment on the four-minus-one status of The Beatles, while the opener 'Too Many People' was, as Paul later admitted, a "dig" at John and Yoko. But more importantly, the whole album is awash with tuneful numbers, from the silly nonsense of 'Monkberry Moon Delight', and the ambitious 'Uncle Albert/ Admiral Halsey – a montage of song snippets and sound effects, often compared to The Beatles' medleys on *Abbey Road* – to the near-innuendo of the faux-rockabilly 'Eat at Home', on which Linda's vocal contribution is particularly effective. Indeed, her background support on the entire album inspired Elton John to describe her singing as the best he'd heard in a long time – an element evident right though to the uplifting closing track, 'Back Seat of My Car'. Unlike on *McCartney*, six of the 12 tracks are credited as co-compositions by Paul and Linda, and the album as such was billed as being by Paul and Linda McCartney.

On its release, *Ram* did as well as Paul might have hoped for, and certainly better than the naysayers predicted, making #2 on the US album chart (where it spent five months in the Top 10 and earned a platinum disc) and #1 in the UK. And while 'The Back Seat of My Car' was a UK-only single that just scraped into the Top 40 at #39, in America, the sound-collage 'Uncle Albert/ Admiral Halsey' hit the *Billboard* #1 spot, giving Paul his first chart-topping single since the days of The Beatles.

Some latter-day reviews have been as fulsome in their praise for the album as they were once in contempt, with *Rolling Stone* describing it as, "A grand psychedelic ramble full of divine melodies and orchestral frippery," while a BBC online review concluded, "Slaughtered at birth, *Ram* has lived on to fight."

Previous page Paul and Linda McCartney in the "heart of the country" in 1973.
Opposite Paul and Linda on horseback, from the same promotional 1973 shoot.

HEART OF THE COUNTRY

RECORDED: NOVEMBER 16, 1970
STUDIO: STUDIO B, COLUMBIA RECORDING, NEW YORK
PRODUCERS: PAUL MCCARTNEY, LINDA MCCARTNEY
COMPOSERS: PAUL MCCARTNEY, LINDA MCCARTNEY
RELEASED: MAY 17, 1971 (US) (ALBUM), MAY 21, 1971 (UK)
(ALBUM), AUGUST 13, 1971 (SINGLE)

"I'd been serious long enough with the Beatles, and I wanted to see if I could do something that played more into my love of the surreal."

Paul McCartney

'Heart of the Country' was a lilting, country-flavoured number that opened side two of Paul's second solo album, *Ram*. Billed as being written by Paul and Linda McCartney, the song was a celebration of Paul's retreat to the Scottish countryside after the emotional chaos following the break-up of the Beatles – a stark contrast to his lifestyle at the cutting edge of the rock business.

What should be remembered is that Paul had owned this property, High Park Farm in Campbeltown, on the Mull of Kintyre, since 1966. That said, it was only after marrying Linda that he began to develop the farm, as he told biographer Barry Miles: "Linda said, 'We could do this place up!' And I'd never thought of that, I thought it just stayed how you bought it. I just wasn't enterprising enough to actually think, 'We could clean this place up!' Linda really turned me on to it."

The finger-picking tune, an acoustic good-time rocker, was accompanied by a promotional film shot on January 2, 1971. It featured Paul and Linda enjoying the wild Scottish landscape, both on horseback and on the tranquil shores of Campbeltown Loch, on the edge of the Kintyre mull.

The full line-up for the *Ram* sessions, as well as Paul and Linda, included David Spinozza and Hugh McCracken on guitars, and Denny Seiwell on drums, but only McCracken and Seiwell appeared on 'Heart of the Country'. Recording and mixing sessions for the album lasted from October 1970 through until March 1971, at Columbia Recording and A&R Recording in New York City, and Sound Recording in Los Angeles. 'Heart of the Country' itself was laid down at Studio B, Columbia Recording, on November 16, 1970.

Ram was released in May 1971, and 'Heart of the Country' (as the B-side of 'The Back Seat of My Car') on August 13, 1971.

WILD

LIFE

MUMBO

BIP BOP

LOVE IS STRANGE
(MICKEY BAKER, SYLVIA VANDERPOOL, ETHEL SMITH)

WILD LIFE

SOME PEOPLE NEVER KNOW

I AM YOUR SINGER

TOMORROW

DEAR FRIEND

(All songs written by Paul McCartney and Linda McCartney,
except where indicated)

Paul McCartney (vocals, guitar, bass guitar, piano, keyboards, recorder, percussion),
Linda McCartney (vocals, keyboards, piano, percussion), Denny Laine (guitars, bass
guitar, percussion, keyboards, vocals), Denny Seiwell (drums, percusssion)

WILD LIFE

RECORDED: JULY 25–AUGUST 2, 1971 // STUDIOS: ABBEY ROAD STUDIOS, LONDON
PRODUCER: PAUL MCCARTNEY // RELEASED: DECEMBER 7, 1971

In the wake of the release and success of *Ram*, on August 2, 1971 McCartney announced to the press that he and Linda were forming a new permanent group. In fact the line-up had already been decided, and the completion of a new album was well underway.

Paul and Linda had rehearsed the group at their farmhouse studio in Scotland; it comprised Denny Seiwell – the drummer they had recruited in New York for the *Ram* sessions – and Denny Laine, late of the UK band The Moody Blues. Paul recognized Laine as something of a kindred spirit, who could sing and play good, reliable rock guitar. Prior to the group getting together in Scotland, Paul had also taught Linda the basics of playing the piano and keyboards, and during that time the couple had come up with a collection of songs that would provide the backbone for a new album.

Booking the band into Abbey Road Studios in London, Paul already had a clear vision for his next project. He'd talked with

Bob Dylan in New York during the *Ram* sessions, and was impressed by the fact that Dylan had made an album in a series of almost live takes – an almost spontaneous approach, without complicated layers of instruments or overdubs – that Paul now hoped to emulate. He reflected, "The early albums by The Beatles hadn't taken long… and it seemed to me that Dylan was getting to that. I was a great admirer of his – and still am to this day – so I thought, 'Well, if it's good enough for him, let's do it.'"

The album opens with Paul addressing engineer Tony Clarke – "Take it, Tony" – into 'Mumbo', a raucous improvisation of nonsense rock 'n' roll lyrics, complete with Little Richard-style screams and yells. Apparently, this was just a jam that Clarke decided to

"We were not trying to follow The Beatles or The Moody Blues,
we were just trying to do our own thing."

Denny Laine

record for fun. "Just hope they don't ask for the sheet music," Paul commented years later. The definitively low-fi, bluesy pickin' piece 'Bip Bop' follows, confirming the genuinely ad lib feel of much of the album, as does a reggae reworking of the old 1950s Mickey and Sylvia hit 'Love Is Strange', with some upfront harmonies by Paul, Linda and Laine. The track was earmarked for release as a single, but was cancelled after poor sales of the album.

The title track, 'Wild Life', is a recounting by Paul of a visit to a safari park in Kenya, which obviously moved him to write this gentle protest at the treatment of animals, a cause that he and Linda would long be identified with. And 'Some People Never Know', was, in Paul's words, "Just me and Linda's love song, us against the world." Likewise, on the next track, Linda takes some of the lead vocals in 'I Am Your Singer', establishing her place in the band, regardless of critics' reservations about her playing abilities. And the backing vocals on 'Tomorrow' are shared by all three, both McCartneys and Denny Laine, recounting the simple life of bread-and-cheese lunches on holiday in the South of France. The final track, 'Dear Friend' – Paul's rebuttal of John Lennon's put-downs of his music at the time – was an altogether more "produced" affair, supporting the suspicion that it was a left-over from the *Ram* sessions concluded earlier in the year, though subsequent accounts by the participants, including engineer Tony Clarke, refute this.

On November 8, 1971, Paul and Linda held a press launch for *Wild Life* at the Empire Ballroom in London, at which they also introduced for the first time the name of their new band, Wings. The album was released a month later, to what could only be generously called a lukewarm reception. In a comprehensive review, *Rolling Stone*'s John Mendelsohn slated the album, calling it, "Vacuous, flaccid, impotent, trivial and unaffecting," while condescendingly adding, "It's also unpretentious… melodically charming in several places, warm and pleasant. Mostly, it's nicely… executed pop music, and should be taken or left on that basis alone."

Nevertheless, *Wild Life* did a bit better than its detractors anticipated, making the #11 spot in the UK album chart and #10 in the United States, where it went on to earn a (albeit relatively modest) gold disc for selling over half a million copies. And unexpected, though muted, praise came from John Lennon in February 1972, when he was asked by a member of the TV studio audience on the *Mike Douglas Show* what he thought of the album: "I quite enjoyed it. I think [Paul] is going in the right direction!"

Previous page Linda and Paul in 1973.

Opposite Linda and Paul flanked by Denny Seiwell (left) and Denny Laine (right) at the launch of Wild Life at London's Empire Ballroom, Leicester Square.

Above Denny Laine performing with Wings at the Cow Palace, Daly City, California.

DEAR FRIEND

RECORDED: JULY 25, 1971
STUDIO: ABBEY ROAD STUDIOS, LONDON
PRODUCER: PAUL MCCARTNEY
COMPOSER: PAUL MCCARTNEY
RELEASED: DECEMBER 7, 1971

With the release of *Wild Life* in December 1971, many critics immediately interpreted the closing track, 'Dear Friend', as Paul's riposte to John Lennon's acerbic put-down in *Imagine,* 'How Do You Sleep,' released in the September. That, however, was clearly far from the truth.

Wild Life had been recorded through July and August of that year, and some accounts – including those of drummer Denny Seiwell – claim that 'Dear Friend' was actually recorded at the tail end of the sessions for Paul's previous album *Ram*, which went through late 1970 to March 1971. Seiwell said, "The track was recorded at Armin Steiner's [Sunset Sound] studios in Los Angeles... I believe that I did play trumpet near the end of the song but they replaced it with a proper horn section when they sweetened it." The Los Angeles recording was more likely to have been a demo, however: Tony Clark, the engineer on *Wild Life*, confirmed that the song was recorded (or re-recorded?) early in the sessions at Abbey Road Studios.

Whatever the details of its creation, while not a reply to 'How Do You Sleep', 'Dear Friend' was certainly written in the context of the war of words the two ex-Beatles were conducting at the time, triggered in part by Lennon's notorious 1970 interview with Jann Wenner in *Rolling Stone*. As Paul reflected in 1994, "'Dear Friend' was written about John, yes. I don't like grief and arguments, they always bug me. Life is too precious, although we often find ourselves guilty of doing it. So after John had slagged me off in public I had to think of a response, and it was either going to be to slag him off in public – and some instinct stopped me, which I'm really glad about – or do something else."

In keeping with the conciliatory nature of the lyrics, 'Dear Friend' is a sombre, some would say mournful, recording. With just Denny Laine and Denny Seiwell accompanying Paul throughout, and some horns and strings added later, the sparseness of the sound matches the stark message. It's a plea in which McCartney questions his old comrade as to his true position – whether, deep down, this can really be the end of their friendship.

Paul vamps lonely chords on the piano, an isolated voice in the echo. Minimal touches of percussion and bass, then strings, a vibraphone and some horns, gradually support the vocal with a subtlety that renders the track the most "professional" on an otherwise largely off-the-cuff album.

Right Paul playing guitar on stage with Wings in 1972.

"I thought the 'Hi, Hi, Hi' thing could easily be taken as a natural high, could be taken as booze high and everything. It doesn't have to be drugs, you know..."

Paul McCartney

HI, HI, HI [SINGLE]

RECORDED: NOVEMBER, 1972
STUDIO: ABBEY ROAD STUDIOS, LONDON
PRODUCER: PAUL MCCARTNEY
COMPOSERS: PAUL MCCARTNEY, LINDA MCCARTNEY
RELEASED: DECEMBER 1, 1972 (UK), DECEMBER 4, 1972 (US)

After it was banned by the BBC, Paul conceded that 'Hi, Hi, Hi' was "a bit of a dirty song," while adding the proviso, "…if sex is dirty and naughty." It wasn't the first post-Beatles McCartney song that "the Beeb" had deemed unsuitable for broadcasting. Earlier in 1972, 'Give Ireland Back to the Irish' was also on the Corporation's forbidden listed, for political rather than puritanical reasons.

The third single by Wings – after 'Give Ireland…' and 'Mary Had a Little Lamb' – it was written by Paul (and, according to the composer credit, Linda) while on holiday in Benidorm, Spain, in June 1972. The song was first performed on the band's European tour in the August, a frantic closing number to their main set before the inevitable encores.

The studio recording took place at Abbey Road Studios, towards the end of Wings' November sessions for the *Red Rose Speedway* album, which would appear in April 1973. Although basically a 12-bar rock 'n' roll number, it took a surprisingly long time to complete. According to guitarist Henry McCullough, "That was a very difficult 12-bar to get down. I think we did something like 50 takes of it!"

Prior to the single's release in December 1972, Paul had predicted there might be a problem with the song's title, and other presumed drug references. Given his brushes with the authorities, both after a Wings gig in Gothenburg, Sweden in August and on his Scottish farm just a few weeks later, Paul rightly anticipated that a song called 'Hi, Hi, Hi' might draw attention, especially given his open advocacy of marijuana. Perhaps naively, he hoped that a degree of ambiguity would prevail, as with the case of Bob Dylan's 'Rainy Day Women #12 & 35'. He said, "It was like 'Ooh, what does Dylan mean? Does he mean you get high? Or does he mean getting stoned, like drunk?' So there was the ambiguity, and I assumed the same would apply to me."

But title aside, it was the sexual nature of some of the lyrics that attracted the attention of the BBC. And the song is replete with "naughty" innuendos that far outweigh any "druggy" lyrics. However, Paul claimed that the line the broadcaster objected to was in fact misconstrued. Northern Songs, the publishers, had sent a copy of the lyrics to the BBC and managed to get one line wrong, misinterpreting "Get ready for my polygon" as "Get ready for my body gun" – the latter being a far more effective image.

Opposite Paul relaxing backstage during the Wings tour of the United Kingdom in 1973.

Right Wings in New York, November 1972, with Jimmy McCulloch (left), Denny Seiwell (top centre), Denny Laine (bottom centre), Paul and Linda.

C MOON [SINGLE]

RECORDED: NOVEMBER, 1972
STUDIO: MORGAN STUDIOS, LONDON
PRODUCER: PAUL MCCARTNEY
COMPOSERS: PAUL MCCARTNEY, LINDA MCCARTNEY
RELEASED: DECEMBER 1, 1972 (UK), DECEMBER 4, 1972 (US)

Released with 'Hi, Hi, Hi' as a double A-side single, C Moon was an excursion into reggae territory for Wings. And as with the flipside, the writing was credited to both Paul and Linda. The song was recorded around the same time as 'Hi, Hi, Hi', at the tail end of the *Red Rose Speedway* sessions, but relocated on this occasion to Morgan Studios in London. McCartney debuted both songs during Wings' 1972 European tour, first performing 'C Moon' on August 19 in Groningen, Holland.

The title was inspired by a reference in the 1965 rock 'n' roll hit 'Wooly Bully' by the American band, Sam the Sham and The Pharaohs. In that song, the line 'Let's not be L-7' signified "let's not be square" – "L" and "7" making a square when formed by the fingers on one hand against the other. 'C Moon' came from a similar contrivance, as Paul explained: "I thought of the idea of putting a C and a moon together (a half-moon) to get the opposite of square. So 'C Moon' means cool, in other words." It's the eternal teenager's lament, struggling not to fall into the generational trap of the "L-7s", concluding that "cool" is the answer:

The somewhat whimsical intro with some extended piano vamping and background giggling from Linda was clearly a false start, which was deliberately kept in the final pressing. A gentle take on the reggae format, 'C Moon' features the instrumentalists switching from their usual roles, with Henry McCullough on drums, Denny Laine on bass, and regular drummer Denny Seiwell playing xylophone – plus overdubbed cornet parts by Seiwell and Paul.

In the UK, with 'Hi, Hi, Hi' banned by the BBC, 'C Moon' got all the airplay and made it to #5 in the singles chart as a consequence. Though both were recorded during the same album sessions, neither track appeared on *Red Rose Speedway*.

RED ROSE

SPEEDWAY

BIG BARN BED

MY LOVE

GET ON THE RIGHT THING

ONE MORE KISS

LITTLE LAMB DRAGONFLY

SINGLE PIGEON

WHEN THE NIGHT

LOUP (1ST INDIAN ON THE MOON)

(All songs written by Paul McCartney and Linda McCartney)

Paul McCartney (vocals, guitar, bass guitar, piano, keyboards, Mellotron, Moog synthesizer), Linda McCartney (vocals, keyboards, piano, percussion), Denny Laine (vocals, guitars, bass guitar, harmonica), Henry McCullough (guitars, vocals, percussion), Denny Seiwell (drums, percussion), Hugh McCracken (guitar), David Spinozza (guitar)

RED ROSE SPEEDWAY

RECORDED: MARCH–JUNE, SEPTEMBER–DECEMBER 1972 // **STUDIOS:** ABBEY ROAD STUDIOS, LONDON;
OLYMPIC SOUND STUDIOS, LONDON; MORGAN STUDIOS, LONDON; TRIDENT STUDIOS, LONDON; ISLAND STUDIOS, LONDON
PRODUCER: PAUL MCCARTNEY // **RELEASED:** APRIL 30, 1973 (US), MAY 4, 1973 (UK)

In the early months of 1972, Paul decided to expand the personnel of Wings
by adding guitarist Henry McCullough to the line-up. They also began touring,
initially on an almost ad hoc basis, playing at small halls, mainly at UK universities,
and usually unannounced. That way they hoped to avoid the close attention of
the music media while they "got it together" on the road.

Just prior to the tour, on February 1, the band recorded what many felt was an ill-advised release. Reacting passionately to shootings in Belfast by British soldiers, McCartney had quickly penned 'Give Ireland Back to the Irish', which was released at the end of the month. The single was met with mixed reactions – political protest wasn't a natural genre for McCartney – although it did get into the UK Top 20, despite being banned from airplay by the BBC. It did, however, top the charts in the Republic of Ireland. Denny Laine for one, had his doubts, recalling in 1993, "I wasn't happy about the song, although it was heartfelt. I thought it was too political… I'm not criticizing Paul, he did it in all innocence."

Similarly, Wings' next release seemed equally against the grain for a time-served rocker like McCartney. A reworking of the childrens' nursery rhyme, 'Mary Had a Little Lamb', many thought it was a deliberate answer to the criticism he'd received for addressing such a serious issue on the previous release. In fact, the recording had originated some time before the '…Irish' single, and Paul insisted it was just an attempt at making a record for children. Released in May 1972, the single reached #9 in the UK chart but, for many, hinted at a lack of direction on the part of McCartney and Wings.

Meanwhile, recording was underway for Wings' next album. Sessions stretched through March to June 1972, and after a break for a 'Wings Over Europe', resumed in September, with sporadic recording until the end of the year. The original intention was to make a double album, with around 30 songs being considered for inclusion, but given what they felt was the disappointing performance of Wings' debut LP and subsequent singles, EMI persuaded McCartney to cut it down to a single disc.

The bass-dominant 'Big Barn Bed' opens the album, rich with overdubbed harmonies, an insistent beat, and a soulful "amen-style" final chord. The memorably romantic 'My Love' follows, the one big hit from *Red Rose Speedway,* which was released ahead of the album on March 23, 1973. Recorded back in 1970 at sessions for *Ram,* with Paul, Linda and Denny Laine being joined by David Spinozza on guitar, the third track, 'Get on the Right Thing', was slipped into this otherwise Wings album – a pure example of McCartney melodic pop.

'One More Kiss' is a good-time, innocuous ditty with the feel of a standard pop tune of a bygone era, on which McCartney, Seiwell and McCullough (with Laine on bass) are simply flawless. Similarly light in texture, and another basic track recorded in 1970, 'Little Lamb Dragonfly' recalls Paul witnessing the death of one of his lambs on his farm in Scotland. The six-minute-plus track has a three-part structure of unrelated segments, not unlike some classics from his days as a Beatle.

Opening the second side of the original vinyl record, 'Single Pigeon' is a typical slice of McCartney observational lyrics, this time a short snapshot of a London Sunday morning. The short track is pared down to just Paul dominant on piano, and a brief

trumpet section taking things to a melancholic conclusion. 'When the Night' is another track that illustrates McCartney's genius at delivering a timeless melody, while 'Loup (1ˢᵗ Indian on the Moon)' is the complete opposite – a quasi-instrumental (with some ethereal chanting) with Paul's bass leading a "lunar" collage of guitars, organ and various sound effects.

The album ends with an 11-minute medley comprising four songs. The repetitious 'Hold Me Tight' ends up as something of a singalong, before segueing into the languid 'Lazy Dynamite'. The jaunty 'Hands of Love' takes over after a somewhat abrupt guitar break, with the track finishing on 'Power Cut', inspired by the 1972 UK miners' strike and consequent power cuts.

The release of *Red Rose Speedway* at the end of April 1973 was preceded by the single 'My Love' – backed by 'The Mess', recorded live during Wings' 1972 summer European tour – which topped the *Billboard* 100 chart. The album fared equally well, hitting #1 in the States and #5 in the UK. Perhaps predictably, the hip rock press was almost unanimous in its castigation of the album, one critic from a fashionable paper calling it "quite possibly the worst album ever made by a rock and roller of the first rank". There were exceptions however. In the UK, the *New Musical Express's* Tony Tyler declared, "I for one am bloody pleased to discover a lightweight record that not only fails to alienate, but actually succeeds in impressing, via good melodic structure, excellent playing and fine production."

Previous page: Wings performing on the ATV television special *James Paul McCartney*, first broadcast in April 1973 in the US, and on May 10 in the UK.

Opposite Paul and Linda with the 'Wings Over Europe' bus, July 1972.

Above The front cover image for *Red Rose Speedway*, with photo of Paul by Linda. The motorbike was transported from the United States specifically for the shoot.

MY LOVE

RECORDED: OCTOBER, 1972
STUDIO: ABBEY ROAD STUDIOS, LONDON
PRODUCER: PAUL MCCARTNEY
COMPOSERS: PAUL MCCARTNEY, LINDA MCCARTNEY
RELEASED: MARCH 23, 1973 (SINGLE), APRIL 30, 1973, (US)
(ALBUM), MAY 4, 1973 (UK) (ALBUM)

Despite being castigated by many critics at the time, particularly in the fashionable rock press, 'My Love' shot to the top of the US *Billboard* chart on its release in March 1973. Paul wrote the number as a love song to Linda in the first year or so of their marriage, and it featured in the Wings' repertoire after their debut tour in 1972.

The recording of 'My Love' took place at Abbey Road Studios towards the end of the sessions for *Red Rose Speedway*, with a full 50-piece orchestra as backing. The sound was much in the manner of some of McCartney's latter-day Beatles' tracks, with his keyboard accompaniment (in this case, a Fender Rhodes electric piano) supported by a lush string section. In fact, for the orchestral parts, Paul engaged the composer/arranger Richard Hewson, who had previously worked on The Beatles' *Let It Be* tracks 'I Me Mine' and 'The Long and Winding Road'.

The recording was not without incident. McCartney wanted a certain sound, and it took what seemed like innumerable takes on the part of the session players to achieve it. Similarly, Paul had a clear idea in his head about what he wanted for a guitar solo, played by Henry McCullough, and was taken aback when the Northern Irishman offered his own version: "I can't remember what it was I was asked to play, but whatever it was I refused and said that I was going to change the solo. So Paul says, 'Well, what are you going to play?' I said, 'I don't know.' Well, that put the fear of God in him, I think. Because there I am, just me and a 50-piece orchestra in the studio...".

By his own admission slightly phased by McCullough's offer of his own version for the solo, Paul nevertheless let the guitarist give it a try, and was delighted with the result – after just one take. "I'd sort of written the solo, as I often did write our solos," McCartney later recalled "...and he walked up to me right before the take and said, 'Hey, would it be alright if I try something else?' And I said, 'Er... yeah.' It was like, 'Do I believe in this guy?' And he played the solo on 'My Love', which came right out of the blue. And I just thought, 'fucking great.'"

Released a few weeks ahead of *Red Rose Speedway*, on which it was the second track, the song was greeted with derision by many reviewers, who felt it confirmed the widely felt view that McCartney's songwriting was going soft. Others, however, felt it exemplified Paul's talent for and emotive simplicity in lyrics rather than over-complicated flamboyance. Chris Welch, the highly-respected *Melody Maker* writer, felt its appeal was "timeless... among his seemingly unstoppable flow of classics", a view reflected

> "My Love' was my definitive one for Linda, written in the early days of our relationship, and that came easily."

Paul McCartney in a *Billboard* interview, 2001

in McCartney's best-yet chart performance for a post-Beatles single. As well as topping the *Billboard* Hot 100 and Easy Listening listings, it made the Top 10 in half a dozen other countries around the globe including Australia, Canada and the UK.

Written as a genuine love song for Linda, 'My Love' became a true elegy to her memory after his wife's tragic death from cancer in 1998. Indeed, Paul chose the song for two memorial services for Linda, one in London, where it was performed as a string piece by the Brodsky Quartet, and one in New York, where a similar interpretation was provided by the Loma Mar Quartet. And the song became among the most-covered from Paul's post-Beatles repertoire, with Tony Bennett, Cher, Corinne Bailey Rae and jazz singer Nancy Wilson among the prestigious names who have recorded versions.

LIVE AND LET DIE [SINGLE]

RECORDED: OCTOBER 19, 1972
STUDIO: AIR STUDIOS, LONDON
PRODUCER: GEORGE MARTIN
COMPOSERS: PAUL MCCARTNEY, LINDA MCCARTNEY
RELEASED: JUNE 1, 1973 (UK), JUNE 18, 1973 (US)

For many purist fans, the idea of Paul McCartney creating the theme song for a James Bond movie was another step in what they felt was the wrong direction for a former Beatle. For others, it was confirmation that his artistic ambition in the pop music arena was not constrained by the expectations of a strictly rock audience. Previous performers of hit Bond anthems included Shirley Bassey (with 'Goldfinger' in 1964, and 1971's 'Diamonds Are Forever') and Tom Jones singing 'Thunderball' in 1965 – both big voices handling strident, dramatically arranged material.

While writer Tom Mankiewicz was still completing the screenplay for *Live and Let Die*, which starred Roger Moore as Bond, the film's producers Harry Saltzman and Albert R. Broccoli invited Paul to write the theme song. After reading the original Ian Fleming novel, he accepted the commission, and recorded it with Wings the following week. And with George Martin on board as arranger of the entire movie score, the old McCartney–Martin team was back together, just like during the days of the Beatles.

Initially, producer Saltzman had envisaged having either Shirley Bassey or Thelma Houston performing the theme song for the soundtrack, but on Paul's insistence it could only be used if a recording by Wings could be used over the opening credits.

So Wings subsequently recorded the number, with the addition of percussionist Ray Cooper and a full orchestra,

Opposite Many of Paul McCartney's most memorable songs were inspired by his wife Linda, seen here in 1978.

Above Paul and Linda (right) with Wings and partners, at the London premier of *Live and Let Die*, July 5, 1973.

Left The original movie poster for *Live and Let Die*.

"I remember a thing in *Rolling Stone*... that said 'McCartney's going to do *Live and Let Die*, so it's come to that, has it?' I thought, you silly sods. Because we were talking to another paper and when I said I was going to do *Live and Let Die*, the 007 thing, the reporter said, 'Hey man, that's real hip.' So it just depends which way you look at it."

Paul McCartney

during the sessions for *Red Rose Speedway* in October, 1972. As drummer Denny Seiwell recalled, "We were at AIR Studios with a 40-piece orchestra. We knew our parts well, and had a few rundowns with the orchestra, and it took only a few takes to get the master. I remember finishing the track in about three hours. The percussion was done by Ray Cooper, he played the tympani part and also the duck call on the reggae bit… great fun!" According to Mark Berry, the uncredited assistant engineer on the recording, the orchestra numbered even more than Seiwell recollected. He said, "They had a 63-piece orchestra in there, and I felt I had emptied every ashtray known to man before the end of that one."

As Paul later recalled, when he and George Martin first played the actual track to the film producers, the latter still assumed it was a demo: "After the record had finished they said to George, 'That's great, a wonderful demo. Now when are you going to make the real track, and who shall we get to sing it?' And George said, 'What? This is the real track!'"

Although as highly charged as anything Paul had ever produced, in keeping with the flash-bang-wallop dynamic of much of the action in the Bond movie, the song opens with a slow intro before breaking into a bombastic up-tempo chorus befitting its subject. Typical of McCartney compositions of the era, the mood again changes abruptly with a reggae-flavoured break before reverting to the signature ballad-plus-chorus. With its in-built sense of drama, it was inevitable the song would remain a firm favourite with Paul's concert audiences over the years.

Despite reservations in some quarters about McCartney accompanying Bond, the single was generally well received, with Paul Gambaccini describing it in *Rolling Stone* as "the best record Paul McCartney has made since 'Let It Be'." Appearing in June 1973 to coincide with the release of the movie, it hit the top spot in two of the three major US charts, *Cash Box* and *Record World*, and #2 in the *Billboard* Hot 100. It was also the most successful James Bond theme at the time, with an Academy Award nomination for Best Original Song in 1974.

In October 2012, Broadcast Music Inc. (BMI), the international music rights body, presented McCartney with their Million-Air Award, marking over four million US broadcasts of 'Live and Let Die'. It wasn't the first such award for Paul, who has to date received over 70 during his career, including one in 1988 for five million plays of The Beatles' 'Yesterday' – a record-breaking figure which now exceeds the 10 million mark. At the ceremony marking the 'Live and Let Die' award, the BMI President Del Bryant was fulsome – in fact some may have said a touch over the top – in his praise for the song: "*'Live and Let Die' shows the incredible magnitude and cultural impact of a single song, both as a musical composition and an integral piece of cinematic history.*"

HELEN WHEELS [SINGLE]

B-SIDE: 'COUNTRY DREAMER'
RECORDED: AUGUST–SEPTEMBER 1973
STUDIO: EMI STUDIOS, LAGOS, NIGERIA
PRODUCER: PAUL MCCARTNEY
COMPOSERS: PAUL MCCARTNEY, LINDA MCCARTNEY
RELEASED: OCTOBER 26, 1973

Recorded during the *Band on the Run* sessions in Lagos, Nigeria, 'Helen Wheels' –with Paul and Linda co-credited as writers – never made it to the album itself as released in the UK, although Capitol Records persuaded Paul to add it to the track listing on the US version.

A straightforward hard-edged rocker, the song featured the core three-piece line-up of Paul, Linda and Denny Laine who performed on the majority of the album, with McCartney himself multi-tracked on drums, guitar and bass. The Wings line-up that had performed on the previous album, *Red Rose Speedway*, was now minus guitarist Henry McCullough and drummer Denny Seiwell, both of whom had quit the band just prior to the recording sessions in Nigeria.

The title is derived from the expression "hell on wheels", affectionately referring to the tough Land Rover 4x4 vehicle that the McCartneys used on trips to their farm in Scotland. The lyrics describe the journey down to London via Glasgow, Carlisle, Kendal, Liverpool and Birmingham, ending up in London where the faithful roadster has a check-up before making the next trip North.

In a highly effective promotional film, sequences of the trio playing (including Paul on drums, lead guitar and bass guitar) were intercut with shots of them travelling in the Land Rover. It was directed by Michael Lindsay-Hogg, who had also directed the Beatles' fly-on-the-wall studio documentary *Let It Be* in 1969.

The single sold well, hitting #10 and #12 in America and the UK respectively, and also made the top five in Canada. *New York Times* reviewer Loraine Alterman described it as "a raucous rocker – its relentless energy is perfect for Top 40 format radio". It confirmed, as so many songs would over subsequent years, that Paul McCartney has always been a straight-from-the-hip rock 'n' roll musician at heart.

The B-side song was 'Country Dreamer', which was originally recorded for *Red Rose Speedway* and featured the earlier Wings personnel, including Henry McCullough and Denny Seiwell.

In 2014, British heavy metal band Def Leppard included a cover of the song on *The Art of McCartney* tribute album, which included over 30 tracks by artists as diverse as Bob Dylan, Billy Joel, Doctor John and BB King.

Opposite A spectacular production number from the *James Paul McCartney* TV special, with Paul singing 'Gotta Sing, Gotta Dance' with a Busby Berkeley-style routine featuring dancers in half-man / half-woman costumes.

BAND

ON THE

RUN

BAND ON THE RUN

JET

BLUEBIRD

MRS VANDERBILT

LET ME ROLL IT

MAMUNIA

NO WORDS
(PAUL MCCARTNEY, DENNY LAINE)

PICASSO'S LAST WORDS (DRINK TO ME)

NINETEEN HUNDRED AND EIGHTY FIVE

(All songs written by Paul McCartney, except where indicated)

Paul McCartney (vocals, bass, guitars, piano, keyboards, drums, percussion),
Linda McCartney (vocals, organ, keyboards, percussion), Denny Laine (vocals, guitars,
drums, percussion), Howie Casey (saxophone), Ginger Baker (percussion),
Remi Kabaka (percussion)

BAND ON THE RUN

RECORDED: AUGUST–OCTOBER, 1973 // **STUDIOS:** EMI STUDIOS, LAGOS, NIGERIA; ARC STUDIO, IKEJA, NIGERIA; AIR STUDIOS, LONDON
PRODUCER: PAUL MCCARTNEY // **RELEASED:** DECEMBER 5, 1973 (US), DECEMBER 7, 1973 (UK)

A summer UK tour by Wings heralded a major fracture in the band in 1973 when, as soon as the trek was over, Henry McCullough announced he was leaving. They were at Paul's studio in Scotland working on some material for the next album when the guitarist's frustrations came to a head. Back in London, McCartney decided the new album should be recorded at a location outside the UK – the world was literally his oyster – and EMI had a string of studios dotted around the globe.

Paul opted for a studio in Lagos, Nigeria, where he was aware there was a lively music scene. But just as he, the band and the rest of the McCartney family – plus engineers and roadies – were about to depart early in August, Denny Seiwell also quit Wings, so the line-up was reduced to just Paul, Linda and Denny Laine.

As soon as they arrived at the EMI studio in Lagos, they realized things were not going to be as idyllic as they imagined. Conditions in the city were tense, with rife corruption and a military government in control. The studio itself was well below the standard they had expected, with out-of-date equipment, some of which was faulty. And to add to a sense of discomfort, the well-known local musician and activist Fela Kuti began a campaign insisting that McCartney was just there to "steal" African music.

Eager to explore the local night life, one evening Paul and Linda ventured out against advice and were robbed at knifepoint, the muggers making off with all their valuables, which included a bag containing a notebook full of lyrics and songs, plus cassettes of demos for the forthcoming sessions.

Somewhat bizarrely, the ex-Cream drummer Ginger Baker (who Denny Laine had played with in Baker's band Air Force) insisted they use his own ARC Studio on the outskirts of the city, in the suburb of Ikeja. That arrangement lasted for just one day (and one song, 'Picasso's Last Words (Drink to Me)'), before Wings resumed work on the rest of the album in the EMI set-up.

Most of the album tracks (plus 'Helen Wheels', which was omitted from the initial UK release) were laid down in Lagos over the six weeks that the McCartney party were in the Nigerian capital, with further overdubs and mixing completed at George Martin's AIR Studios in London. Along with 'No Words', 'Jet' – the second track on the LP – was recorded in its entirety in London, and was the first track from the album to be released as a single, in January 1974. Likewise, the album opener and title track would also see life as a follow-up single in the US and UK, the following April and June respectively.

Tenor saxophone player Howie Casey, who Paul had known since their early days in Liverpool, recalled how he got the gig: "At that particular time I'd done a few sessions with Tony Visconti, and he was called in to help out on *Band on the Run*, and then they wanted a horn section, four saxes, for 'Jet' – I think it was two baritones, two tenors – anyway, Tony mentioned me to Paul, so I did three tracks. The other guys did the 'Jet' one, then I did the solo on 'Bluebird' and 'Mrs Vanderbilt', so that was it really, and I didn't think much about it. I got my 30 quid, and went off and did other things."

The third track on the album, 'Bluebird' is thought to have been written back in late 1971 while Paul was on vacation in Jamaica. The laid-back, sun-kissed track is the only one that boasts a Nigerian musician on the session – percussionist Remi Kabaka (recruited via Ginger Baker), who Paul invited to London to the overdub sessions. A highlight of the track is certainly Howie Casey's sultry sax solo, a smoky interlude in keeping with the nuance of the song. And with its "hey ho" chorus, perfect for sing-alongs anywhere in the world, 'Mrs Vandebilt', which also benefited from some punchy sax overdubs by Casey, was a surprise favourite among teenagers in the Soviet Union before the fall of the Iron Curtain.

From its opening bars, 'Let Me Roll It' reminds many listeners of nothing less than John Lennon's best post-Beatles tracks, with the same tape echoes, and distorted vocals and guitar parts. Indeed, Paul's guitar is nothing short of sensational in its simple impact, as engineer Geoff Emerick recalled: "It's even more amazing considering that it was double-tracked. Paul played that, and he did an excellent job of doubling the part with exactly the same phrasing and attitude."

Opening side two on the original vinyl LP, 'Mamunia' was the first track to be recorded during the sessions in Lagos. With the title inspired (though misspelled) by the luxury hotel where he'd stayed on holiday the previous February – the Mamounia in Marrakesh, Morocco – the track exudes a happy, tropical beat. It reflects, one could assume, an early optimism about the whole Nigeria experience, which wouldn't last.

'No Words' was the first published track to be written by Paul and Denny Laine, as the latter remembered: "Writing with [Paul] wasn't a chore. Nothing negative. He'd come up with an idea and so would I. I wasn't as prolific, but that's beside the point. I wasn't thinking at the time. I had bits. But he was always encouraging me to put bits together, so we did."

In his exhaustive chronicle, *Paul McCartney: Recording Sessions (1969–2013)*, Luca Perasi recounts the origin of 'Picasso's Last Words (Drink to Me)'. Earlier that year, Paul was visiting the Hollywood actor Dustin Hoffman at his house in Jamaica, and Hoffman challenged him whether he could write a song "about anything". When Paul answered in the affirmative, his host picked up a copy of *Time* magazine, pointing to an article entitled 'Picasso's Last Days and Final Journey', about the recent death of the great artist. To Hoffman's delight, Paul picked up a guitar and began strumming, then sang a line of Picasso's last words 'Drink to me...' as reported in the magazine.

He finished the song over the next few days, after which it was more or less untouched until he brought it to the one-day session at Ginger Baker's ARC Studio on September 1. There, Baker himself joined in a "percussion section" along with other studio folk, shaking little cans of gravel from the dirt road outside, using them as maracas. But the finished track, as it appears on the album, was fundamentally created after some extensive overdubbing and production work back in London.

The resulting collage begins with a straightforward tribute to the venerated painter, before taking on a myriad of elements, including clips from 'Jet' and 'Mrs Vanderbilt', some orchestral

insertions masterminded by arranger Tony Visconti, and seemingly random radio commentaries in French. It ends with an equally unrelated fade-out chant.

The closing song, 'Nineteen Hundred and Eighty Five', is as direct in its impact as the previous track is obtuse. With a solid bedrock of piano and bass, McCartney's strident vocal is matched by a stunning guitar solo, and an epic orchestral fade that finishes with a brief excerpt from 'Band on the Run', bringing the whole album full circle.

On its release, *Band on the Run* was greeted by most critics as the post-Beatles Macca album the world had been waiting for. In *Melody Maker*, Chris Welch concluded a glowing review, "And with this album, Wings prove they are not just a flutter, or plaything, but a highly valued addition to the ranks of music makers." And the often acerbic Charles Shaar Murray told readers of the *New Musical Express*: "*Band On The Run* is a great album. If anybody ever puts down McCartney in your presence, bust him in the snoot and play him this. He will thank you for it afterwards."

Although initial sales of the album were disappointing, its eventual performance was aided by the two hit singles, 'Jet' and 'Band on the Run'. It went on to top the charts in six countries, including, crucially, the UK and the US, and sold six million copies worldwide.

Opposite Paul, Linda (holding a copy of *Band on the Run*) and family (left to right: Stella, Mary and Heather), departing for Jamaica from London's Heathrow Airport, December 3, 1973.

Above Wings with their platinum discs for *Band on the Run*: Denny Laine and Jimmy McCulloch (second and third from left), Geoff Britton (centre back), Paul and Linda, and behind Linda session conga player Kenneth "Afro" Williams.

JET

RECORDED: OCTOBER, 1973
STUDIO: AIR STUDIOS, LONDON
PRODUCER: PAUL MCCARTNEY
COMPOSERS: PAUL MCCARTNEY, LINDA MCCARTNEY
RELEASED: DECEMBER 5, 1973 (US) (ALBUM),
DECEMBER 7, 1973 (UK) (ALBUM), JANUARY 28, 1974 (US)
(SINGLE), FEBRUARY 15, 1974 (UK) (SINGLE)

Another tough-sounding rocker that immediately found its way into the McCartney on-stage repertoire, and has stayed there ever since. Unlike the rest of *Band on the Run*, 'Jet' was recorded solely at AIR Studios in London after the band's return from Nigeria. As well as Paul on bass, drums, guitar and Moog synthesizer, and Linda on keyboards and Moog, the track features Denny Laine on guitar, Howie Casey fronting a four-piece sax section, and the Beaux Arts Orchestra providing string backing, arranged by Tony Visconti.

Despite its hard-rock dynamic, the recording has a tantalizingly psychedelic edge to it, with electronically distorted vocals and some hard-to-fathom stream-of-consciousness lyrics. Regarding the words, the title is generally agreed to have been named after a black Labrador puppy of Paul's, Jet.

Alternatively, McCartney later told *GQ* magazine: "I was in a songwriting mood and I was up in Scotland. I just thought, 'OK, I just gotta go somewhere and try and write a song.' We happened to have a little pony that was called Jet on the farm. I took my guitar and hiked up this great big hill. I found myself a place which was in the middle of nature, and just sat there and started making up a song."

The rest of the song is lyrically more obscure, with McCartney himself admitting that references like "suffragette" were there purely because they sounded right, rather than having any deeper significance. "I make so much stuff up" he admitted, "…but if I'm asked to analyze it, I can't really explain what it is."

To add to the confusion for would-be McCartney analysts, on at least one occasion Paul suggested the lines referencing a "sergeant major" were inspired by his meeting Linda's father, which he admitted was somewhat intimidating at the time.

As the first British and American single to be released from *Band on the Run*, the song made the #7 position in both the US and UK charts, as well as charting across Europe and elsewhere, including Canada, Japan and New Zealand

Below Paul and Linda on stage during the 1976 Wings tour.

Opposite Producer Tony Visconti, who provided some of the orchestral arrangements for *Band on the Run*, here with his wife, the Apple Records protégé Mary Hopkin, leaving for a tour of New Zealand.

"He wanted that one to be totally mad. Paul's had a lot
of practice in the studio. He's done some very trippy things.
Every now and then he remembers how much he loves it."

Linda McCartney, 1976

BAND ON THE RUN [SONG]

RECORDED: SEPTEMBER–OCTOBER 1973
STUDIO: EMI STUDIOS, LAGOS, NIGERIA; AIR STUDIOS, LONDON
PRODUCER: PAUL MCCARTNEY
COMPOSERS: PAUL MCCARTNEY, LINDA MCCARTNEY
RELEASED: DECEMBER 5, 1973 (US) (ALBUM),
DECEMBER 7, 1973 (UK) (ALBUM), APRIL 8, 1974 (US) (SINGLE),
JUNE 28, 1974 (UK) (SINGLE)

An audacious composition in three parts, the song was the opener and title track of Wings' most successful album. The first section is in a reflective ballad-style, bemoaning being stuck inside four walls, and setting the scene for the theme running throughout. That scene is of prisoners escaping from their fate, either literally – as per the album cover with Wings and assorted celebrity friends in prison garb, caught in their captors' searchlight – or metaphorically. Driving rock provides a short bridge leading into a country-flavoured chorus proclaiming the anthemic 'Band on the Run' theme.

At the time of the album's release, Paul had inferred that the lyric alluding to a release from captivity was inspired by a remark George Harrison had made during one of The Beatles' interminable business meetings, when the fate of the band and their Apple company was being decided. But the broader analogy of escape from imposed restriction could be interpreted as the band being outlaws to convention – as rock 'n' roll performers had often been regarded over the years – or even obliquely referencing the drug laws that the McCartneys had fallen foul of more than once.

Recording of the song initially took place during the almost-aborted album sessions in Lagos, Nigeria, after the theft of the original demo tapes at knifepoint. The first two parts of the track were laid down there, the third after the return to London in October 1973, at AIR Studios. Released as a US single in April 1974, with the album-closer 'Nineteen Hundred and Eighty-Five' as the flipside, 'Band on the Run' became Paul's third non-Beatles single to top the American charts. And as *Rolling Stone* reflected: "The whole world decided to run along with him, taking the song to the top of the pop charts…. no one dismissed him as lightweight after this."

Above Linda, Paul and Denny Laine in the studio, London 1974.
Opposite Paul in AIR studios, London, during final recordings for *Band on the Run*.

"The song not only anchors McCartney's best album (which is co-credited with Wings), it gave new life to a singer and songwriter many had given up on."

Ultimate Classic Rock

JUNIOR'S FARM [SINGLE]

RECORDED: JULY 16–18, 1974
STUDIO: SOUND SHOP STUDIOS, NASHVILLE
PRODUCER: PAUL MCCARTNEY
COMPOSERS: PAUL MCCARTNEY, LINDA MCCARTNEY
RELEASED: OCTOBER 25, 1974

In the wake of the success of *Band on the Run* and the subsequent title track single, and after auditioning for a new Wings drummer (Denny Seiwell having left, along with Henry McCullough, before the Nigeria recordings), the McCartneys took a holiday in the United States, which also involved some recording with the new line-up. Their vacation in Nashville lasted six weeks from early June, during which time the band laid down what would be the two sides of their next single.

They were all staying at a rented 133-acre farm in Lebanon, Tennessee, belonging to a local session musician and songwriter, Norbert "Curly" Puman Jr., best known for penning country hits such as 'The Green, Green Grass of Home'. With their host's name as inspiration for the title – as well as, according to Paul, Bob Dylan's 'Maggie's Farm' – the lyrics of 'Junior's Farm' were the kind of "nonsense" verse Paul was adept at.

As he later pointed out, "I wasn't trying to say anything… it has silly words and basically all it says is, 'Let's get out of the city… let's go out to Junior's Farm or Strawberry Fields or whatever…' As for reading deep meanings into the words, people shouldn't bother, there aren't any."

The song is an archetypal McCartney rock number, with more than a passing resemblance to the Beatles' 'Get Back', the closing track on their final album *Let It Be*. One of those rock 'n' roll recordings whose magic hinges on its sheer simplicity, the performance of Wings is enhanced by the contribution of the two newcomers: Jimmy McCulloch, whose guitar punctuates throughout with inspired economy; and drummer Geoff Britton, who Paul lauded as a fine rock 'n' roll drummer, but only lasted with Wings until the following January.

The actual recording in Nashville was facilitated by Buddy Killen, the owner of the Sound Shop Studios. Killen was a client of lawyer Lee Eastman, Paul's father-in-law, who had asked him a few weeks earlier if he would host the McCartney family on what would turn out to be a working holiday. "He wasn't supposed

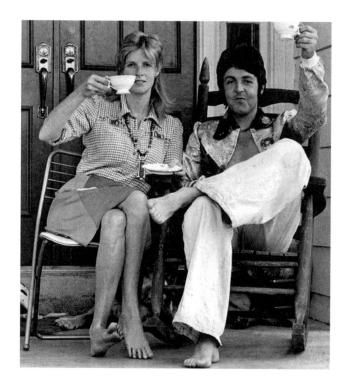

Above Linda and Paul relaxing outside the farmhouse of Norbert Puman Jr (inspiration for 'Junior's Farm') in Lebanon, Tennessee.

Opposite above The celebrated Skull's Rainbow Room venue in Nashville, where Paul was inspired to write 'Sally G'.

Opposite below Jimmy McCulloch in concert with Wings.

to be recording, because he didn't have a green card. But it just worked out because I had that studio there. They weren't trying to break the law." The head engineer at The Sound Shop was Ernie Winfrey, who recalled the sessions with McCartney: "As a vocalist, he was a true artist. His instrument was so well-tuned it was amazing. Seeing him standing at the microphone, like you recall seeing him on The Ed Sullivan Show, I thought, 'Am I really sitting here doing this?'"

The photograph on the sleeve of one of the single's releases had the band dressed as characters from the lyrics, with Denny Laine as an "eskimo", Paul as a farmer and Geoff Britton as a poker dealer. With 'Sally G' on the flipside the single was a worldwide hit, making #3 in the US charts, and the Top 10 in New Zealand, South Africa, Canada and Norway.

"I rather fancy the place [Nashville]. It's a musical centre.
I've just heard so much about it that I wanted to see for myself."

Paul McCartney

SALLY G [SINGLE]

RECORDED: JULY 16–18, 1974
STUDIO: SOUND SHOP STUDIOS, NASHVILLE
PRODUCER: PAUL MCCARTNEY
COMPOSERS: PAUL MCCARTNEY, LINDA MCCARTNEY
RELEASED: OCTOBER 25, 1974

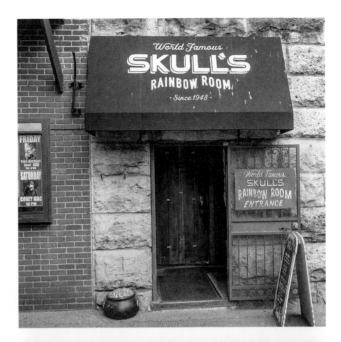

One of Paul's most successful ventures into country music, 'Sally G' was directly inspired and executed during the 1974 working holiday in Nashville. After arriving in "Music City", he was soon exploring the clubs and bars where live music proliferated, and the song was born during one such visit to the Printer's Alley district, a hub of musical nightlife.

He was drinking in Skull's Rainbow Room, one of the most famous venues in the area, where the singer Diane Gaffney was performing that night. According to the club's owner, after hearing Gaffney sing, McCartney found a piano at the back of the club and promptly wrote the song, initially naming it after the vocalist. It was only when he later found out that Gaffney had once sued a magazine for using her name without permission, that he decided to change the title to 'Sally G'. It's thought that Paul may have chosen 'Sally' as a substitute after the pre-war song 'Sally in Our Alley' made famous by the UK star, Gracie Fields. After establishing the factual background to the song, the narrative is one of love gone wrong, a frequent theme in country music.

And for the subsequent sessions at Sound Shop Studios, a week before he cut 'Junior's Farm' there, McCartney recruited top-of-the-line Nashville musicians to add a genuine down-home feel to the recording. Pedal steel and dobro guitar parts, key elements in country music, were provided by Lloyd Green, a long-time star session man who had accompanied The Byrds, Johnny Cash and Bob Dylan, among many others. Johnny Gimble was a renowned fiddle player, who had been recording with the best for decades, notably through the 1950s with the legendary Bob Wills and his Texas Playboys. And fellow fiddler Wills himself, the "King of Western Swing" through the 1940s and '50s, was on hand to complete a truly Nashville sound, just a year before his death in 1975.

As the B-side to 'Junior's Farm', the song didn't seem to get the exposure it deserved, although many American radio stations picked up on it and it became a minor hit in its own right on various country charts. This led to Paul re-releasing it as the A-side in February 1975, when it got to #17 on the *Billboard* Hot 100, and the same paper's Easy Listening chart at #7.

WALKING IN THE PARK
WITH ELOISE [SINGLE]

(AS THE COUNTRY HAMS)

RECORDED: JULY 16, 1974
STUDIO: SOUND SHOP STUDIOS, NASHVILLE
PRODUCER: PAUL MCCARTNEY
COMPOSERS: JAMES 'JIM' MCCARTNEY
RELEASED: OCTOBER 18, 1974

While on his Nashville sojourn in 1974, Paul hooked up with a number of local musicians, some huge stars in their own right. Inevitably, they jammed, and some of it ended up in the recording studio. One idea being kicked around the McCartney camp at the time was an album of songs that Paul had left off previous albums, or had yet to be earmarked at all.

Although the album project never materialized, one such number that would have been included was 'Walking in the Park With Eloise'. During a conversation with the legendary country guitarist Chet Atkins, the subject of their respective fathers came up, and out of that conversation came Paul's suggestion they try a song written many years before (in the pre-Beatles days of his childhood, or possibly earlier) by his father Jim McCartney. In fact, McCartney senior had played trumpet and piano, leading Jim Mac's Jazz Band, in the 1920s.

The result was a 1920s-inspired jazz age instrumental, featuring a Wings line-up of Paul, Denny Laine and drummer Geoff Britton, augmented by a local horn section of clarinet, trombone and trumpet, a banjo (always a must in Dixieland-style music), plus country superstars Atkins and pianist Floyd Cramer. The Americans were intrigued by Paul playing a washboard on the track but for a UK musician of his generation it was no big deal – it had been a trademark during the 1950s DIY skiffle craze that launched the careers of thousands of British rock musicians, including The Beatles.

The track has never been strictly classed as an official McCartney release, because Paul decided to credit it as a single to The Country Hams, along with the instrumental B-side, co-written with Linda, 'Bridge on the River Suite'. Although 1920s pastiches by outfits like The Temperance Seven and The New Vaudeville Band had enjoyed novelty chart success from time to time, as the single was not promoted as a McCartney or Wings release, it disappeared without trace sales-wise.

It would appear under the McCartney banner later, however, when both sides of the single (along with 'Sally G') were included as bonus tracks on the 1993 CD reissue of 1976's *Wings at the Speed of Sound*. And the single itself was released again on March 3, 1982, after Paul had picked it as one of his eight choices on the BBC radio programme *Desert Island Discs*.

"I actually did a song of his [my dad] with Chet Atkins and Floyd Cramer called 'Walking in the Park With Eloise'. I said to my dad, 'Do you know you wrote that song?' and he said, 'I didn't write it. I made it up.' I said, 'I know what you mean, but we call that writing these days, Dad!'"

Paul McCartney

Above The legendary country superstar guitarist Chet Atkins, who appeared as one of The Country Hams on 'Walking in the Park With Eloise'.

Opposite Paul with his father Jim McCartney (composer of 'Walking in the Park With Eloise') outside Paul's London home in St John's Wood.

VENUS

AND MARS

(All songs written by Paul McCartney and Linda McCartney,
except where indicated)

Paul McCartney (vocals, bass, guitars, keyboards, piano, percussion), Linda McCartney
(vocals, keyboards, percussion), Denny Laine (vocals, guitars, keyboards, percussion),
Jimmy McCulloch (guitars, vocals, percussion), Joe English (drums, percussion),
Geoff Britton (drums), Kenneth "Afro" Williams (congas), Allen Toussaint (piano),
Dave Mason (guitar), Tom Scott (soprano saxophone)

VENUS AND MARS

RECORDED: NOVEMBER 5–13, 1974, JANUARY 16–FEBRUARY 24, 1975 // **STUDIOS:** ABBEY ROAD STUDIOS, LONDON; SEA-SAINT STUDIOS, NEW ORLEANS; WALLY HEIDER STUDIOS, LOS ANGELES // **PRODUCER:** PAUL MCCARTNEY // RELEASED: MAY 27, 1975

Early in 1975 Paul, Linda and the rest of the band were on another trip of transatlantic discovery, this time in the "Crescent City" of New Orleans. The birthplace of jazz at the dawn of the 20th century and, more recently, a hotbed of its own brand of rhythm and blues and rock 'n' roll, "The Big Easy" was home to a number of key studios – including Sea-Saint Studios, at 3089 Clematis Street in the Gentilly section of town. The studio was founded in 1973 by the eminent musician, songwriter and producer Allen Toussaint, a mainstay of the New Orleans music scene, and had a growing reputation as a cutting-edge facility boasting state-of-the-art equipment. Paul decided to record his album there.

The Wings party had only been in the city a couple of days, during which time they had recorded one jamming-style instrumental, 'Lunch Box/Odd Sox', when drummer Geoff Britton left the group. Paul had to move quickly – he had an album to make – and on the recommendation of trombonist Tony Dorsey, brought in Joe English to occupy the vacant drum stool.

"I was rehearsing with Bonnie Bramlett [of Delaney and Bonnie]," Joe explained in a UK interview a few months later, "…and I was thinking of going on the road with her band when I received a call from Paul in New Orleans asking me to play on the album. Fortunately, I was able to find Bonnie a replacement drummer pretty quickly, and there were no hang-ups as far as she was concerned." English remained a member of Wings until 1977.

It was at that stage that there was a decision to form a horn section for the touring version of Wings, and again Dorsey helped pull it together. "So he pulled in local musicians," Howie Casey explained. 'Well, one was a New Orleans player, one was from Dallas and lived in New Orleans, Thaddeus Richard was from that area, then Tony Dorsey was from Atlanta. They did both sessions, and there was another sax player. But when the tour came up, Paul actually asked for me, he said 'We'll take the other American guys, but I'd like Howie to do it.' So I got into that, and of course that went on for a few years, a few albums."

Simply McCartney at his most romantic, the opening title track was inspired by the two neighbouring planets, Venus and Mars, representing two lovers (though not Paul and Linda, as some listeners speculated). It also reflected the fashion for astrology from the late 1960s, in America particularly. Paul also explained that the reference to someone following the stars could be interpreted as a groupie or an astrologer. The track leads directly into 'Rock Show', a direct celebration of

what Paul always claimed as his first instinct, performing live. References to actual venues like Madison Square Garden and the Hollywood Bowl give the lyrics an authentic edge, while instrumentally, the frantic rocker is enhanced by some dazzling guitar breaks from McCulloch and Laine, and a lengthy fade-out led by the funky piano of Allen Toussaint.

Recorded initially at Abbey Road Studios before the sessions in New Orleans, 'Love in Song' began life as an acoustic ballad, showcasing Paul's genius at delivering a powerful lyric with suitably restrained emotion. The theme is one repeated in much of the McCartney songbook, that of love and happiness being a universal goal, but to be essentially found much closer to home.

The superbly crafted 'You Gave Me the Answer' is one of Paul's light-hearted excursions into the retro territory he clearly has great affection for, but his detractors always find irksome. In the context of The Beatles of course, songs like 'Your Mother Should Know' were deemed perfectly acceptable, but apparently not when McCartney indulged himself under his own name. Performing it in concert, he often dedicated the number to the doyen of 1930s movie musicals, Fred Astaire.

A fine piece of rock-solid storytelling, inspired by the Marvel Comics superheroes and villains, Paul voices the adventure of 'Magneto and Titanium Man' (and their sidekick, Crimson Dynamo) over some great instrumental and backing vocals. In many ways, the song is reminiscent of the classic 1950s narratives of songwriters Leiber and Stoller, on their hits by The Coasters (such as 'Riot in Cell Block #9' from 1954, when they were still called The Robins). And there's some great punctuating guitar from Jimmy McCulloch, too.

Paul has been quoted as naming 'Letting Go' as his favourite track on the album. A heavy number compared to much of his

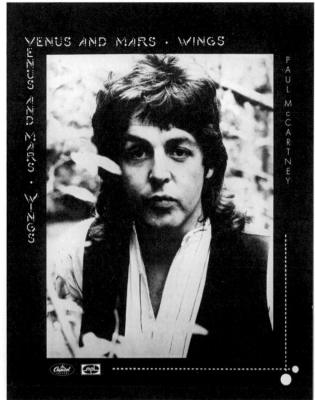

"We just wanted to record in America and find a musical city. There's not that many. Only New York, Nashville, and LA, and I'd never been to New Orleans, except on tour when we [The Beatles] never saw anything except the inside of a trailer. The only thing I remembered about New Orleans was the vibrator bed in the motel."

Paul McCartney

output at the time, with an insistent beat and a rich, overdubbed horn section, it closes the first vinyl side as an epic, dramatically voiced statement, both vocally and instrumentally. Which takes us to the reprised version of 'Venus and Mars', on which Paul's voice and the instrumental backing are given an ethereal feel with lots of echo and reverb, a space-age take on the main theme of the title track.

'Spirits of Ancient Egypt' is an oddity, sounding like it started as a conventional slice of McCartney up-tempo songwriting before being bathed in quasi-Oriental musical motifs. As in many of Paul's songs, the lyrics sound almost accidental, rhymes arrived at to fit the melody rather than the other way round. Nevertheless, it adheres to a formula that has produced a million classic songs since the dawn of pop music.

Along with both 'Love in Song' and 'Letting Go', 'Medicine Jar' was basically recorded at Abbey Road Studios in November 1974, prior to Paul and company recording in New Orleans in January

and February '75. A hard-riffing rocker, the song was written by Jimmy McCulloch and the British drummer and songwriter Colin Allen. With a scorching solo from McCulloch, the lead guitarist was also the principal vocalist on the track, with Paul, Linda, and Denny Laine all credited as contributing 'backing vocals'.

Paul was firmly in his Little Richard-inspired blues-shouting mode on 'Call Me Back Again'. With McCartney vamping six-to-the bar on the piano, the layers of brass (arranged by trombonist Tony Dorsey) fill out the bare bones of a simple blues-based rock ballad to a spectacular production number. Add to the mix some fine guitar from McCulloch, and you have one of the most satisfying rock 'n' roll tracks on the album.

Previous page McCartney in concert with Wings, at Hammersmith Odeon, London, September 18, 1975.

Above left The celebrated New Orleans pianist, songwriter, producer – and founder of Sea-Saint Studios – Allen Toussaint.

Above right A publicity poster, promoting *Venus and Mars* in May 1975.

'Listen to What the Man Said' was the hit track on *Venus and Mars*, preceding the release of the album by just 11 days and selling over a million copies in the US alone. And the penultimate track, 'Treat Her Gently – Lonely Old People', was in fact two sections of what was essentially the same number. It originated as a simple piano, bass, drums and guitar recording, before an extravagant string arrangement was overdubbed, played by a 23-piece orchestra. The opulent embellishments made the lyrics, touching on loneliness and old age, all the more poignant.

Why the group opted to end the album with a short instrumental cover of the theme from the UK soap opera *Crossroads* was a mystery to many. But this guitar-dominant version of the tune – written by songwriter Tony Hatch, famous for 'Downtown' among many other hits – *was* actually used occasionally at the close of the show, usually when there was some dramatic 'cliffhanger' ending.

The reaction to the album, though sometimes muted compared to the acclaim that had greeted *Band on the Run*, was generally favourable. Inevitably, some hard-bitten rock critics could see no good in it, like Charles Shaar Murray in the *New Musical Express* who, after extolling its predecessor, called it "a terrible album." But the public had the last say, and *Venus and Mars* followed *Band on the Run* to the top of the LP charts in the US, UK and at least five other countries, selling over four million copies worldwide.

Below Wings pictured together at Abbey Road Studios to record *Venus And Mars*, London, 15 November 1974. Left to right: Geoff Britton, Paul McCartney, Linda McCartney, Denny Laine and Jimmy McCulloch.

Opposite The acclaimed UK rock guitarist Dave Mason, one of the guest musicians on *Venus and Mars*.

LISTEN TO WHAT THE MAN SAID

RECORDED: JANUARY 16–FEBRUARY 24, 1975
STUDIO: SEA-SAINT STUDIOS, NEW ORLEANS
PRODUCERS: PAUL MCCARTNEY, LINDA MCCARTNEY
COMPOSERS: PAUL MCCARTNEY, LINDA MCCARTNEY
RELEASED: MAY 16, 1975 (SINGLE), MAY 27, 1975 (ALBUM)

The band were well into the sessions at Sea-Saint Studios when Paul decided to tackle 'Listen to What the Man Said'. He'd been keen on the song for some time, but never found the right inspiration to commit it to disc. And at first, things certainly didn't look they were getting anywhere. Despite some great vocal harmony and incisive rhythm section takes, the music wasn't quite gelling to his satisfaction, until he decided to bring in some extra instrumental voices. First of all, former Traffic guitarist Dave Mason was added to overdub guitar parts, but there was still something missing. McCartney was looking for a special sound for the solo break, and they hadn't found it. "We thought it would be great to have a very technical musician and do a great lyrical solo," he recalled. "Someone said 'Tom Scott [a jazz musician] lives near here.' We said, 'Yeah give him a ring, see if he turns up,' and he turned up within half an hour!" The result was the icing on the cake McCartney was searching for, with Scott's sensational first take on soprano sax being the one they settled on.

The song itself is a heartfelt celebration of love as a basic virtue in itself. Each verse is a little romantic vignette full of optimistic one-liners, as if pulled from a collection of Valentine cards. Released as a single just 11 days before *Venus and Mars*, the song met with almost universal acclaim, critics applauding it as pure pop music of the finest calibre. As *Rolling Stone* would later conclude, "It wasn't quite 'The Hustle', but 'Listen to What the Man Said' – with its silky, seductive groove spotlighting session pro Tom Scott's zesty sax – proved that McCartney would have no trouble fitting into the dawning disco age." With its insistent, catchy riff and slick harmonies punctuating the verses, the singalong ditty was an almost guaranteed hit. And you can hear the sound of a kiss, planted on a microphone by Linda, if you listen carefully. It quickly hit the #1 spot in the *Billboard* Hot 100, as well as topping the Canadian chart, and making the top 10 in Norway, New Zealand and the UK.

One sad postscript to the recording sessions at Sea-Saint Studios came in 2005 – by which time the studio had hosted numerous world-class acts including Paul Simon, Joe Cocker and Elvis Costello, as well as local heroes like Dr John and The Meters – when the whole complex was destroyed by Hurricane Katrina, as it rampaged through the Crescent City.

"My stuff is never 'a comment from within'. Basically, I'm saying, 'Listen to the basic rules, don't goof off too much.' But if you say 'The Man', it can mean God, it can mean 'women, listen to your man', it can mean so many things."

Paul McCartney

WINGS AT THE SPEED OF SOUND

LET 'EM IN

THE NOTE YOU NEVER WROTE

SHE'S MY BABY

BEWARE MY LOVE

WINO JUNKO
(JIMMY MCCULLOCH, COLIN ALLEN)

SILLY LOVE SONGS

COOK OF THE HOUSE

TIME TO HIDE
(DENNY LAINE)

MUST DO SOMETHING ABOUT IT

SAN FERRY ANNE

WARM AND BEAUTIFUL

(All songs written by Paul McCartney and Linda McCartney,
except where indicated)

Paul McCartney (vocals, bass, guitars, keyboards, double bass), Linda McCartney
(vocals, keyboards), Denny Laine (vocals, guitars, piano, harmonica), Jimmy
McCulloch (vocals, guitars), Joe English (drums, percussion), Tony Dorsey (trombone),
Thaddeus Richard (saxophone, flute), Steve Howard (trumpet, flugelhorn), Howie
Casey (saxophone), George Tidwell (trumpet), plus uncredited session musicians

WINGS AT THE SPEED OF SOUND

RECORDED: AUGUST–OCTOBER, 1975; JANUARY–FEBRUARY 1976 // **STUDIOS:** ABBEY ROAD STUDIOS, LONDON
PRODUCER: PAUL MCCARTNEY // RELEASED: MARCH 25, 1976

The fifth studio album by Wings, *Wings at the Speed of Sound* was recorded while the band was undertaking its hugely successful 'Wings Over the World' tour. Although the tour was a sell-out at every venue, there was a growing criticism among some McCartney-watchers that he was treating the band as just a backing outfit rather than an integrated group in its own right. Consequently, when they got into the studio during a break in the gruelling schedule on the road, the roster of tracks for the new collection included every band member taking the lead vocals on at least one song.

Sax player Howie Casey recalled how the sessions were typical of the working style at a McCartney recording: "You know Paul, bless him and all that, but he doesn't write [music], so for instance when we did *Speed of Sound*… (on *Band on the Run*, I don't think there were any charts, we just busked it, there was only 'Jet'… But on *Speed of Sound*, there were those like 'Silly Love Songs' and 'Let 'Em In', so what we did, there were charts. And they were for the live gigs… and they wanted us to dispense with them as soon as possible, so we weren't looking down at the music. So you learn them.

"When we got called in to do the *Speed of Sound* album, we just stood around the piano, and Paul would be at the piano and he'd say, "I'd like this" (singing the riff for 'Silly Love Songs') for instance. We [the horns] voiced it between ourselves, and the same with 'Let 'Em In', we voiced that ourselves. He said what he wanted, but we jotted it down for our own memory's sake, and then that was it. That was the way it worked.

"And it worked very well," Casey continued. "With Paul, he knew what he wanted; you were allowed a little leeway, you know, you'd say, 'How about if we did that there?', or sometimes I'd drop a little lick in, where there was a gap, and he'd say, 'Oh yeah, we'll keep that.' So it was like that, it was loose, but it was tight, it had to be tight, 'cos Paul wants things exact. And the other thing was solos… if you did a solo on an album, a top of the head thing, he'd want you to play that live, you had a little leeway but not a lot, you couldn't just go off on a tangent… and I suppose the punters are the same [imitating a fan], 'That's not like on the record.'"

The album opens with the welcoming sound of Paul's (actual) doorbell, inviting us to savour the delights to come. 'Let 'Em In' was a huge success, both as a feature on the American leg of the world tour that followed a month or so after the album's release, and later in the year when it was a chart hit as a stand-alone single.

A vehicle for Denny Laine as lead vocalist, 'The Note You Never Wrote' is a plaintive ballad written in 3/4 waltz time, with a delicate basic backing of piano and acoustic guitar. A subsequent overdubbing of an orchestral arrangement, by members of the Gabrieli String Quartet, serves to add to the melancholy feel of an emotionally stark song.

Originally written by Paul during the emotionally fraught period following the break-up of The Beatles, 'She's My Baby' consists of brief statements, snapshots of his ongoing daily life with Linda during a period when at times it might have seemed like it was a case of 'us against the world'. The result, nevertheless, as honed in the studio in early 1976, is a warm, lightly pitched celebration of domestic intimacy.

Paul and Linda shared the lead vocals on 'Beware My Love', a tough-sounding rocker that in its powerful dynamic sounds somewhat at odds with the feel of the album as a whole. Linda handles the deliberately understated intro and outro parts, with Paul singing the main body of the song with the thrusting urgency we associated with tracks like 'She's a Woman' a decade earlier. The track later appeared as the flip-side to the single release of 'Let 'Em In', in July 1976.

Written by Jimmy McCulloch and Colin Allen, who had been the co-writers of 'Medicine Jar' on the previous Wings album, 'Wino Junko' gives the vocal spot to McCulloch. An easy-going rock song that fitted into the typically laid-back ambience of the mid-1970s mainstream, the main highlight is McCulloch's well-rounded guitar solo that rides the number out.

The perfectly accomplished 'Silly Love Songs' opens the second vinyl side. With its smooth harmonies, slick horn parts and overall disco ambience, it was destined to top the charts effortlessly, when released as a single a week after the album.

With the sounds of food cookin' in the frying pan, Linda's vocal vehicle is another piece of McCartney domesticity, an upbeat

Previous page Paul during a 1977 interview in London.

Above Ticket stub for the "Wings Over America" concert, at New York's Madison Square Garden, May 24, 1976.

Right Nam Sound-check for "Wings in Concert" at the Empire Pool, Wembley, London; October 19, 1976.

jaunt with the horns busking merrily. Written on the Australian leg of the grand tour, Paul recounted how the song was born in the kitchen of their rented house in Adelaide: "They had these pots of sage and onions… all the condiments. I took everything I saw and tried to work it into a song. Every line in the song was actually in the kitchen."

'Time to Hide' was Denny Laine's major personal contribution, as both writer and lead singer. There's a bluesy feel to the track, some harmonica from Laine, and a solid bass line from Paul that carries it along faultlessly. As part of his ambition to democratize the share of vocals on the album, after the backing track to 'Must Do Something About It' had been recorded, with himself singing lead, Paul decided to instead hand Joe English the mike. A creditable performance, but it would be the only time the drummer took the front vocal spot on a Wings record.

On 'San Ferry Anne', Paul indulges his love for a lightly-sketched folksy ballad, here embellished with some ad-libbing from the horn section, which fades all too quickly. The album's closer, 'Warm and Beautiful', is a love song in a tradition by this time well established by McCartney, a heartfelt paean to Linda. An interesting instrumental voicing, arranged by the composer Fiachra Trench, was in the use of two tenor horns as well as the Maggini string quartet. Assessments of the song have been mixed over the years, but many would go on to agree with Elvis Costello's contention that 'Warm and Beautiful' was one of McCartney's finest love songs.

Critical reaction to the album was mixed. While Barbara Charone called it a "major disappointment" in *Sounds* magazine, *Melody Maker*'s Chris Welch concluded his review with: "Much good music then on an album that will engender fierce comparisons with the past two albums, but will undoubtedly increase the growing worldwide appeal of Wings." And once again, much of the press assessment of the album was contradicted by the public's support at the cash desks of record stores worldwide. *Wings at the Speed of Sound* reached the #1 spot in the *Billboard* chart, and #2 in the UK, as well as topping the charts in Canada and France.

"Family man? Most people are family people. That's not soft. Every man must have a home especially if you come from a big family like Paul's. There's nothing wrong with a family life."

Linda McCartney

LET 'EM IN

RECORDED: FEBRUARY 3, 1976
STUDIO: ABBEY ROAD STUDIOS, LONDON
PRODUCERS: PAUL MCCARTNEY, LINDA MCCARTNEY
COMPOSERS: PAUL MCCARTNEY, LINDA MCCARTNEY
RELEASED: MARCH 25 1976 (ALBUM), JULY 23, 1976 (SINGLE)

Although a master of the narrative ballad, Paul McCartney's best-known "story" songs have usually been strictly observational – the desolate 'Eleanor Rigby', the distraught mother in 'She's Leaving Home', the lonely office girl of 'Another Day'. Rarely did he venture into autobiographical territory – his cast of characters were typically third-person creations. With 'Let 'Em In', however, he describes a gathering of real-life heroes, friends and relatives, who've all come a-knocking at his door and ringing the bell.

The run-down of personalities range from close family members, such as his paternal aunt Gin and brother Michael. They also include the world famous – 'Martin Luther' references the civil rights leader Dr King, and 'Brother John', President John F. Kennedy (although an alternative interpretation claims it referred to John Lennon). Don and Phil, the Everly Brothers, are there, as is 'Uncle Ernie', a character played by Ringo Starr in the stage version of The Who's *Tommy* with the London Symphony Orchestra.

The track opens with the sound of a doorbell. It transpired that the eight-note Big Ben chimes (officially known as the Westminster Quarters or Westminster Chimes) were from an actual doorbell given to the McCartneys by drummer Joe English, as Paul explained in *Melody Maker*: "Well, as it happens, it is our actual doorbell which our drummer bought us, so it has a group significance. And it seemed a good introduction to the album." It was sound effects like that, and the opening and closing of a door, that helped earn the song a Grammy Award nomination for Best Arrangement of the Year.

With a gentle opening, the song builds up layer by layer, while retaining a laid-back aura until the ending, which turns out to be a false fadeout ending abruptly for the final two notes of the track. As well as the Wings line-up, a horn section consisting of sax players Howie Casey and Thaddeus Richard, Steve Howard on trumpet, and trombone man Tony Dorsey – the latter providing an emotive solo break – was also augmented by the sound of flutes and military drumming throughout.

'Let 'Em In' was the opening track of what became Paul's most successful chart album since his days with The Beatles. And when it was released as a single five months later, it reached #2 in the UK, #3 in the *Billboard* Hot 100, and #1 in the American *Cashbox* Top 100. It also earned a Gold Disc in America for sales of over a million copies.

Opposite above Wings on stage at Ahoy in Rotterdam, Netherlands, March 25, 1976. Left to right: Jimmy McCulloch, Denny Laine, Linda McCartney, Paul McCartney.

Opposite below Paul with his brother Mike, also known as 'Mike McGear' at the time, who he collaborated with on the 1974 album *McGear*, and name-checked on 'Let 'Em In'.

SILLY LOVE SONGS

RECORDED: JANUARY 16, 1976
STUDIO: ABBEY ROAD STUDIOS, LONDON
PRODUCER: PAUL MCCARTNEY
COMPOSERS: PAUL MCCARTNEY, LINDA MCCARTNEY
RELEASED: MARCH 25 1976 (ALBUM), APRIL 1, 1976 (SINGLE)

One of the main criticisms aimed at Paul McCartney during the early 1970s, in the wake of the break-up of The Beatles, was that he had become a purveyor of frothy love songs and little more. Tired of proving the opposite by example on numerous occasions, with 'Silly Love Songs' he went out on a limb in defence of the romantic pop number, which in fact was the mainstay of most popular songwriting of the 20th century. And as many fans were quick to glean, it could also be read as a direct response to comments made by John Lennon, to the effect that Paul's output now amounted to just lightweight pop ditties.

"Originally I wrote this song at about the time when the kind of material I did was a bit out of favour," he explained in 1984, "…and you had Alice Cooper doing 'No More Mr Nice Guy' and that kind of hard parody. I rather picked up a feeling in the air that ballads were being regarded as soppy and love songs as too sentimental. I thought – so what's wrong with silly love songs? I was striking a blow for nice sentimental love songs."

Recorded with Wings and the horn section that would accompany them on tour, the track exemplified a classic disco sound with its out-in-front bass and drums, embellished by swirling string effects, cool harmonies and soulful interjections from the horns. It caught the mood of the era perfectly, and on its release, first as an album track and a single just a week later, it almost instantly proved to be one of Paul's most successful songs. It spent five weeks in a row at the top of the *Billboard* Hot 100, and was the #1 pop song on the magazine's Year-End Chart for 1976, selling over a million copies in the US alone. It was released in the UK at the end of April, where it peaked at #2 in the singles chart.

And despite Paul not always being flavour of the month among the press reviewers, the song was generally well-received, with *Rolling Stone*'s Stephen Holden acknowledging it as "a clever retort whose point is well taken".

In retrospect, the song has been recognized as a classic example of McCartney's commercial songwriting. "Hate all you want. McCartney's fifth #1 (credited to Wings) is a solid piece of pop songcraft by a guy who knows a few things about the subject," was the verdict of *Ultimate Classic Rock* in 'Top 10 Paul McCartney Songs', published in 2013. And *Rolling Stone* concluded in 'Paul McCartney's Greatest Solo Songs': "After years of doing his best to ignore critics who saw him as a starry-eyed fool for love, McCartney struck back with this disco smash."

SEASIDE WOMAN [SINGLE]

(AS SUZY AND THE RED STRIPES)

RECORDED: NOVEMBER 27, 1972
STUDIO: AIR STUDIOS, LONDON
PRODUCER: PAUL MCCARTNEY
COMPOSER: LINDA MCCARTNEY
RELEASED: MAY 31, 1977 (US), AUGUST 10, 1979 (UK)

A heartfelt slice of reggae magic from Linda McCartney, which was born partly out of the pressures of litigation. There was a lawsuit in progress challenging Paul's naming of his wife on songwriting credits – specifically 'Another Day' – in order to transfer 50 per cent of the publishing royalties to his own McCartney Music company. The claim was based on the assertion that Linda was not an actual songwriter, and that her contribution was minimal. The family were on holiday in Jamaica in 1971 when she wrote the song, inspired by the reggae music all around, and spurred on by Paul, as she explained in 1974: "'Seaside Woman' is very reggae-inspired. That's when ATV was suing us saying I was incapable of songwriting, so Paul said, 'Get out and write a song.'"

With a similar feel to the 1972 Wings single 'C Moon', and recorded at the same November sessions that year, Linda's song evoked the sun-kissed spirit of Jamaica that the couple loved so much, and its ever-present music. "I was so in love with reggae music when I heard the Wailers that I wrote a reggae song," she would enthuse. The result was a glimpse of an uncomplicated life by the ocean, in a joyous mini-celebration of the island and its culture, in a series of simple images.

Wings had first performed the number during their UK University Tour in February 1972, and it was recorded in the November during the *Red Rose Speedway* sessions. With Linda singing lead, Paul on back-up vocals and the rest of Wings backing, Linda decided to release the song under a fictitious band name, Suzy and The Red Stripes. "When we were in Jamaica, there had been a fantastic version of 'Suzie Q', so they used to call me Suzy. And the beer in Jamaica is called Red Stripe, so that makes it Suzy and The Red Stripes."

It would be five years, in November 1977, before the recording was released in the United States, and a further two years before it appeared in the UK, with its Paul-and-Linda flipside (without Wings) 'B-Side to Seaside'. And both tracks appeared on the Linda McCartney posthumous album *Wide Prairie*, released in 1998.

Top Linda and Paul with Heather, Mary and Stella, about to board a flight at London's Heathrow airport around the time of the recording of 'Seaside Woman'.

Above Pioneering 1950s doo-wop vocal group The Penguins, who McCartney would cite as a key influence.

Opposite Paul and Linda attending the Knebworth Fair pop festival (as audience, not performers), August 21, 1976; The Rolling Stones headlined.

"We went in to do a B-side for it of something I'd written in Africa, some chords I wrote in Africa, and we just talked over it. It's very sort of 50s R&B, the Doves, the Penguins. I love that, that was my era. I'm New York, you know, Alan Freed and the whole bit."

Paul McCartney

MULL OF KINTYRE [SINGLE]

RECORDED: AUGUST 9, 1977
STUDIO: SPIRIT OF RANACHAN STUDIO,
CAMPBELTOWN, SCOTLAND
PRODUCER: PAUL MCCARTNEY
COMPOSERS: PAUL MCCARTNEY, DENNY LAINE
RELEASED: NOVEMBER 11, 1977

If one song typified Paul McCartney's populist instinct, often in the face of critical opprobrium, 'Mull of Kintyre' was that song. And on this occasion, as on many others, his instinct was right on the mark. The genesis of 'Mull of Kintyre' goes back as far as 1974, when it appeared in a home demo with Paul playing piano, with only the chorus more or less as it would end up in the finished song three years later.

The song's lyrics, a celebration of the natural beauty of the Kintyre peninsula where Paul had his High Park farm, were completed with Wings guitarist Denny Laine in 1976, the only successful collaboration between the two. "Paul and I were very into folk music… I was into bluegrass… I like Django Reinhardt. 'Mull of Kintyre' came about [when] we were in Scotland. I went round to Paul's one day and he had the chorus. That's the song, I think. The chorus. We were inspired by Scotland, so I helped with the lyrics." It was eventually recorded in August 1977,

during a break in the band's sessions for the album *London Town*, necessitated by Linda's advanced pregnancy.

The key factor in the final production, however, was Paul's decision to add the traditional sound of Scottish bagpipes. To that end he engaged 14 members – seven pipers and seven drummers – of the local Campbeltown Pipe Band, for what would be the record's atmospheric selling point. One of the young pipers – most of them were teenagers, still in school – recalled how after weeks of rehearsing, they went into McCartney's studio on his farm, to make the record. "It took an hour to record the song. We then had something to eat – sandwiches and beer for the boys – and we had a party. But we couldn't stay long because we had school in the morning…"

Much of the recording actually took place in the open air, with a mobile studio and the control room set up in one of the farm's outhouses. Paul's vocals and acoustic guitar were taped outside the barn, and some inevitable wind noise had to be shielded (in the absence of a proper filter) by someone's sock over the microphone! After overdubbing back at Abbey Road Studios, the track was ready to be pressed, but Paul still had some serious doubts about its suitability as a single. It was 1977, and punk had become dominant on the UK music scene, which was a far cry from the reflective lyrics and evocative bagpipes of 'Mull of Kintyre'.

A bagpipe-assisted pub singalong in praise of the gorgeous, remote part of western Scotland where McCartney's farm is located, Mull of Kintyre' is a footnote for most US fans. But it was an unstoppable phenomenon in Britain..."

Rolling Stone

Erring on the side of caution, Paul decided to release the song as a double-sided single with 'Girl's School'. He should have trusted his original instinct – purely on the strength of 'Mull of Kintyre', the single shot to the top of the UK charts after its November 11 release, just in time for the Christmas market. It stayed at #1 for the next nine weeks, selling two-and-a-half million copies before the end of January 1978.

Perhaps predictably – it was, after all, a very "British" anthem – the single only made it to #33 in the American chart, but sold over 10 million copies worldwide and went on to be the UK's best-selling single of all time. That achievement was previously held by The Beatles' 'She Loves You', released in 1963, and was only replaced in the record books by the Band Aid single 'Do They Know It's Christmas?' in 1984.

Paul has only played 'Mull of Kintyre' occasionally in live concerts over the years, and never in the US, the Far East or South America. It has appeared on playlists at performances in British Commonwealth countries including Canada, Australia and New Zealand, Wings' 1979 UK tour, and a few UK gigs since including Glasgow, Liverpool and London. Poignantly, the refrain of 'Mull of Kintyre' was played at the beginning of the London memorial service for Linda McCartney, in June 1998.

Top Denny, Linda and Paul strolling in the heather, during shooting of the promotional film for 'Mull of Kintyre'.

Above The Mull of Kintyre, and the Kintyre peninsula, Argyll and Bute, southwest Scotland.

Opposite Paul, Linda and Denny Laine backed by the Campbeltown Pipes Band on *The Mike Yarwood Christmas Special*, BBC TV, December 1977

LONDON
TOWN

LONDON TOWN
(PAUL MCCARTNEY, DENNY LAINE)

CAFÉ ON THE LEFT BANK

I'M CARRYING

BACKWARDS TRAVELLER

CUFF LINK

CHILDREN, CHILDREN
(PAUL MCCARTNEY, DENNY LAINE)

GIRLFRIEND

I'VE HAD ENOUGH

WITH A LITTLE LUCK

FAMOUS GROUPIES

DELIVER YOUR CHILDREN
(PAUL MCCARTNEY, DENNY LAINE)

NAME AND ADDRESS

DON'T LET IT BRING YOU DOWN
(PAUL MCCARTNEY, DENNY LAINE)

MORSE MOOSE AND GREY GOOSE
(PAUL MCCARTNEY, DENNY LAINE)

(All songs written by Paul McCartney, except where indicated)

Paul McCartney (vocals, guitars, bass, keyboards, drums, percussion, violin, flageolet, recorder), Linda McCartney (vocals, keyboards, percussion), Denny Laine (vocals, guitars, bass, flageolet, recorder, percussion), Jimmy McCulloch (guitars, percussion), Joe English (drums, percussion, harmonica)

LONDON TOWN

RECORDED: FEBRUARY 1977–JANUARY 1978 // **STUDIOS:** ABBEY ROAD STUDIOS, LONDON; RECORD PLANT MOBILE STUDIO ON *FAIR CAROL*, OFF WATERLEMON CAY, VIRGIN ISLANDS // **PRODUCER:** PAUL MCCARTNEY // **RELEASED:** MARCH 31, 1978

1977 looked like it would be a good year for Wings. *Wings at the Speed of Sound* had done well in the charts worldwide the previous year, and the Wings Over the World tour had been a triumph. Quite simply, the band were riding high, and things augured well for a new album. With that in mind, they began recording at Abbey Road Studios that February, the sessions running through until the end of March.

The plan was to break for another US tour, but that had to be put on hold when Linda found herself pregnant. So, with time unexpectedly on their hands, Paul decided to relocate the sessions to sunnier climes – namely, the Caribbean, where they rented some yachts off Waterlemon Cay in the Virgin Islands. As he later recalled in the McCartneys' in-house fanzine *Club Sandwich*: "We recorded *London Town* in the Caribbean, in the Virgin Islands. There was a little vogue going around – people still do it, they go

to Montserrat and places like that, which is nice work if you can get it. Some people called Record Plant in LA, got some equipment and put it on a boat in the Virgin Islands, so we recorded that whole album on a boat." The mobile studio was set up on one of the yachts, the *Fair Carol*, where they recorded the basic tracks for eight of the songs that would appear on *London Town*.

After the party returned to the UK at the end of May, the sessions were again deferred on account of Linda's pregnancy,

resuming in the autumn. In the meantime, both Joe English and Jimmy McCulloch had left the band, English because he wanted to spend more time at home in America, McCulloch because he joined a reformed version of the Small Faces. Soon after Linda gave birth to baby James in September, recording continued until the end of 1977, with just the basic trio of both McCartneys and Denny Laine (plus some unnamed session players on the final track, 'Girlfriend'). In all, the much-anticipated new album from Wings had taken nearly a year to complete.

As the opener and title track, 'London Town' sets a restrained mood for what is to come. Another 'travelogue' song follows, snapshots of Paris centred on the 'Café on the Left Bank'. It was the first recording made on the yacht in the Virgin Islands, and at the overdub sessions at Abbey Road Studios, Paul decked the studio in striped café umbrellas and such, to give a *rive gauche* ambience to proceedings.

'I'm Carrying', a gentle romantic song that some might feel verges on the sentimental, has Paul's voice set against only a light acoustic guitar, some synthesized effects, and overdubbed strings. Acting as an unfortunately too-brief bridge, the energetic 'Backwards Traveller', a potentially strong rock number, takes the listener into the instrumental 'Cuff Link' – a less-than-inspiring venture into synth-based electronic sounds, which was clearly part of a longer jam between Paul, Denny and Linda.

'Children, Children' is a post-hippy 'fairy tale' folk song from the pens of Paul and Denny Laine. With the instrumental support including flute, violin and autoharp, it's a trip into the ethereal world of child-like make-believe championed a few years earlier by the likes of Donovan and the Incredible String Band.

A light, poppy song that Paul delivers with an infectious falsetto that sounds tailor-made for Michael Jackson's style of high-pitched delivery, which it was – Jackson covered it on his album, *Off the Wall,* a couple of years later. The next track, 'I've Had Enough' shows the complete contrast in vocal style that Paul has always been capable of, on a tough rocker that confirms that his reputation for hard-bitten rock 'n' roll is second to none.

When it was released as a single 10 days before the album, 'With a Little Luck' was a soft-rock smash in the States, his seventh #1 on the charts (and #5 in the UK), aided no doubt by lots of AOR radio play. 'Famous Groupies' has Paul in exclamatory mode, his voice distorted in "character" style while he recounts a saga of the groupies who were a celebrated (and sometimes notorious) part of the 1960s rock scene.

A driving ballad, with powerful Spanish guitar breaks and a rolling, infectious rhythm, 'Deliver Your Children' is the second track sung by Denny Laine, and co-written with McCartney – a dramatic narrative of goodies, baddies and desperate choices, through the prism of protecting the innocence of children. Slapped-bass rockabilly has Paul in early Elvis mode in 'Name

Previous page Paul, Linda and Denny promoting *London Town*.
Above Paul and Linda on the *London Town* Thames river cruise, March 22, 1978.
Opposite Wings in 1979, including guitarist Laurence Juber (bottom left) and drummer Steve Holley (bottom right).

and Address', coming over as something akin to the British rock revival specialists, Shakin' Stevens et al, who were rampant on the UK scene in the late 1970s. One writer has suggested that its inclusion was probably influenced by the death of Elvis Presley, in August 1977.

A light waltz-time folk indulgence, with Paul and Denny on Irish tin whistles to give it an essential Gaelic flavour, 'Don't Let It Bring You Down' is as relaxed as anything on the album. The laid-back atmosphere reflects the easy-going stance in the lyrics, exuding hope in the most negative of circumstances. The album rides out with some more McCartney experimentation, this time a folk-inclined saga of disaster at sea that's punctuated throughout with an electronic evocation of the Morse code rhythms of the title, developing a frightening traction as a marine catastrophe looms.

London Town was generally greeted enthusiastically, marking as it did a move by Paul into slicker, soft-rock territory, with synth-orchestral parts aplenty giving a glossy overall feel to the production. As one retrospective review described it: "A distinctly European flavour, a feeling that intensifies when the lyrics are taken into the equation... a different flavour than almost any other record in his catalogue." And the album did well, making the top five in more than a dozen album charts worldwide – including #2 and #4 in the US and UK respectively.

LONDON TOWN [SONG]

RECORDED: FEBRUARY 7–MARCH 31, 1977
STUDIO: ABBEY ROAD STUDIOS, LONDON
PRODUCER: PAUL MCCARTNEY
COMPOSERS: PAUL MCCARTNEY, DENNY LAINE
RELEASED: MARCH 31, 1978

A somewhat retrospective opener for the *London Town* album, released by Wings in March 1978. Paul, Linda and Denny Laine created the first musical sketches for the song in 1975 in Perth, Australia, during the 'Wings Over the World' tour, and the composition was completed later by McCartney and Laine, in Scotland. "Linda and I were sitting in the hotel in Perth, which is a big Sheraton hotel," he told Paul Gambaccini on BBC radio, "…and we came up with the opening lyrics. I hung around for a little while, I just had that first bit. Then I got together with Denny in summer 1976 in Scotland. We sat up [late], we finished it all and arranged it up a little bit."

One of the first songs to be recorded for the album, it featured Jimmy McCulloch on guitar and drummer Joe English, before both left the band.

Set against the lonely landscape of a *'purple afternoon'*, it's a bleak evocation of McCartney's "lonely people", including a street musician, the out-of-work actor, even a policeman ("rozzer"), all with their own brand of isolation. With a melodic structure not dissimilar to Paul's 'Fool of the Hill', recorded by The Beatles in 1967, the song was met with praise by many reviewers, who welcomed it as an expressive piece that skilfully conjured up the personal solitude that's all-too-possible in a metropolis such as London. In its 'Top Single Picks', *Billboard* described it as "a melodic, atmosphere ballad about the city of London," adding "…as usual Paul McCartney's voice is standout."

As the third single taken from *London Town*, the title track failed to make much of an impression, just scraping into the top 40 in America at #39, and a mediocre #60 in the UK.

Below Paul with Melvyn Bragg at the recording of *The South Bank Show*, 1978.

Opposite Linda and Paul as proud parents of new-born James Louis McCartney, September 12, 1977.

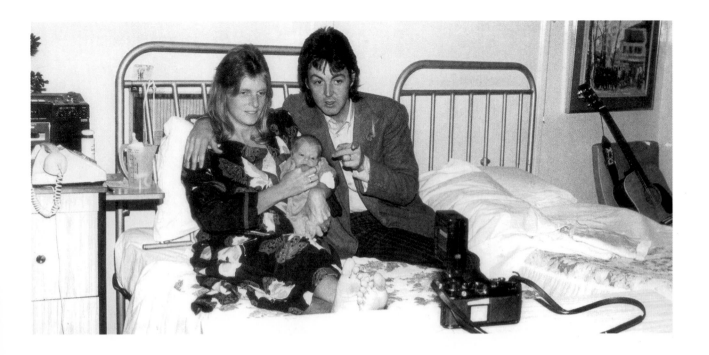

GOODNIGHT TONIGHT [SINGLE]

RECORDED: FEBRUARY 6, 1978; JANUARY 23–FEBRUARY 9, 1979
STUDIO: RUDE STUDIOS, CAMPBELTOWN, SCOTLAND; REPLICA STUDIO, LONDON
PRODUCER: PAUL MCCARTNEY
COMPOSER: PAUL MCCARTNEY
RELEASED: MARCH 23, 1979

'Goodnight Tonight' was one of Paul McCartney's most successful hits of the disco era. Yet the recording, with its infectious beat, upfront dancefloor-perfect bass line and flamenco-flavoured guitar breaks, almost didn't see the light of day. "I'm making records, I'm not running a record store," was his alleged reaction when his new label Columbia proposed putting the song on his forthcoming *Back to the Egg*, as he didn't think it fitted with the overall feel of the album.

The origins of the song actually dated back to the last of the *London Town* sessions in early 1978. It was the height of the disco boom, and Paul had been at a club. Inspired by the dance sounds that night, he laid down an instrumental track, building up the tempo by using a drum machine. A year later, when Wings were looking for a single to promote their new album, *Back to the Egg*, he pulled it out and began embellishing it with the full Wings sound. In Paul's London studio, beneath his offices in Soho Square, Denny Laine and Laurence Juber added electric guitars, and Steve Holley percussion. He said, "I had just spent some time

in Morocco and brought some clay hand drums back with me. I added those to Paul's drum track and drum machine percussion. I believe we all sang the chorus as well."

At one stage, the track was nearly aborted. "We scrapped the whole thing," Paul recalled. "A week later, I played the record again and thought, 'That's crazy.'" So the band finished perfecting what would be one of McCartney's biggest hits. Released as a single, the seven-minute track was edited down to four, with the full version being made available as a 12-inch. And, in keeping with Paul's imaginative work on his music videos, the promotional film featured the band as a 1930s-style dance outfit, complete with bow ties, tuxedos and slicked-back hair.

The lyrics were simplicity itself, tailored to the sensibilities of the dance audience it was clearly aimed at. With that in mind, although Columbia still wanted the track on *Back to the Egg* as intended, Paul was having none of it. It went out as a single in its own right, despite some heated resistance from the record executives.

The record was a big hit worldwide, making the top 10 sales charts in more than half a dozen countries, and hitting the #5 spot in both the UK and US. It did appear on later McCartney compilation albums, *All the Best* in 1987, *Wingspan: Hits and History* (2001) and *Pure McCartney* in 2016. And in 2007, the seven-minute version was included as a bonus track on the iTunes digital release of *Back to the Egg*.

"That was all based round some rhythm. I do like dance records: when you listen to records, you're often down a club and want to dance with someone – I like dancin', actually!"

Paul McCartney

BACK TO THE EGG

RECEPTION

GETTING CLOSER

WE'RE OPEN TONIGHT

SPIN IT ON

AGAIN AND AGAIN AND AGAIN
(DENNY LAINE)

OLD SIAM, SIR

ARROW THROUGH ME

ROCKESTRA THEME

TO YOU

AFTER THE BALL / MILLION MILES

WINTER ROSE / LOVE AWAKE

THE BROADCAST

SO GLAD TO SEE YOU HERE

BABY'S REQUEST

(All songs written by Paul McCartney, except where indicated)

Paul McCartney (vocals, bass, guitars, keyboards, concertina, piano, harpsichord),
Linda McCartney (keyboards, vocals), Denny Laine (vocals, guitars), Laurence Juber
(guitars, synthesizer, bass), Steve Holley (drums, percussion), Howie Casey (sax),
Tony Dorsey (trombone), Steve Howard (trumpet) Thaddeus Richard (sax)
Black Dyke Mills Band (horns, 'Love Awake')

plus with 'Rockestra' ('Rockestra Theme' and 'So Glad You're Here'): David Gilmour,
Hank Marvin, Pete Townshend (guitars), John Bonham, Kenney Jones (drums), John Paul Jones,
Ronnie Lane, Bruce Thomas (basses), Gary Brooker, John Paul Jones (pianos), Tony Ashton
(keyboards), Speedy Acquaye, Tony Carr, Ray Cooper, Morris Pert (percussion)

BACK TO THE EGG

RECORDED: JUNE 29, 1978–FEBRUARY, 1979 // **STUDIOS:** SPIRIT OF RANACHAN, CAMPBELTOWN, SCOTLAND; LYMPNE CASTLE, KENT; ABBEY ROAD STUDIOS, LONDON; REPLICA STUDIO, LONDON // **PRODUCERS:** PAUL MCCARTNEY, CHRIS THOMAS // **RELEASED:** JUNE 8, 1979

The final album by Wings, *Back to the Egg* introduced two new members of the band, guitarist Laurence Juber, who was already a respected name on the London session scene, and drummer Steve Holley. Howie Casey, who played on the album with the touring Wings band, had sensed things weren't OK with Jimmy McCulloch. "I don't know why Jimmy McCulloch left, he threw a wobbly I think. He wanted to do his own thing, and the same with Joe English. I was talking to Jimmy in America about it, I said, 'You know, there are gaps between the tours, and recording, you can go and do your own thing then. Nobody's stopping you.' But he got this bee in his bonnet..."

For the project, Paul also brought in Chris Thomas as co-producer. Thomas had already worked with McCartney on The Beatles' 'White' album in 1968, as an assistant producer to George Martin. Now he brought a contemporary edge to the Wings project, reflecting his more recent background in punk and new wave, including records by The Sex Pistols and The Pretenders.

As was by now something of a pattern during the summer months, in 1978 Paul hunkered down in his Scottish retreat to work on new material, laying down basic tracks with Wings for what would be their next album. During June and July the band completed taping six songs that were destined for *Back to the Egg*, at the Spirit of Ranachan Studio, which McCartney had established adjacent to his farm estate outside Campbeltown.

Most of the remaining tracks for the album, however, were recorded after the band had changed location to the medieval environment of Lympne Castle in Kent (not far from Paul's other rural address near Rye), on the south-east coast of England. There, with the back-up of the RAK Mobile Studio, they taped another half dozen items through the month of September.

The album opens with 'Reception', a minute-long collage of bass-backed sound effects imitating the tuning of a radio, which many listeners simply found bewildering. It serves as a link to 'Getting Closer', a driving, powerful number that became the most successful of three singles released from the album, though hardly what used to be called a smash hit.

The delicate acoustic guitar backing on 'We're Open Tonight', courtesy of Laurence Juber, belies the suggestive nature of Paul's lyrics, referencing an invitation to a brothel. Talking to *Goldmine* magazine in 2001, Juber explained that the "natural echo" of a spiral staircase in the castle was perfect for the effect he wanted. Nearer to the raw punk that Paul was obviously aware of at the time, "Spin It On" is a hectic rocker with the

simple structure and frenetic drumming that characterized much of the late-1970s New Wave.

Another nod in the direction of the new blood emerging on the music scene, the Denny Laine composition 'Again and Again and Again' has echoes of groups such as The Stranglers and The Clash – bands who, although promoted as punks, displayed an accomplished style lacking in the back-to-basics musical shortcomings of the likes of the Sex Pistols.

Paul decided to put out 'Old Siam, Sir' as the lead single to promote *Back to the Egg* in the UK, a week before the album's release. Coming out of a jam, based on a keyboard riff by Linda, its composition was the result of a joint effort by all, with a middle eight by Steve Holley and final touches by Denny and Paul. Despite this, the credit line was just 'McCartney'. In any case, the single failed to live up to expectations, hitting just #35 in the UK chart.

A throbbing synthesizer riff is the bedrock for 'Arrow Through Me', a fine up-tempo ballad reminiscent of Stevie Wonder's best of the period – right down to some incisively clipped horn parts from the on-stage team of Casey, Richard, Howard and Dorsey. That closed the first side of the vinyl original, with the flip heralded by the rousing 'Rockestra Theme'. A total indulgence on Paul's part, but one that came off magnificently, the conceit of 'Rockestra' was putting together a marathon supergroup. The resulting ensemble was certainly impressive, including The Shadows' Hank Marvin and The Who's Pete Townshend on guitar, and no fewer than two members of Led Zeppelin – bassist John Paul Jones and drummer John Bonham. The track went on to be cited the Best Instrumental Track of the Year 1979 at the subsequent Grammy Awards.

The first track to be recorded at the *Back to the Egg* sessions, on June 29, 1978, at the Ranachan Studio in Scotland, 'To You' is one of the strongest songs on the album. With a caustic lyric regarding an unfaithful lover, Paul's delivery is as tough, expansive

Previous page Paul in the recording studio, June 12, 1979, straight after the release of *Back to the Egg*.

Above Paul and Linda prior to Wings playing in Liverpool, November 23, 1979.
Left Paul promoting *Back to the Egg* in June 1979.

and dramatic as it ever has been. 'After the Ball', by contrast, has a soulful McCartney singing a traditional-sounding pop song, along the lines of dramatic ballads of yesteryear. The evocative melody (played in a seductive ¾ time), like all great pop, sounds like it has always been there, before it segues into the equally magnificent 'Million Miles', with just Paul's lone voice graced by his self-accompanying concertina.

Another medley follows, with the peaceful snowscape of 'Winter Rose' sketched delicately by acoustic guitar, piano and harpsichord, before the more fulsome textures of 'Love Awake' take its place.

'The Broadcast' links us to the opening track, inasmuch as it conjures up the illusion of a radio broadcast. This time, it's a reading of two pieces of drama – from plays by Ian Hay and John Galsworthy respectively – delivered by the owner of Lympne Castle where the track was recorded, with Paul providing atmospheric piano, Mellotron and guitar backing. Many felt this was a piece of McCartney eccentricity. On the penultimate track, we're treated to another roaring slice of the Rockestra in full flight with 'So Glad to See You Here', before the closer, 'Baby's Request'. This was initially written by Paul for the veteran vocal group The Mills Brothers, after he'd heard them at a concert in the south of France, and it concludes the album in the casual lounge-jazz style of a by-gone musical era.

As the final studio album produced with Wings, *Back to the Egg* was a disappointment commercially, "only" reaching the lower half of the Top 10 in both the UK and USA – but selling a million or so copies (in America alone) in the process. In retrospect, history has dealt it a more reasonable judgement than critics at the time. As one online reviewer concluded in 2015, "It's too bad *Back to the Egg* marked the end of Paul McCartney and Wings. Awash with keen ideas, vital energy and songs that clicked, it appeared as if there was a sense of rejuvenation going on. But it was not to be…"

GETTING CLOSER

RECORDED: OCTOBER 10, 1978
STUDIO: ABBEY ROAD STUDIOS, LONDON
PRODUCERS: PAUL MCCARTNEY, CHRIS THOMAS
COMPOSER: PAUL MCCARTNEY
RELEASED: JUNE 5, 1979 (US), AUGUST 16, 1979 (UK)

Released in America as a lead-on to *Back to the Egg*, and the first single extracted from the album, 'Getting Closer' had gestated from a series of demos recorded by Paul back in the earlier years of the decade. It was originally delivered at a slower tempo, before developing into the frantic rock number that appeared as the first actual song (as opposed to the experimental collage 'Reception') on the collection.

From its explosive opening, we know it's going to be a classic piece of McCartney power pop. The finely orchestrated instrumental layers are supported by an insistent riff of guitar and Mellotron, while the flawless vocals – which originally appeared on demos as a duet with Denny Laine – are carefully crafted to the point of technical perfection. And with Chris Thomas sharing the production responsibilities with Paul, the influence of punk and New Wave music was very apparent, as it was through most of the album.

Most reviewers welcomed 'Getting Closer'. Mitchell Cohen in *Creem* magazine enthused, while reviewing the album as a whole: "There is some dandy material on side one (designated as "sunny side up"), especially the jaunty new 45 'Getting Closer'." Nevertheless, the single didn't live up to the expectations of either Macca or the new American label bosses at Columbia. Backed with 'Spin It On' in the US, 'Getting Closer' reached #20 in both the Billboard and Cashbox charts. In the UK it fared even worse. Following 'Old Siam, Sir' (which reached #35) as the second single from the album, it wasn't released until the August as a double A-side with 'Baby's Request'. It only made it to the #60 spot.

WONDERFUL CHRISTMASTIME [SINGLE]

RECORDED: JUNE–JULY, 1979
STUDIO: HOME STUDIO, PEASMARSH, EAST SUSSEX;
SPIRIT OF RANACHAN, CAMPBELTOWN, SCOTLAND
PRODUCER: PAUL MCCARTNEY
COMPOSER: PAUL MCCARTNEY,
RELEASED: NOVEMBER 16, 1979

One of several songs by McCartney that have provoked particularly strong reactions, both for and against ('Mull of Kintyre' and 1984's 'We All Stand Together', both UK hits, immediately spring to mind), 'Wonderful Christmastime' is as familiar to the general public as anything he has ever recorded.

Recorded completely solo during the session that made up his next album, *McCartney II*, the idea of a Christmas record for Paul was not unprecedented. But whereas The Beatles had produced quirky, jokey 'special editions' on an annual basis, intended solely for their fan club members and distributed accordingly, Paul decided on a straightforward Christmas song aimed at the mainstream commercial marketplace.

He recorded the basic instrumental backing track at his home studio in Sussex, then added vocals at his Spirit of Ranachan set-up in Scotland. The layers of instruments included guitar, synthesizers, tambourines and sleigh bells, with a solo halfway produced on a Mellotron that sounds somewhere between a sax and guitar.

The single was credited just to Paul McCartney, with a cover illustration of him in a Santa Claus outfit, referencing the iconic image of Bing Crosby from his album *Merry Christmas*. And although the other members of Wings didn't contribute a note to the recording, the promotional video featured the band as if playing the number, including film of them at the Hippodrome Theatre, Eastbourne, where they were rehearsing for their upcoming UK tour.

With scant support from the music press, the single didn't make the impact that Christmas that Paul and the record company probably hoped for. While in the UK it did reasonably well, peaking at #6 in the charts, it failed miserably in the United States, where it made just #83 in *Cash Box* while not even making the Hot 100 in *Billboard*.

Over the years, however, the song has proved a huge seasonal success, featuring on festive radio playlists and in-store Yuletide background music with seemingly unstoppable regularity. In 2010, Paul's earnings from the song, including cover versions, were estimated at £300,000 (about $400,000) a year, which would make his accumulated income from the song about £14.5 million (about $20 million) to date. Not bad for a song which a *Rolling Stone* writer described as, "A holiday song that would barely pass muster as an advertising jingle."

Below Wings 1979, (left to right) Denny Laine, Steve Holley, Laurence Juber, Linda and Paul.
Opposite Paul in full flight at a Wings gig, 1979.

MCCARTNEY

II

COMING UP
TEMPORARY SECRETARY
ON THE WAY
WATERFALLS
NOBODY KNOWS
FRONT PARLOUR
SUMMER'S DAY SONG
FROZEN JAP
BOGEY MUSIC
DARKROOM
ONE OF THESE DAYS

(All songs written by Paul McCartney)

Paul McCartney (vocals, guitars, bass, piano, electric piano, synthesizer,
keyboards, drums, sequencer, percussion), Linda McCartney (vocals)

MCCARTNEY II

RECORDED: JUNE–JULY 1979 // **STUDIOS:** HOME STUDIO, PEASMARSH, EAST SUSSEX; SPIRIT OF RANACHAN, CAMPBELTOWN, SCOTLAND
PRODUCER: PAUL MCCARTNEY // **RELEASED:** MAY 16, 1980

During the early summer months of 1979, McCartney retreated once again to his farm in Scotland, to indulge in some creative home taping. *Back to the Egg*, which transpired to be Wings' final album, had just come out to a mixed reception. But seemingly unfazed by bad press notices, Paul forged ahead in his home studios in Campbeltown and Peasmarsh, Sussex, literally "doing his own thing".

Initially he was spending his time just experimenting with synthesizers and other electronic devices, with no intention of his doodlings going any further. Gradually, something approaching songs emerged, almost by accident in most instances. "I wasn't trying to do an album," he recalled. "It was just for my own satisfaction." Often a song would develop from just a drum track – or an electronic "rhythm box" – with Paul overdubbing instruments one by one.

Eventually, over six or seven weeks through June and July, he had recorded 19 songs in this way, tracks that he now felt were good enough to develop into material for an album. So, *McCartney II* was created, with basically the same DIY approach as its predecessor, *McCartney,* a decade earlier.

The lead track to the album, 'Coming Up', was released in April 1980. A huge hit on either side of the Atlantic and around the

world, it was a perfect, contemporary opener for the collection. 'Temporary Secretary', which follows, is a synth-dominated free-form piece which, when released as a 12-inch single, made no impression on the charts. Paul said he treated it as purely experimental – when the track ended up in *Rolling Stone*'s list of his '40 Greatest Solo Songs' in 2020, and something of a cult classic, he was probably as surprised as anyone.

It was after seeing a TV blues documentary, *The Devil's Music*, that Paul was inspired to add some vocals to some instrumental busking he'd had on tape for a while. The resultant 'On the Way' is a rare excursion on his part into pure blues territory. And the only song on the album that McCartney had already written before his *McCartney II* sessions, 'Waterfalls' would become a minor classic.

Proving that electronic experiments aren't always ventures in the outer reaches of the avant garde, 'Nobody Knows' is at

heart a basic rock 'n' roll number, albeit raggedy in structure and delivery. In total contrast, 'Front Parlour' was the first of the home recordings that would end up on the album, a somewhat repetitive instrumental that at three-and-a-half minutes could have been edited to advantage. Likewise, 'Summer's Day Song' was also intended to be an instrumental track, a laid-back synth and Mellotron ballad that had some stunning harmony vocals added at the later mixing stages in October, at Paul's Replica Studio under his offices in London's Soho Square.

On another instrumental, 'Frozen Jap' has Paul on some upfront drumming and a faux-Japanese melody. Like much of the synthpop of the album, he later acknowledged that his electronic experimentation was influenced by composers such as John Cage, Cornelius Cardew and, on the fringes of the new wave rock scene, Talking Heads' David Byrne. Again, the focus is adjusted with 'Bogey Music', a distortion-laden version of good-time boogie music, inspired by the Raymond Briggs childrens' book *Fungus the Bogeyman*, published a couple of years earlier.

The lyrics of the penultimate track 'Darkroom', like 'Temporary Secretary' early on in the album, have a slightly sinister, sexual ambiguity that Paul was well aware of, describing it as having a 'double meaning'.

But far more straightforward was the message in the closing song, 'One of These Days', worthy of comparison as one of the great McCartney ballads, voiced with a simple acoustic guitar. Paul described how the song came about after he had been talking to a member of the Hare Krishna sect, giving him pause for reflection. "The song seemed right as a very simple thing and it basically just says, 'One of these days I'll do what I've been meaning to do the rest of my life.' I think it's something a lot of people can identify with."

The album was greeted with derision by many reviewers, though none as drastic as Stephen Holden in *Rolling Stone*, who described it as "an album of aural doodles designed for the amusement of very young children." But given the relatively inaccessible nature of some of Paul's musical approaches, the album fared very well sales-wise – probably a lot better than many in the music press anticipated. It topped the LP chart in the UK, made #3 in the US, and did well worldwide. Over the years, since its 1980 release, it has been named as an influence on bands as diverse as Kraftwerk, The Pet Shop Boys, and Japan's Yellow Magic Orchestra.

And it's worth remembering, as a footnote to the *McCartney II* sessions in June and July 1979, that it was during those home studio tapings that Paul also produced 'Wonderful Christmastime', one of the Christmas record favourites around the world. Nothing could be further from the generally esoteric experiments of the album. Significantly, those same critics who derided *McCartney II* for being too obscure, "to clever by half", were by and large the ones who scorned 'Christmastime' for its accurate connectivity to the popular zeitgeist.

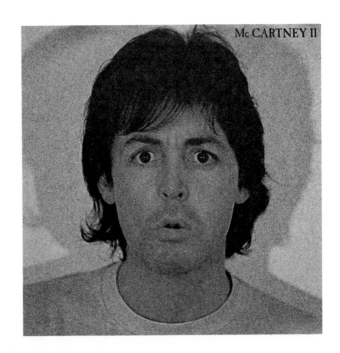

COMING UP

RECORDED: JUNE–JULY, 1979
STUDIO: HOME STUDIO, PEASMARSH, EAST SUSSEX; SPIRIT OF RANACHAN, CAMPBELTOWN, SCOTLAND
PRODUCER: PAUL MCCARTNEY
COMPOSER: PAUL MCCARTNEY,
RELEASED: APRIL 11, 1980 (SINGLE), MAY 16, 1980 (ALBUM)

The personnel line-up for 'Coming Up' says it all: "Paul McCartney – vocals, backing vocals, bass, electric guitars, electric piano, synthesizer, Mellotron, drums, percussion, tambourine", with the addition of Linda on backing vocals. The opening track on *McCartney II*, like the rest of the album – and its 1970 predecessor *McCartney* – was a totally solo effort, apart from Linda's vocal contributions.

It was recorded with the rest of the album in the summer of 1979, not long after Paul had disbanded the latest (and final) version of Wings, which bowed out after the release of their album, *Back to the Egg*. He was at his farm in Scotland when he started work on the song, and like other tracks on the album it took full advantage of current technology, with a synthesized sound that allowed him (among other tricks) to vary the pitch of the vocals.

"I went into the studio each day and just started with a drum track. Then I built it up bit by bit without any idea of how the song was going to turn out," he explained in *Rolling Stone*. "I was working with a vari-speed machine with which you can speed up

Previous page Paul at the Abbey Road Studios promoting *McCartney II* in 1980.

Above Front cover for *McCartney II*. The photograph, by Linda McCartney, has often been likened to a police mugshot.

Opposite The inside gatefold sleeve for *McCartney II*.

your voice. It's been speeded up slightly and put through an echo machine I was playing around with."

The song was a piece of perfectly crafted, disco-pitched contemporary pop. The slick, artificial feel to the voice matched the energetic backing perfectly, with tight horn parts (also a synthesized confection) interjecting seamlessly. The lyrics, though sounding lightweight in the context of the upbeat melody, nevertheless carried an optimistic message, opening up from the personal to the universal.

Key to the single's success was the accompanying promotional video, in which Paul played 10 different members of a fictional band, The Plastic Macs (referencing John Lennon's Plastic Ono Band, as McCartney readily admitted). Linda was also on hand to play the male and female members of a back-up vocal duo. Some of the characters were impersonations of real-life musicians, including guitarist Hank Marvin from the Shadows, keyboard player Ron Mael of Sparks, and a drummer thought to be based on the late John Bonham of Led Zeppelin.

When it was released as a single in April 1980, as a trailer for *McCartney II*, 'Coming Up' shot to #2 in the UK charts. For the American market, Columbia Records (against McCartney's better judgment) released a live version, recorded in Glasgow, Scotland, in December 1979. That version, complete with the Wings touring horn section, was released as the B-side of the single. In America, it was the live side that was promoted – the company felt the public would want to hear Paul's "real" voice – and subsequently went to #1, followed by the studio version, which also topped the chart. It was the only time two versions of the same song have followed each other to the *Billboard* top spot.

Above Paul as one of the fictional band members featured in the promo video for 'Coming Up'.

Opposite left Paul on *The Tomorrow Show*, US, 1979.

Opposite below Paul giving his trademark thumbs-up to the press at his farmhouse near Rye, East Sussex in 1980.

WATERFALLS

RECORDED: JUNE–JULY, 1979
STUDIO: HOME STUDIO, PEASMARSH, EAST SUSSEX;
SPIRIT OF RANACHAN, CAMPBELTOWN, SCOTLAND
PRODUCER: PAUL MCCARTNEY
COMPOSER: PAUL MCCARTNEY,
RELEASED: MAY 16, 1980 (ALBUM), JUNE 13, 1980 (SINGLE)

A genuinely minimalist performance that proves that less can indeed be more, 'Waterfalls' is McCartney at his romantic best. Recorded solo on electric piano, synthesizer and with an acoustic guitar break, Paul had already written the number when he 'got a bit bored' in the middle of recording *McCartney II*. "I decided to do a song that was already written, a track left over from the last Wings album, and that was my favourite at the time. That's why it's included."

The title itself comes from the Waterfalls Estate, where Paul has a house near Rye, East Sussex, but is used as one of a series of metaphors against taking too many risks in life – especially where matters of the heart are concerned. As he would later explain, the lyrics described a caution that was born out of experience. "'Waterfalls' is basically saying, 'Don't go doing a load of dangerous stuff, 'cause I need you.' And that's a kind of a more mature thought for me than I would have been able to have 20 years ago, 'cause I just didn't realize that it's not all gonna be here for ever. That's the kind of thing you realize when you pass 30."

Like much of *McCartney II*, the magic of 'Waterfalls' is in the sparseness of the instrumentation, starkly clean arrangements unhindered by any of the orchestral embellishments that could always be a temptation, given the technology at hand.

When released as a single, the song was greeted enthusiastically by many reviewers, with *Billboard* enthusing: "McCartney's second single from his latest runaway LP places his inimitable, creamy vocals in the center stage. There's a subtle oriental flavour sprinkled throughout this ballad." In the United States, however, the single simply bombed, not even making it into the *Billboard* Hot 100. But it did manage to fare much better in Britain, where it made it to #9 in the singles chart, despite reservations of writers like *Sounds*' Phil Sutcliffe: "Overall the thing is ridiculously attractive, charming… I'd say beautiful, if it wasn't so insubstantial."

"I got into all sorts of tricks, and I can't remember how I did half of them, because I was just throwing them all in and anything that sounded good, I kept. And anything I didn't like I just wiped."

Paul McCartney

T U G

O F   W A R

TUG OF WAR
TAKE IT AWAY
SOMEBODY WHO CARES
WHAT'S THAT YOU'RE DOING?
(PAUL MCCARTNEY, STEVIE WONDER)
HERE TODAY
BALLROOM DANCING
THE POUND IS SINKING
WANDERLUST
GET IT
BE WHAT YOU SEE
DRESS ME UP AS A ROBBER
EBONY AND IVORY

(All songs written by Paul McCartney, except where indicated)

Paul McCartney (vocals, guitars, bass, piano, drums, synthesizer, percussion, vocoder),
Linda McCartney (vocals), Denny Laine (guitars, synthesizer, bass), Eric Stewart (guitar,
vocals), Ringo Starr (drums), Steve Gadd (drums, percussion), George Martin (piano,
Fender Rhodes), Stanley Clarke (bass), Stevie Wonder (vocals, synthesizer, piano,
Fender Rhodes, drums), Campbell Maloney (drums), Adrian Brett (pan pipes),
Andy Mackay (lyricon), Jack Brymer (clarinet), Adrian Sheppard (drums, percussion),
Carl Perkins (vocals, guitar), Dave Mattacks (drums, percussion)

TUG OF WAR

RECORDED: DECEMBER 1980; FEBRUARY–DECEMBER, 1981 // **STUDIOS:** AIR STUDIOS, LONDON; AIR STUDIOS, MONTSERRAT
PRODUCER: GEORGE MARTIN // **RELEASED:** APRIL 26, 1982

After a hiatus, a pared-down version of the Wings line-up (basically Paul, Linda and Denny Laine) reconvened in the latter half of 1980, and rehearsed a number of songs for future use, some of which would end up on *Tug of War* and its successor, *Pipes of Peace*. But things weren't going as well as planned, until Paul called in George Martin to take over production. "I wanted to work with George Martin again. I called him on the phone, asking him if he was interested, he accepted and we decided to make a very professional album. It was the first time that George Martin produced me since 'Live And Let Die.'" And with the involvement of the former "fifth Beatle", things really began to gel.

Tragedy struck, however, on December 8, 1980, with the murder of John Lennon in New York City. After winding up some sessions already scheduled at the AIR Studio in London, McCartney and Martin agreed to shelve any more recording for a while, resuming in early February 1981.

It was decided to reconvene at Martin's AIR Studio in Montserrat, where Paul, Linda and Denny Laine were joined by various world-class guests who were engaged for different tracks. These included Ringo Starr, bass player Stanley Clarke, rockabilly pioneer Carl Perkins, and the biggest name in contemporary soul music, Stevie Wonder.

On its release in April 1982, the album was immediately hailed by many as a return to form by McCartney right from the get-go, with the sensational opening title track. That was followed by 'Take It Away', a strident, melodic rocker with the double-up support of two drummers, Steve Gadd and Ringo, plus 10cc's Eric Stewart on backing vocals, George Martin helping out on piano, and an overdubbed horn section. As a single, the track made it to the Top 10 in the United States. A flamenco-tinged acoustic guitar forms the intro to 'Somebody Who Cares', a typically tender ballad that features an effective pan flute from Adrian Breet, and bass from supremo Stanley Clarke.

The first of two tracks with Stevie Wonder, 'What's That You're Doing?' has a signature Wonder riff over some funky rhythm from Paul behind the drum kit. Andy Mackay, sax man with Roxy Music, fills in with the lyricon, the first electronic wind instrument, developed in the early 1970s.

"With George Martin, it was 'Oh, come on, let's really get it right,' and that attitude really made the album enjoyable, because you know that by the time you finish the album, you're going to have an album that you started off wanting."

Paul McCartney

With just McCartney on acoustic guitar and a string quartet (echoes of The Beatles' 'Yesterday') arranged by George Martin, 'Here Today' is a heartfelt tribute to his old compadre John Lennon. As he recalled in 1982, the tragedy touched more than one song on the album. "John was killed. I can't believe it to this day, I can't even say those words… but 'Here Today' is the only song specifically about that. Obviously, 'Tug of War' ties in… and so does 'Somebody Who Cares'. I remember being aware of John's death while writing it."

A rollicking evocation of the dance hall culture that was a part of growing up in 1950s England, 'Ballroom Dancing' moves along like a rock 'n' roll-powered juggernaut, complete with a brief excerpt from a "real-life" TV dance contest, as effervescent as a revolving mirror ball.

A slightly doom-laden intro preludes 'The Pound is Sinking', an oddly inspired song prompted by the then-recent 1970s financial crisis. 'Wanderlust' had an equally unlikely inspiration, the name of one of the boats on which Wings recorded their *London Town* sessions in 1977.

Paul and the rest of The Beatles were in awe of all the old rock 'n' roll pioneers, and rockabilly hero, Carl Perkins, was no exception. "Anyone who was a legend in our formative years is still a legend…" McCartney enthused, talking about the guest player and vocalist on the lightly country-fied 'Get It'. "Carl is still the guy who wrote 'Blue Suede Shoes' and he can never do any wrong."

Perkins' raucous laughter at the end fades nicely into 'Be What You See', one of Paul's experimental pieces, a 30-second indulgence of voice, acoustic guitar and vocoder (an electronic device that synthesizes the human voice), more fitting of *McCartney II*.

'Dress Me Up as a Robber' is a hard up-tempo rocker backed with a disco-orientated drum machine, an electric guitar riff overlaid with frantic flamenco-tinged acoustic guitar, and McCartney's voice in its finest falsetto mode.

For the final track, and the biggest-selling single from the album, 'Ebony and Ivory' has Paul teaming up with Stevie Wonder for a song that some felt was too casually superficial for its serious message.

Tug of War was accorded mixed reviews. Nick Kent verged on the pompous in a *New Musical Express* piece headlined "Macca Makes Good Album – Well, Almost", declaring, "McCartney at last appears to be up for making music worthy of the attentions of a thinking audience." In *Rolling Stone*, Stephen Holden was rather more generous, reflecting what many were thinking by calling it, "The masterpiece everyone has always known Paul McCartney could make". The album sold several million copies across the globe, topping the LP charts in at least nine countries including the US and UK, and confirmed McCartney as a major player when his reputation might otherwise have been on the wane.

Previous page Linda and Paul in 1982, shortly before Paul's 40th birthday.

Above The shock headline in the *Liverpool Echo*, announcing the death of John Lennon on December 8, 1980.

Opposite left Ringo Starr on *Good Morning America* in February 1981, while he was recording with Paul for *Tug of War*.

Opposite right Rockabilly guitar legend Carl Perkins who, like Ringo, made a guest appearance on *Tug of War*.

TUG OF WAR [SONG]

RECORDED: DECEMBER 16 AND 18, 1980
STUDIO: AIR STUDIOS, LONDON
PRODUCER: GEORGE MARTIN
COMPOSER: PAUL MCCARTNEY
RELEASED: APRIL 26, 1982 (ALBUM),
SEPTEMBER 6, 1982 (SINGLE)

The title song and opener on Paul's hugely successful album, 'Tug of War' can be read as a simple comment on complex relationships, a plea for a more peaceful world (*Rolling Stone* drew a parallel with John Lennon's 'Imagine') or, as some have suggested, reflections after the death of his former Beatle partner less than two months earlier.

One of the most evocative of Paul's songs of the period, there was an in-built rhythm implicit in the title, the to-and-fro of an actual tug of war. "I wanted to do the whole album around that theme," he explained. "The idea was conflict – that everything is a tug of war." Developing the song from an acoustic beginning, with just the hint of an orchestra in the background, the track concludes with a full ensemble, driven by the military sound of a marching band snare drum, played by Campbell Maloney, who was the drum major with the Campbeltown Pipe Band on the recording of 'Mull of Kintyre'.

The lyrics lay bare the sometimes fractured realities of relationships, whether between lovers, nations or former estranged colleagues, while leading to a hopeful conclusion played out "on a different drum". The track has an epic quality that resonates throughout, from the understated opening to the full-on majesty of the orchestra, plus the guitars of Paul, Denny Laine and 10cc's Eric Stewart. The track is simply among Paul McCartney's greatest triumphs.

The album as a whole was well received, 'Tug of War' in particular. As Nick Kent, in an otherwise muted appraisal in the *New Musical Express*, had to concede: "The title track… is arguably as fine a piece of work as McCartney has ever put his name to, a beautiful, sombre melody bolstered by a quite splendid arrangement that bears testament to McCartney's formidable sense of pop dynamics."

In retrospect, the song didn't work that well as a single, reaching just #53 in both the US and UK charts. Considering the New Wave and disco landscape of the early 1980s, radio exposure would have certainly been more sympathetic in another era, and the track might have achieved the classic status of certain other stand-out McCartney songs. It definitely deserved to.

EBONY AND IVORY

RECORDED: FEBRUARY 27–28, 1981
STUDIO: AIR STUDIOS, MONTSERRAT
PRODUCER: GEORGE MARTIN
COMPOSER: PAUL MCCARTNEY
RELEASED: MARCH 29, 1982 (SINGLE),
APRIL 26, 1982 (ALBUM)

It was during the closing days of the Montserrat sessions that the two tracks with Stevie Wonder were laid down – 'What's That You're Doing', and the biggest hit to appear on the *Tug of War* album, 'Ebony and Ivory'.

The basic metaphor of the song, of the black and white keys of a piano representing racial harmony, was not new. In the 1930s, the African black activist James Aggrey had used the analogy for the title of the progressive journal *The Keys,* while Paul claimed to have been directly inspired by the words of the UK comedian Spike Milligan: "Black notes, white notes, and you need to play the two to make harmony, folks!"

While writing the song, Paul had decided it seemed a natural duet, and had a clear idea who he wanted as a partner: "My first thought was Stevie." The lyrics certainly fitted in with the American's campaigning stance on the issue of race relations and civil rights. If anything, the language verges on the bland compared to some of Wonder's more militant musical statements on the subject, such as his 1973 tour de force 'Living For the City'.

Despite being savagely dismissed by many critics, and described variously as 'soggy', 'saccharine' and 'sugary', many conceded that the song had its virtues given the racial climate at the time. "Although some considered it saccharine, his duet with Paul McCartney on 'Ebony and Ivory' sounded a note of reconciliation as racial relations continued to worsen in Ronald Reagan's America," wrote Craig Werner in *Goldmine* magazine, while Carol Cooper in the UK's trend-leading *The Face* admitted, "It was nevertheless the perfect sop to allay fears of Wonder becoming dangerously militant."

And regardless of the finely-tuned reactions of the critical cognoscenti, 'Ebony and Ivory' worked for millions of fans around the world, topping the charts in at least eight countries, with the album performing in a similar way. It spent seven consecutive weeks in the American #1 spot, was the fourth-biggest US hit of 1982, and was the 28th song by Paul McCartney to top the US *Billboard* chart.

Opposite above Stevie Wonder and Paul McCartney during the 'Ebony and Ivory' recording sessions at the AIR studios in Montserrat.

Opposite below Stevie Wonder and Paul McCartney at the Forum in Inglewood, California, performing 'Ebony and Ivory'. It was their first time on stage together.

"I listened to the song, and I liked it very much. I felt it was positive for everybody. I won't say it *demanded* of people to reflect upon it, but it politely asks the people to reflect upon life in using the terms of music... this melting pot of many different people."

Stevie Wonder

PIPES OF PEACE

SAY SAY SAY
(PAUL MCCARTNEY, MICHAEL JACKSON)

THE OTHER ME

KEEP UNDER COVER

SO BAD

THE MAN

SWEETEST LITTLE SHOW

AVERAGE PERSON

HEY HEY
(PAUL MCCARTNEY, STANLEY CLARKE)

TUG OF PEACE

THROUGH OUR LOVE

(All songs written by Paul McCartney, except where indicated)

Paul McCartney (vocals, bass, guitars, piano, keyboards, synthesizer, drums),
Linda McCartney (vocals, keyboards), Michael Jackson (vocals), Denny Laine (guitar, keyboards, vocals),
Eric Stewart (guitar, vocals), Hughie Burn (guitar), Geoff Whitehorn (guitar), David Williams (guitar),
Stanley Clarke (bass, vocals), Nathan Watts (bass), Chris Hammer Smith (harmonica), Bill Wolfer
(keyboards), Gavyn Wright (violin), Jerry Hey (strings, French horn), Gary Herbig (flute), Andy Mackay
(saxophone), Ernie Watts (saxophone), Gary Grant (horns), Ringo Starr (drums), Ricky Lawson (drums),
Steve Gadd (drums), Dave Mattacks (drums), James Kippen (tabla), Pestalozzi Children's Choir (vocals)

PIPES OF PEACE

RECORDED: OCTOBER–DECEMBER 1980; FEBRUARY–MARCH 1981; MAY 1981; AUGUST–DECEMBER 1981; APRIL 14–16, 1982; SEPTEMBER–OCTOBER 1982; FEBRUARY AND JULY 1983 // **STUDIOS:** ABBEY ROAD STUDIOS; AIR STUDIOS, LONDON; AIR STUDIOS, MONTSERRAT; CHEROKEE STUDIOS, LOS ANGELES; RUDE STUDIOS, CAMPBELTOWN, SCOTLAND; THE MILL, RYE, EAST SUSSEX **PRODUCER:** GEORGE MARTIN // **RELEASED:** OCTOBER 17, 1983

After the plea for racial harmony of 'Ebony and Ivory' in *Tug of War*, Paul's next album would be the conduit for another hopeful message of peace and love, most specifically in the opening title track. The album was another exercise in a variety of collaborations, most famously with Michael Jackson – then enjoying superstar status – who, like Stevie Wonder on the previous album, featured on two tracks, 'Say Say Say' and 'The Man'.

A number of the songs on *Pipes of Peace* were recorded during the same 1981 sessions that produced *Tug of War*, and there were consequent similarities between the two albums. Both were produced by George Martin, the collaborations continued the involvement of both Ringo Starr and Eric Stewart, and both collections represented the last McCartney sessions to include former Wings guitarist Denny Laine.

Following the message-establishing opener, 'Say Say Say' quickly introduces us to Paul's high-profile collaboration with Michael Jackson, and another hit in its own right. 'The Other Me' is a lighter song, though with serious intent – nothing less than a lover's confessional. Pitched as a totally solo effort, it takes advantage of much overdubbing from the McCartney box of tricks, including guitar, bass, piano, synth and percussion.

After a languid introduction, 'Keep Under Cover' breaks into a frantic plea highlighting daily comforts being used as a cushion against the harsher realities of life. Any message here, however, is somewhat lost in a busy arrangement. Originally written during the *Tug of War* sessions, but with a final recording in October 1982, 'So Bad' is a powerful love song with a riveting upper-range delivery by Paul. Rich harmonies with Linda and Eric Stewart ensure a brand of textural perfection, on a number sometimes dismissed by critics as an example of soft-centred McCartney.

The other vehicle for Michael Jackson, 'The Man' is a harmless slice of ineffectual 1980s pop, and certainly more Michael than Macca. 'Sweetest Little Show' is another seemingly solo exercise on Paul's part, though credits for some of the percussion contributions are unclear. The track has him delivering a strident statement of musical intent – complete with an elegant acoustic guitar break – that elicits a round of applause from the studio workforce.

The jaunty Chas 'n' Dave-style piano backing to 'Average Person' is strangely at odds with the potential for melancholy in the subject matter. More of Paul's "lonely" people figure in the urban landscape, including a failed boxer and a would-be film actress. Its followed by a filler of sorts, 'Hey Hey', and this instrumental, featuring fusion jazz bass maestro Stanley Clarke, works on just that level. Clarke, drummer Steve Gadd and McCartney– and possibly Denny Laine – indulge in three minutes of virtuoso jamming. But regardless of its musical virtues, many thought the track simply ill-placed.

Then on to 'Tug of Peace'. A slightly spooky jungle rhythm haunts this crossbreed of 'Pipes of Peace' and the majestic title track from the previous album. As one writer commented, it evokes "an awful sense of *déjà vu*." Apart from Paul, the only other recorded participant seems to have been George Martin, with the two of them thrashing the studio floor with bunches of garden canes!

The final track, 'Through Our Love', takes us back into the thankfully familiar realm of Paul McCartney as the gifted songwriter, here extolling the virtues of love itself as a transcendental state. A lush orchestral backing, courtesy of the studio talents of George Martin, gradually lifts the song from an elegant acoustic ballad to a majestic finale, closing what is otherwise a mixed bag of an album.

Once again, the press reaction to a new album by Paul McCartney was characterized by less than unanimous acclaim, although none went quite as near to the jugular as the writer in *Musician* magazine, who began his review: "Just when you thought it was safe to like Paul McCartney again, along comes an album that makes *Ram* look like *Abbey Road*." Many thought it sounded too much like a left-over legacy from its successful predecessor, which indeed a number of tracks were. It only made it to #15 in the American charts, although it managed to score a healthier #4 position in the United Kingdom.

Previous page Paul relaxes during a visit to Liverpool, September 1983.

Opposite The enigmatic, surrealist-flavoured cover artwork for *Pipes of Peace*.

Above Paul during the recording of *Give My Regards to Broad Street*, which included just two originals; 'No More Lonely Nights' was the most successful.

PIPES OF PEACE [SONG]

RECORDED: SEPTEMBER 10, 1982
STUDIO: AIR STUDIOS, LONDON
PRODUCER: GEORGE MARTIN
COMPOSER: PAUL MCCARTNEY
RELEASED: OCTOBER 17, 1983, DECEMBER 5, 1983 (SINGLE)

For the opening title track on *Pipes of Peace*, McCartney utilized a line-up consisting of himself on piano, synthesizer, drums and other percussion instruments; Linda McCartney and Eric Stewart on backing vocals; James Kippen on the tabla (a pair of Indian hand drums) and Adrian Brett on Pan flute. Initially, Paul had planned a more exotic arrangement featuring various Indian instruments, but after most were unavailable he settled on the tabla, with George Martin contacting his friend, the Canadian percussionist Kippen. "He used his hands on my drums to tap out a kind of rhythmic feel," Kippen explained, 'And he was also speaking simple syllables (a bit like scat singing in jazz) in imitation of the drum syllables used by tabla players."

The addition of marching drums and a children's choir enhanced the backing on a truly inspiring track, which, when released as a single in December 1983, shot to the top of the UK charts.

With an overtly anti-war message, the song pleads for human understanding, metaphorically represented by the 'pipes of peace' in the title. And an even more direct statement of the message came in the accompanying video, in which the British and German armies face each other over the World War I trenches. Paul plays the dual roles of a combatant from each side, re-enacting the legendary real-life instance when, on Christmas day, the warring troops exchanged gifts and pictures of their loved ones, and played an impromptu game of football, before returning to their lines to commence hostilities. The emotive film, produced by Hugh Symonds, was shot on Chobham Common in Surrey, and employed more than 100 extras. At the 1984 Brit Awards it went on to win the Best Video category, with Paul being cited as Best British Male Solo Artist.

Opposite A scene from Paul's evocative World War I-themed video film for 'Pipes of Peace'.

Above The flipside to 'Pipes of Peace' – 'So Bad' – featured (left to right) Ringo Starr, Eric Stewart, Linda and Paul.

"I recall that AIR [Studios] had a video game machine there and guess what? Paul was having a go on the '80s ultimate game – *Space Invaders*. We chatted a bit and then he confessed, 'I'm addicted to this game... I just can't stop playing it!'"

James Kippen

SAY SAY SAY

RECORDED: MAY 1981 AND APRIL 1982
STUDIO: AIR STUDIOS, LONDON; HOLLYWOOD SOUND
STUDIOS, LOS ANGELES; CHEROKEE STUDIOS, LOS ANGELES
PRODUCER: GEORGE MARTIN
COMPOSERS: PAUL MCCARTNEY, MICHAEL JACKSON
RELEASED: OCTOBER 3, 1983 (SINGLE), OCTOBER 17, 1983

By the time 'Say Say Say' was released in October 1983, Michael Jackson was at the height of his success in the wake of his mega-selling album, *Thriller*. The LP had spent 37 weeks at the top of the *Billboard* album chart (and many more bestseller lists worldwide), spawning no fewer than six hit singles in the process. Paul McCartney had guested on the album, singing 'The Girl Is Mine', which made #2 in the *Billboard* singles chart on its release in October 1982.

But McCartney and Jackson had already collaborated before this, when they first laid down recordings for 'Say Say Say', back in May 1981, during the sessions for *Tug of War*. Apparently, Jackson wrote the majority of the lyrics before giving them to Paul to work around. The resulting demo for the song – with both stars singing, and Paul playing acoustic guitar – then languished on the proverbial studio shelf until the following April, when Jackson gave it to some of his regular session men to work on.

"Michael came over and we sat around upstairs on the top floor of our office in London, and I just grabbed a guitar and 'Say Say Say' came out of it."

Paul McCartney

NO MORE LONELY NIGHTS

ALBUM: *GIVE MY REGARDS TO BROAD STREET*
RECORDED: JUNE–JULY 1984
STUDIO: ELSTREE STUDIOS, BOREHAMWOOD
PRODUCER: GEORGE MARTIN
COMPOSER: PAUL MCCARTNEY
RELEASED: SEPTEMBER 24, 1984

The location was Cherokee Studios in Los Angeles, and the musicians involved included Nathan Watts on bass, Bill Wolfer on keyboards and Ricky Lawson on drums. In a 2011 interview, Watts – a long-time musical associate of Stevie Wonder – recalled how he laid down what he assumed was a demo bass part, expecting McCartney to overdub it with his own version, "but when it got to Paul, he said he liked the feel so much he was leaving it the way it was. Now *that* was a complement!"

Jackson went on to add a horn section led by Jerry Hey, and a harmonica solo by Chris Smith, both key elements in the final arrangement that Michael Jackson took back as a 24-track tape to London, for McCartney to assess. It wasn't just Watts' bass part that impressed Paul – he decided that they would keep the entire backing track as was, with the addition of some more vocal parts by himself, Jackson, Linda, and Eric Stewart.

The record's publicity was supported by a heavily narrative video, with McCartney and Jackson playing two 1930s snake-oil con men, "Mac and Jack". Like many such TV marketing promotions at the time, the onscreen story being acted out bore little (or arguably, no) relationship to the music, which in this case was a thrusting disco beat dominating a fairly trite song, with the aforementioned interjections of horns and harmonic giving the finished product its instrumental strength. Add in the undoubted vocal confidence of both leads, the perfectly crafted backing vocal arrangements, and slick production courtesy of George Martin, and you had a faultless, but ultimately superficial, dance track.

Regardless of some critical lambasting (*Rolling Stone* described it as an "amiable though vapid dance groove… froth-funk that tends toward… banality"), 'Say Say Say' was a huge commercial success. As the lead single for *Pipes of Peace* and released two weeks before the album, in America it topped the *Billboard* chart, and remained in pole position for the next six weeks. It was also #1 in Norway, Sweden, Spain, Canada, Italy and France, reached the #2 position in the UK, and the top five in Australia, Ireland and South Africa. There was also a 12-inch "disco" edition, remixed by the noted dance music producer John "Jellybean" Benitez, which ran two minutes longer.

Opposite Paul McCartney and Michael Jackson during their studio collaboration in 1981 that resulted in two tracks on *Pipes of Peace*.

Although the majority of the music on the soundtrack of Paul's 1984 feature film *Give My Regards to Broad Street* was retrospective, 'No More Lonely Nights', one of just two original songs in the production, was a significant success in its own right. It was recorded after the actual filming was completed – there was still another song needed to round things off, and act as a signature tune for the whole movie.

Paul had been playing with the idea of a song with the same title as the film, but gave up eventually. What became the film's musical theme was created – like so many inspirations over the years – out of his doodling around in the studio, this time at the Elstree film lot at Borehamwood. "I had been messing around in the studio with a bass thing. And it was just jamming, one day, when I had nothing to do, coming here, just having some fun on some of the equipment."

What he came up with was one of his best McCartney-style ballads, which he acknowledged himself in an interview at the time: "It's a nice track. I think maybe it's as good as the old (Beatles) songs." The sequence featuring the song, with Paul wandering around Broad Street station in London, was initially just accompanied by sound effects, but later became part of the promotional video for the number.

The song was recorded "as live" in a short session at the studio. Paul enlisted the help of Ann Dudley on synthesizer, drummer Stuart Elliott, bass ace Herbie Flowers, and Pink Floyd guitarist David Gilmour, who recalled the session in a 1986 interview for *Q* magazine. "I found it quite amazing doing 'No More Lonely Nights' with Paul McCartney. In one three-hour session with a band we learned it and put it down, and Paul played piano and sang the lead vocal live, and I put the guitar solo down, bang." In a 1990 radio interview, Gilmour, whose solo was a highlight of the track, said he told Paul after the session to give his fee to a charity of his choice.

Released a month before the US screening of the film, and two months ahead of the UK release, the single was far better received than the movie, charting at #2 in the UK and #6 in the United States. In addition, a "playout" version was recorded to run over the credits at the end of the film. Significantly more up-tempo than the ballad, it featured Paul on vocals that he had adapted for a dance re-hash of the song, plus backing vocals by Linda and Eric Stewart, and a five-piece horn section.

PRESS

TO PLAY

STRANGLEHOLD

GOOD TIMES COMING/FEEL THE SUN
(PAUL MCCARTNEY)

TALK MORE TALK
(PAUL MCCARTNEY)

FOOTPRINTS

ONLY LOVE REMAINS
(PAUL MCCARTNEY)

PRESS
(PAUL MCCARTNEY)

PRETTY LITTLE HEAD

MOVE OVER BUSKER

ANGRY

HOWEVER ABSURD

(All songs written by Paul McCartney and Eric Stewart,
except where indicated)

Paul McCartney (vocals, bass, guitars, piano, keyboards, synthesizers), Linda McCartney (vocals),
Eric Stewart (guitars, keyboards, vocals), Pete Townshend (guitar), Carlos Alomar (guitars),
Eddie Raynet (keyboards), Simon Chamberlain (piano), Nick Glennie-Smith (keyboards),
Phil Collins (drums), Jerry Marotta (drums, percussion), Graham Ward (drums, percussion),
John Bradbury (violin), Ray Cooper (percussion), Dick Morrissey (saxophone), Lenny Pickett (saxophone),
Gary Barnacle (saxophone), Gavyn Wright (violin), Kate Robbins (vocals), Ruby James (vocals),
James McCartney, Steve Jackson, Eddie Klein, John Hammel and Matt Howe (spoken word)

PRESS TO PLAY

RECORDED: MARCH–MAY 1985, OCTOBER–DECEMBER 1985 // STUDIOS: HOG HILL MILL, ICKLESHAM, SUSSEX
PRODUCER: PAUL MCCARTNEY, HUGH PADGHAM // RELEASED: AUGUST 25, 1986

It would be nearly three years before Paul McCartney released another solo studio album, after 1983's *Pipes of Peace* (not counting the soundtrack to *Give My Regards to Broad Street*, which was largely a retrospective compilation). Recorded at Paul's brand-new studio located in an old windmill at Hog Hill, Icklesham, near to his home in East Sussex, the album was largely a collaboration with 10cc guitarist, Eric Stewart.

Perhaps anxious to regain some credibility after the disappointing reception accorded the 'Broad Street film, McCartney also engaged the services of Hugh Padgham to co-produce the new project. The award-winning producer had a formidable reputation on the contemporary rock scene, having worked with the likes of Genesis, The Police, The Human League and XTC.

After the tough-sounding opener, 'Stranglehold', the second track is actually one of Paul's familiar medley devices, the summery 'Good Times Coming', which uses a reggae sound to evoke a warm, optimistic holiday feel. It fades appropriately into 'Feel the Sun', which, if anything, is over-layered for what is essentially light subject matter.

Far more experimental, 'Talk More Talk' opens with some sci-fi electronic effects, and atmospheric dialogue read by Linda, Paul's son James, and some of the studio crew. The song proper has McCartney's voice double-tracked on a strident statement, interrupted by more overdubbed voicings, which chat away to form the nebulous conversation that makes up the lyrics.

'Footprints', co-written by Paul and Eric Stewart, is a straightforward acoustic ballad that the pair admitted they wrote in just a few minutes. Despite some perhaps unnecessary instrumental embellishment, the track retains a basic simplicity and, as a bonus, a Spanish guitar solo from McCartney.

Although it was the final number to be taped at the Hog Hill Mill sessions, 'Only Love Remains' appeared halfway through the original vinyl release of *Press to Play*, closing side one. A classic McCartney love song dedicated to Linda, the track builds from a simple piano accompaniment to a full-blown orchestral backing with arrangements courtesy of Tony Visconti. For McCartney traditionalists, it's certainly the stand-out song on the album.

'Press' was released as the lead single from the album, but did little to dent the charts in its own right, reaching #21 in the US and #25 in the UK. A frantic rocker, Paul went on to explain – not for the first time – that textual references were often there in the lyrics purely because they sounded right: "'Oklahoma was never like this.' That can mean whatever you want it to mean. To me, when you're writing songs, you often get a line you assume you're going to edit later… But every time I came to that line, I couldn't sing anything else – just scanning, the way it sang. People would have understood it if it was 'Liverpool was never like this', but it wouldn't have sung the same. It's a symbol for the provinces, the sticks, the out of the way places."

Although it was released as a single, 'Pretty Little Head' is in many ways the most experimental track on the album, with repetitive percussion, ambient instrumental sounds, and a knocked-back vocal that makes Paul sound strangely unearthly.

'Move Over Busker' was basically taped "as live" in the studio, a back-to-basics rock 'n' roller that must have been fun to record – although most of the instruments were Paul accompanying himself. Some genuine sounding honky-tonk piano adds to the fun of the proceedings, as do back-up vocals from Eric Stewart, Ruby James and Paul's cousin, Kate Robbins.

In 'Angry', a staccato vocal from Paul is backed with a suitably frantic Pete Townshend on guitar and Phil Collins on drums. With an uncompromising dynamic reminiscent of The Beatles' 'Helter Skelter', it's a musical rant that moves from the personal – railing against the unfairly bad press he'd received over the years –

to the more broadly political: "Britain's attitude towards apartheid at the moment is just so crazy," he would tell *Rolling Stone*, "It's so insane. Couldn't they just wise up?"

Described by Paul as deliberately surrealist, 'However Absurd' elicits comparison to 'I Am the Walrus' and other Sergeant Pepper-era flights of fancy. Even the fade-out ending sounds more '67 than '86, the year *Press to Play* was released. "It did suggest the epic finale – which is why it's at the end of the album!" he recalled. "For me, it was another thing you start off and think, 'Ooh no, that's too Beatley, so I won't do it.' So I resisted it for a while, but I kept coming back to 'why? Tell me one good reason why you're resisting this Beatles influence?'"

Although many of the reviews for *Press to Play* were highly favourable – the *Chicago Tribune* called it "McCartney's most rocking album in years" – sales-wise, the album was a let-down for Paul. It briefly graced the UK chart, climbing to #8, but in the US it just reached #30, and sold only a quarter of a million copies at the time. And more recently, the album has enjoyed a reassessment, with a recognition that it represented musical directions that McCartney would develop in subsequent years.

Previous page Paul pictured at his offices in London's Soho in 1985.

Opposite Paul and Linda with a copy of *Press to Play*, at a launch event for the album at the Radio City Music Hall in New York City: August 22, 1986.

Above Eric Stewart, best known for his work with 10cc, who collaborated closely with McCartney – including on much of the songwriting – on *Press to Play*.

STRANGLEHOLD

RECORDED: MARCH–MAY, 1985
STUDIO: HOG HILL MILL, ICKLESHAM, SUSSEX
PRODUCERS: HUGH PADGHAM, PAUL MCCARTNEY
COMPOSERS: PAUL MCCARTNEY, ERIC STEWART
RELEASED: AUGUST 25, 1986 (US), SEPTEMBER 1, 1986 (UK)

The opening track from *Press to Play*, 'Stranglehold' was co-written by McCartney and guitarist Eric Stewart. Paul would describe how they bandied the words about to fit the rhythm, reminiscent of the way he and John Lennon used to work, facing each other with acoustic guitars, reacting to what the other was putting down. Stewart in turn was delighted with the ways things went after their first run-through of the number. "The song sounded great with just Paul on bass, me on electrified acoustic guitar, and Jerry [Marotta] on kit. I went home feeling very, very happy and got a call, which my wife Gloria answered. It was Paul and he said, 'Tell that bloke of yours that is bloody good and I'm really looking forward to tomorrow!'"

As with most of the album, however, the track went on to suffer from too much where less would have certainly been better. Between co-producers Hugh Padgham and Paul, the overdubbing of more guitars, vocals and a horn section simply over-egged what was basically a simple, attractive song. Stewart, who had expected to be in on the production in some capacity, was severely disillusioned: "…a great song called 'Stranglehold', which was a beautiful song we'd written together, [they] buggered it all up with ******* saxes going all the way through the verses."

The up-tempo rocker certainly feels like its potential is buried in layers of unnecessary music and recording effects, turning a punchy album intro into a pedestrian disco-orientated track. When it was released as a single exclusively in the United States, it failed to make a big impression, reaching just #81 in the *Billboard* Hot 100.

Above Paul jamming with Tina Turner on 'Get Back', at the 1986 Princes Trust Concert, with an all-star line-up including Elton John, Eric Clapton, Mark Knopfler, Phil Collins and Status Quo.

Opposite (above) Paul on stage at Live Aid with George Michael, Bono, Freddie Mercury and more, 1985; **(Below)** at the 1986 American Music Awards with Roger Daltrey, Bob Geldof and Phil Collins.

"Wait a minute. What did we do? Where did we go wrong?
Most people would give their right arm for the Wings career, to have hits
as big as 'Mull Of Kintyre', 'My Love', 'Band On The Run', 'Maybe I'm Amazed'."

Paul McCartney talking to Chris Salewicz, Q magazine, October 1986

CHOBA

B CCCP

(BACK IN THE USSR)

KANSAS CITY
(JERRY LEIBER, MIKE STOLLER)

TWENTY FLIGHT ROCK
(EDDIE COCHRAN, NED FAIRCHILD)

LAWDY, MISS CLAWDY
(LLOYD PRICE)

BRING IT ON HOME TO ME
(SAM COOKE)

LUCILLE
(RICHARD PENNIMAN, ALBERT COLLINS)

DON'T GET AROUND MUCH ANYMORE
(DUKE ELLINGTON, BOB RUSSELL)

THAT'S ALL RIGHT (MAMA)
(ARTHUR CRUDUP)

AIN'T THAT A SHAME
(FATS DOMINO, DAVE BARTHOLEMEW)

CRACKIN' UP
(ELLAS MCDANIEL)

Paul McCartney (guitar, bass, vocals), Mick Green (guitar), Mick Gallagher (piano, keyboards),
Nick Garvey (bass, vocals), Chris Whitten (drums), Henry Spinetti (drums)

CHOBA B CCCP

(BACK IN THE USSR)

RECORDED: JULY 20–21, 1987 // STUDIO: HOG HILL MILL, ICKLESHAM, SUSSEX
PRODUCER: PAUL MCCARTNEY // RELEASED: OCTOBER 31, 1988 (USSR), OCTOBER 29, 1991 (WORLDWIDE)

Paul McCartney's seventh solo album under his own name was something of an oddity. Completely made up of covers of old songs that Paul had grown up with during his teenage years, the collection was initially only available in Russia, then known as the (USSR), or the Soviet Union.

The tracks came out of two sessions at his Hog Hill studio, during which two quartets of musicians playing guitar, bass, drums and piano/keyboards ran through a bunch of vintage classics, most of which they recorded "as live". Over two days in July 1987, they recorded around 20 songs – mostly rock 'n' roll numbers – on which Paul indulged his love for the music of his youth, an exercise similar to John Lennon's 1975 album *Rock 'n' Roll*.

The opener 'Kansas City' sets the mood perfectly. Paul, in his typical 'Little Richard' vocal style, takes us through the double medley (linking the Leiber and Stoller song with Richard's 'Hey, Hey, Hey') that was a sensation during the Beatles' Cavern Club gigs, and featured on *Beatles for Sale* in 1964. Likewise, Eddie Cochran's 'Twenty Flight Rock', here with bags of echo, has a special resonance in McCartney lore – it was the song he played when offering his services to The Quarrymen skiffle group, on the day he first met John Lennon in 1957.

'Lawdy Miss Clawdy' started life as a 1952 hit for New Orleans rhythm and blues man Lloyd Price, before being covered by Elvis Presley for his debut album in 1956. Mick Green, formerly of Brit-rock pioneers Johnny Kidd and the Pirates, provides some roaring guitar. And Green shines again in a sensational break on Sam Cooke's 'Bring it On Home to Me'.

The entire album is clearly a labour of love. A blistering version of Little Richard's 'Lucille', with Paul's voice sounding stretched but never out of control, pays hectic homage to the master. The first side of the vinyl disc closes with an intriguing R&B-flavoured version of the 1940 Duke Ellington jazz standard 'Don't Get Around Much Anymore'.

It's back to the earliest days of Elvis' recording career with 'That's All Right (Mama)', the Arthur 'Big Boy' Crudup song that Presley covered on Sun Records, and which became one of the templates of rock 'n' roll. The Fats Domino song 'Ain't That A Shame' has Paul introducing some contemporary technical sounds to a well-covered classic, while there's a nod to another of rock's true originals, Bo Diddley, with 'Crackin' Up', credited to his real name Ellas McDaniel.

Another song sharing the title 'Just Because' had appeared on the Lennon *Rock 'n' Roll* album – that was a Lloyd Price number from 1955 – but Paul's cover is of a much older composition, dating from 1929 when it was a country-style hit for Nelstone's Hawaiians, and later a successful 1933 release for its composers, The Shelton Brothers. Paul's high-octane rockabilly version is clearly influenced by the recording by Elvis Presley, dating from his debut album in 1956.

Although the album-closer 'Midnight Special' dates back to the 1920s, it's almost certain that Paul first heard it via Lonnie Donegan, the UK 'king of skiffle' who resurrected it in 1956 when he released the classic 'train song' on an EP, *Backstairs Session*.

In the spirit of *glasnost*, the move towards democracy across the Soviet Union during the late 1980s, Paul decided to release the album exclusively in the USSR as a gesture of goodwill. An agreement was reached with the state record company Melodiya, who licensed 400,000 copies. On its release in October 1988, the first pressing of 50,000 discs sold out in days. The album was entitled *Choba B CCCP* or *Back in the USSR*, echoing The Beatles' track of the same name from their *White* album in 1968.

Since the album had not been released in the West, there was an immediate black market in copies in Europe and the USA, as reported in the *New York Times*:

"Paul McCartney has released an album exclusively in the Soviet Union called *Back in the USSR* as his tribute to Mikhail S. Gorbachev's moves toward openness. The record, believed to be the first Soviet-only release by a Western rock star, has been slipping into the West and has been commanding $100 to $250 a copy in the United States, and is reportedly selling for as much as £500 (about $885) in London."

The album was eventually released worldwide in 1991, where it sold only modestly, with a #109 and #63 position in America and the UK respectively, and a healthier # 48 in Japan.

Previous page Paul in 1988.

Opposite The cover for Paul's 1988 Russia-only release, designed by Michael Ross and evoking the style of Soviet poster art.

Above Paul and his band performing to a huge crowd in Red Square, Moscow, May 24, 2003. It was Paul's first show in Russia.

ONCE UPON A LONG AGO [SINGLE]

RECORDED: MARCH 11–12, 1987; JULY 1, 1987
STUDIOS: HOG HILL MILL, ICKLESHAM, SUSSEX;
ABBEY ROAD STUDIOS, LONDON
PRODUCER: PHIL RAMONE
COMPOSER: PAUL MCCARTNEY
RELEASED: NOVEMBER 16, 1987

In March 1987, Paul invited the producer Phil Ramone – who in a long career had worked with names including Bob Dylan, Aretha Franklin, Stevie Wonder and Frank Sinatra – to his Hog Hill studio. They laid down 10 tracks in all, but it wasn't a successful partnership, and only five ended up being released: 'Once Upon a Long Ago' and its B-side, 'Back on My Feet', later in 1987, and three others in the late 1990s.

Paul's original plan for 'Once Upon a Long Ago' was as a duet with Freddie Mercury, who he'd got to know after the Live Aid concert in 1985. But it never happened due to Mercury's heavy work schedule, and eventually Paul recorded the song himself during the Ramone sessions.

The richness of the melody and instrumental backing belies the seemingly haphazard nature of the lyrics, throwaway images and questions that are arranged, it seems, purely for McCartney's need for a rhyme here, a musical scan there. Nevertheless, the end product is an unquestionably solid ballad, judged by many fans to be one of Paul's finest songs of the 1980s.

The quality of the track was aided in no small part by the musicians playing on it. Paul was on his usual assortment of instruments, including guitars, bass and keyboards, added to which were Linda's contributions, Nick Glennie-Smith on keyboards, Tim Renwick on acoustic guitar, and Henry Spinetti on drums. Extensive overdubs took place at Abbey Road Studios in July. There, with the aid of George Martin, a full orchestra was added, plus some crucial contributions from the celebrated violinist Nigel Kennedy, as well as Stan Sulzmann on tenor sax, and Adrian Brett on flute.

Sulzmann recalled McCartney's exacting requirements regarding solos: "I remember that Paul really just liked solos to stick fairly close to the tune, so I did a soft variation. We tried lots of things but it always came back to the tune. Paul didn't really like improvised solos, he just wanted what he had in his head."

Released in November 1987, 'Once Upon a Long Ago' was a big hit in Europe, making #2 in Italy, #4 in Belgium and #10 in the UK. In the United States it was never released as a single, nor did it appear in the US edition of *All the Best*, the McCartney compilation released two weeks before the single. And 'Back on My Feet', the flipside to the single, was something of a milestone in itself, as the first song co-written by Paul McCartney and Elvis Costello, a songwriting partnership that would go on to bear fruit on Paul's next album release.

Above Paul relaxing on a park bench, in a shot by the Italian photographer Rino Pestrosino, in 1987.

FLOWERS
IN THE
DIRT

MY BRAVE FACE
(PAUL MCCARTNEY, DECLAN MACMANUS)

ROUGH RIDE

YOU WANT HER TOO
(PAUL MCCARTNEY, DECLAN MACMANUS)

DISTRACTIONS

WE GOT MARRIED

PUT IT THERE

FIGURE OF EIGHT

THIS ONE

DON'T BE CARELESS LOVE
(PAUL MCCARTNEY, DECLAN MACMANUS)

THAT DAY IS DONE
(PAUL MCCARTNEY, DECLAN MACMANUS)

HOW MANY PEOPLE

MOTOR OF LOVE

(All songs written by Paul McCartney, except where indicated)

Paul McCartney (vocals, guitars, bass, piano, keyboards, synthesizer, drums, percussion, tambourine, celeste, sitar, wine glass, harmonium, Mellotron, flugelhorn, bongos, violin, woodsaw), Linda McCartney (Minimoog, vocals), Robbie McIntosh (guitars), Hamish Stuart (guitars, percussion, vocals), Chris Whitten (drums, percussion, synthesizer), Paul Wickens (keyboards), Elvis Costello (vocals, keyboards), David Gilmour (guitar), Greg Hawkes (keyboards), David Foster (keyboards), Dave Mattacks (drums), Guy Barker (trumpet), Stephen Lipson (computer programming, guitars, keyboards), Peter Henderson (computer programming), Trevor Horn (keyboards), Nicky Hopkins (piano), Mitchell Froom (keyboards), David Rhodes (guitar), Judd Lander (harmonica), Chris Davis (saxophone), Chris White (saxophone), Dave Bishop (saxophone), John Taylor (cornet), Tony Goddard (cornet), Ian Peters (euphonium), Ian Harper (tenor horn), Jah Bunny (percussion)

FLOWERS IN THE DIRT

RECORDED: OCTOBER 1, 1987–JANUARY 12, 1989 // **STUDIOS:** HOG HILL MILL, ICKLESHAM, SUSSEX; OLYMPIC SOUND STUDIOS, LONDON; AIR STUDIOS, LONDON; HOT NIGHTS STUDIOS, LONDON; MAD HATTER STUDIOS, LOS ANGELES; SOUNDCASTLE STUDIOS, LOS ANGELES
PRODUCERS: PAUL MCCARTNEY, MITCHELL FROOM, NEIL DORFSMAN, ELVIS COSTELLO (DECLAN MACMANUS), TREVOR HORN, STEVE LIPSON, CHRIS HUGHES, ROSS CULLUM, DAVID FOSTER // **RELEASED:** JUNE 5, 1989

Flowers in the Dirt was a landmark release for Paul McCartney, in which he used the talents of several different producers, teamed up with Elvis Costello on a number of tracks, and (apart from the *Give My Regards to Broad Street* soundtrack) had his first UK #1 album since *Tug of War* seven years earlier. And with an eye on an upcoming world tour in September 1989, most of the tracks were planned by Paul with live performances in mind.

As well as the collaborations with Costello, the album also featured musicians that Paul went on to use regularly on the road. These included guitarists Hamish Stuart (best known as part of The Average White Band) and Robbie Macintosh, noted for his work with The Pretenders. Likewise, drummer Chris Whitten also went on to tour with the McCartney line-up. And during the recording sessions Paul invited a number of famous names to sit in the producer's chair, including luminaries such as Trevor Horn, Mitchell Froom, Neil Dorfsman and Steve Lipson.

The opening track, 'My Brave Face', was the first of five songs co-written by McCartney and Elvis Costello, the latter credited as Declan MacManus, his real name. It was also released ahead of the album as a 'trailer' single. And the New Wave producer, Trevor Horn, was at the controls for the second track, 'Rough Ride', a sophisticated arrangement with dominant horns and funky guitar licks.

Another partnership with Costello, 'You Want Her Too', has the pair sharing vocals for much of the song. In complete contrast, 'Distractions' is a laidback piece of smooth McCartney balladeering, with a Latin-tinged, lounge-jazz rhythm and sleek string orchestrations by Clare Fischer. With its sleepy, relaxed ambience, it's one of the most satisfying tracks on the album.

'We Got Married' originated during Hog Hill sessions in 1984, and is another in a long line of Paul's acutely observational songs – this time extolling the simple virtues of love in its early, euphoric stages. With an appropriately 'romantic' Mexican guitar part by McCartney bringing the song in, the track builds layer by layer, with a fading trumpet bringing it to an open-ended conclusion nearly five minutes later.

Another track with its roots in Paul's personal nostalgia, 'Put It There', is an affectionate tribute to his father Jim McCartney, taking one of his dad's much-used sayings as the title. Composed during the winter of 1987, when Paul and his family were on holiday in Zermatt, Switzerland, the gentle texture of the song is maintained by his acoustic guitar backing the track.

Paul used the solid-sounding rocker, 'Figure of Eight', as an opener for the 1989–90 world tour. A good show-starter, the studio track was co-produced by Trevor Horn and Steve Lipson, who also contributed guitar and keyboards respectively, but some think it has a messy ending. An instrumental introduction featuring wine glasses and other extraneous effects brings in 'This One', a Beatle-flavoured slice of sweet and sour reflections. In terms of structure and texture it's another stand-out track on an album full of gems.

'Don't Be Careless Love' is the third song co-written with Elvis Costello. A track that lacks overall direction, it's arguably the weakest of the Macca–MacManus get-togethers on the album. Which is in total contrast to the next track, another collaboration between the pair. 'That Day is Done' is a rousing McCartney gospel-tinged clarion-call, on a par with his magnificent 'Tug of War'. The lyrics sprang from Costello's own memory of his grandmother's funeral and instrumentally, the brass band on the track provides echoes of both industrial northern England and a traditional New Orleans burial. Appropriately, given its inspiration and subject matter, it's one of the most genuinely moving tracks on the album.

One of a number of reggae songs that Paul has penned over the years, 'How Many People' was dedicated to the memory of Chico Mendes, a Brazilian trade union leader and climate-change activist. A militant defender of the Amazon rainforest, Mendes was assassinated in December 1988.

The album closes with 'Motor of Love', a song Paul had been working on for some time before putting it in the hands of Chris Hughes and Ross Cullum during the final stages of the Hog Hill sessions. The Hughes–Cullum partnership had been hugely successful with the UK synth-pop band Tears for Fears earlier in

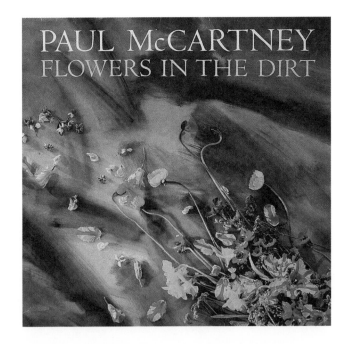

"We enjoy each other, everything seems easy-going. And whenever we sit down and play music, it seems to sound good. This band's good enough to learn a song fairly quickly. In fact, they know them better than I do."

Paul McCartney

the decade, and they brought a new level of high-tech production to the track. The straightforward ballad is delivered against a lush backing of electronic effects which make it more synth-sounding than perhaps McCartney originally intended.

On its release, the album shot to the top of the British charts, with generally positive reviews across the board. Mark Cooper in *Q* magazine called Side One of *Flowers in the Dirt* 'his best work since *Band On The Run*', concluding a glowing assessment: 'against all the odds, he's lovable Paul once again, the master of all affable ceremonies'. And while it didn't do quite as spectacularly in America, reaching #21 in *Billboard*, it featured in the Top Twenty in another dozen countries worldwide – sales that were aided in no small part by the Paul McCartney World Tour, that swung through North America, Europe, Japan and Brazil between September 1989 and the following July.

Previous page Paul during a press showcase performance for *Flowers in the Dirt* at London's Playhouse Theatre, July 27, 1989.

Above left The original album cover for *Flowers in the Dirt*, designed by Paul's friend and collaborator Brian Clarke.

Above right Buggles, the pop duo consisting of Geoff Downes (left) and Trevor Horn, one of various producers on the album.

MY BRAVE FACE

RECORDED: SEPTEMBER–OCTOBER 1988
STUDIO: OLYMPIC SOUND STUDIOS, LONDON
PRODUCERS: PAUL MCCARTNEY, MITCHELL FROOM, NEIL DORFSMAN
COMPOSERS: PAUL MCCARTNEY, ELVIS COSTELLO
RELEASED: MAY 8, 1989 (UK), MAY 27, 1989 (US)

The opener to *Flowers in the Dirt*, 'My Brave Face' was released prior to the album, in May 1989. A demo for the song had already been laid down at Paul's Hog Hill studio the previous year by its two composers, McCartney and Elvis Costello. A strident statement, there's a Beatles-like feel that some ascribe to the fact that Paul – on Costello's suggestion – used his old Hofner "violin" bass for the first time in many years, the same one he'd played on Fab Four classic recordings.

Although the two worked closely on the chord structure and the lyrics, McCartney later smoothed things over a little. He brought the demo to producers Mitchell Froom and Neil Dorfsman at the Olympic Sound Studios, where they all agreed the recording needed some more work.

Using the line-up of guitarists Hamish Stuart and Robbie McIntosh, and drummer Chris Whitten, they re-cut the track, which became a great album opener and a single in its own right. "Well, it seemed like it could be a hit," Mitchell Froom reflected later. "It's a bit of an odd song in some ways, but it was really hooky, it had a great bass line, it was positive and [had] a really cool lyric, great melody, it sort of had all that stuff."

Their collective instinct paid off. 'My Brave Face' made the Top 20 in at least a dozen countries, peaking at #18 in the UK and #25 in the USA, and topped the charts in Japan.

YOU WANT HER TOO

RECORDED: FEBRUARY, 1988
STUDIO: HOG HILL MILL, ICKLESHAM, SUSSEX
PRODUCERS: PAUL MCCARTNEY, ELVIS COSTELLO,
NEIL DORFSMAN, MITCHELL FROOM
COMPOSERS: PAUL MCCARTNEY, DECLAN MACMANUS
RELEASED: JUNE 5, 1989

As well as co-writing four of the songs on *Flowers in the Dirt*, Elvis Costello shared the vocals with Paul on 'You Want Her Too'. Initially the pair had tried to imitate the compositional technique that McCartney and Lennon had used all those years before, exchanging chords, melodies and lyrics as they built on a song. Paul was initially dubious, as he would later admit, about not wanting to duplicate what had been a unique working relationship in the context of The Beatles. Consequently, a preliminary demo recording had just Paul doing both vocal parts.

But as it turned out, the two voices work perfectly, in a song where the statement-and-answer is essential to the narrative of the lyric, and in no way sounds like a reworking of any Lennon–McCartney formula. The track is an imaginary conversation, possibly between a man and his conscience, or is it with a rival, as the title suggests? Costello's is the nagging 'answer' voice, with a nasal delivery that blends effectively with McCartney's smoother texture on the harmony sections. There's a brief hint of The Beatles' 'She's Leaving Home' in the melody, while the end coda fades in surprising fashion with a short 15-second blast of exuberant big band swing (a genre both Paul and Elvis were fond of), orchestrated by arranger Richard Niles.

While reviewing *Flowers in the Dirt*, the *Chicago Tribune* called the track "another stand-out, a rancorous dialogue". Many others agreed, with particular reference to the McCartney–Costello co-writes. Mark Cooper, writing in *Q* magazine, summed up the "deep soul pastiche" of 'You Want Her Too' as the best example of Costello's "sense of drama", saying: "As Elvis and Paul take swipes at one another's personas while they wrestle over a shared lover, McCartney's role as a 'hopeless romantic' gains a contrasting interest against Costello's residual sneer."

Above Singer, songwriter, and *Flowers in the Dirt* collaborator Elvis Costello.
Opposite Paul and Linda photographed by Rino Petrosino in Italy, 1989.

"That's a good old trick. We both love the art of songwriting, we're still intrigued by it. Little things like having a cynical answer to a line – that's the kind of thing I did a long time ago, like in [the 1967 Beatles song] 'Getting Better' where I sing, 'It's getting better all the time', and John sings, 'It can't get no worse.' Otherwise, you're just writing a song straightforward. That's good too, but it's kind of nice to have little things that bounce off each other, that yin-yang thing."

Paul McCartney

OFF THE

GROUND

OFF THE GROUND

LOOKING FOR CHANGES

HOPE OF DELIVERANCE

MISTRESS AND MAID
(PAUL MCCARTNEY, DECLAN MACMANUS)

I OWE IT ALL TO YOU

BIKER LIKE AN ICON

PEACE IN THE NEIGHBOURHOOD

GOLDEN EARTH GIRL

THE LOVERS THAT NEVER WERE
(PAUL MCCARTNEY, DECLAN MACMANUS)

GET OUT OF MY WAY

WINEDARK OPEN SEA

C'MON PEOPLE

(All songs written by Paul McCartney except where indicated)

Paul McCartney (vocals, bass, guitars, piano, keyboards, ocarina, percussion, sitar, drums), Linda McCartney (vocals, autoharp, keyboards, percussion, whistle), Hamish Stuart (vocals, guitars, bass, percussion, piano), Robbie McIntosh (guitars, mandolin, vocals), Paul Wickens (keyboards, piano, accordian, LinnDrum, percussion, vocals), Blair Cunningham (drums, congas, percussion, vocals)

OFF THE GROUND

RECORDED: NOVEMBER 25, 1991–JUNE 30, 1992 // **STUDIOS:** HOG HILL, ICKLESHAM, SUSSEX; HIT FACTORY, LONDON
PRODUCER: PAUL MCCARTNEY, JULIAN MENDELSOHN // **RELEASED:** FEBRUARY 2, 1993

Off the Ground was released to coincide with McCartney's New World Tour, which kicked off on February 18, 1993. The album featured the touring band, with Blair Cunningham a new addition on drums, in place of Chris Whitten who had left to join Dire Straits.

The album was recorded 'live in the studio', with the band running through numbers and then recording them in a single take, rather than making separate instrumental and vocals tracks. "I didn't do serious demos," Paul recalled later, "I just sang the songs with guitar or piano on to a Sony Walkman. The point was to leave room for ideas for the band, and the co-producer, Julian Mendelsohn."

Nevertheless, the perfectionist in Paul certainly appeared in the songwriting process itself. He ran through some of his new lyrics with a friend, the poet Adrian Mitchell, to have a second opinion before finalizing them. In addition, some of the songs were leftovers from *Flowers in the Dirt*, Paul's previous studio album, and included two more compositions written with Elvis Costello.

The album opens with the title track, a smooth up-tempo ballad distinguished by the fact that the backing is almost entirely computer-based. This likeable pop song is then followed by 'Looking for Changes', which takes on a far tougher persona. Much more of a straight rocker, the song addresses the subject of animal vivisection, an issue close to Paul's heart. There's a tangible anger in the lyrics, not least emphasized by his use of some strong language, and in under three minutes he manages to vent in a most effective way against the cruelties of the animal laboratories.

Another social commentary of sorts, but with a more optimistic slant, 'Hope of Deliverance' was released as a moderately successful single ahead of the album, in December 1992. And the first of two co-compositions with Elvis Costello, 'Mistress and Maid', is a gliding waltz-time ballad that tells the story of the trauma felt by a devoted young woman married to an inattentive husband. It's powerful stuff.

'I Owe It All to You' is one in a long line of Paul's love songs addressed directly to his wife Linda. Describing a visit to an exhibition space in France, where images were projected onto rock walls to spectacular effect, he uses the memory as a device to confirm more intensely personal emotions. And there's some typically McCartney-esque punning, exemplified in the song's title, that makes the amusing 'Biker Like an Icon' irresistible to lovers of any kind of word play.

One of the best examples of the 'live in the studio' methodology is 'Peace in the Neighbourhood', which has the feel of a really spontaneous jam. With a beautifully crafted guitar conclusion from Robbie McIntosh, it's a hugely satisfying exercise in relaxed musical excellence.

And 'Golden Earth Girl' is a delicate piano-based ballad that grows in texture with each verse, as backing vocals, flute and oboe help create an ethereal spell.

The second collaboration with Elvis Costello, 'The Lovers That Never Were', was initially destined for *Flowers in the Dirt*, but when it didn't work out on those sessions McCartney decided to shelve it for a while. Recalling the original demo the pair recorded, Costello described Paul's singing as, "One of the great vocal performances of his solo career."

Paul would be the first to admit that straight-ahead rock 'n' roll is often the hardest genre to tackle successfully. But on 'Get Out of My Way' he seems to have no problems. This

is a slice of highly danceable country rock endowed with some great guitar from Robbie McIntosh, honky-tonk piano courtesy of Paul 'Wix' Wickens, and a horn section made up of three saxes and a trumpet.

Like the endless vista of the ocean conjured up in the song's lyrics, 'Winedark Open Sea' casts an almost hypnotic spell featuring Paul's electric piano, Linda's harmonium, and the guitars of McIntosh and Hamish Stuart. And at over seven minutes, 'C'mon People', with its dramatic orchestral build-up and long-fade coda, closes the album in majestic style.

Various singles from the album enjoyed a mixed reception around the world. None performed particularly well in Britain or America, while 'Hope and Deliverance', for instance, made the Top Five in charts across mainland Europe. Likewise, the album itself fared only moderately. In the UK it briefly charted

at #5, while in the US it never got higher than #17 in Billboard. In Germany, on the other hand, it became Paul's best-selling solo album, eventually selling over half a million copies.

Long-term sales, however, must have been influenced by the New World Tour that kicked off just a couple of weeks after the release of the album. As one UK concert review noted: "Vibrant new tunes like 'Hope of Deliverance' and 'Get Out of My Way' made a compelling argument for *Off the Ground* as McCartney's best work in some time."

Previous page Paul performing in Mexico City during "The New World Tour", November 27, 1993.

Opposite The poet, novelist and playwright Adrian Mitchell, who reviewed some of Paul's lyrics for *Off the Ground* before McCartney finalized them.

Above Paul with Linda in the Hog Hill recording studio during sessions for *Off the Ground* in 1992.

HOPE OF DELIVERANCE

RECORDED: DECEMBER 9, 1991–JULY, 1992
STUDIOS: HOG HILL MILL, ICKLESHAM, SUSSEX;
HIT FACTORY, LONDON
PRODUCERS: PAUL MCCARTNEY, JULIAN MENDELSOHN
COMPOSER: PAUL MCCARTNEY
RELEASED: DECEMBER 28, 1992 (UK) (SINGLE),
JANUARY 12, 1993 (US) (SINGLE)

Released as a "trailer" track for *Off the Ground*, 'Hope of Deliverance' was released two months ahead of the album at the end of December 1992. A "social commentary" song in the broadest sense, with a definitely optimistic slant, its Spanish-tinged, hand-clapping rhythms pulsate with a feel-good factor that's infectious – Paul himself would describe it as "An international message with a Latin American flavour."

The song started life as a simple solo busk on a 12-string guitar, in his house in rural Sussex, not far from his Hog Hill studio. From there he took it along to the next studio session where he worked it into a fully-fledged acoustic track with guitarist Robbie McIntosh. The number evolved from there, and as the rest of the band threw ideas around and a definite Latin American sound emerged, the track developed into a joyous sing-along. More exotic colour was added at the overdub stage, with a trio of percussionists called in to contribute bongos, conga drums, tom-toms and a cowbell. By the time of the final takes, a veritable party was happening in the studio.

Critics warmed to the song, with *Billboard*'s singles reviewer commenting: "A soft, acoustic-anchored arrangement clips along at a breezy pace. Spanish cultural influences and handclappin' rhythms give the track a unique and refreshing vibe that will please programmers at pop, AC [Adult Contemporary] and album-rock levels." With the aid of the tour, 'Hope of Deliverance' became a huge international hit, particularly in Latin America, where it became a favourite anthem with audiences.

It was a Top Five hit in Austria, Canada, Norway, Switzerland, Germany and Italy, in the latter two countries peaking at #3 and #2 respectively. It also made the Top 10 in Belgium, Denmark, Iceland, Japan and the Netherlands and, although it didn't fare as well in Great Britain (#18) or the US (#83), it went on to sell over four million copies worldwide.

BIKER LIKE AN ICON

RECORDED: NOVEMBER 25, 1991
STUDIOS: HOG HILL MILL, ICKLESHAM, SUSSEX
PRODUCERS: PAUL MCCARTNEY, JULIAN MENDELSOHN
COMPOSER: PAUL MCCARTNEY
RELEASED: FEBRUARY 22, 1993, NOVEMBER 8, 1993 (SINGLE)

The first number to be recorded at the *Off the Ground* sessions, it was also done – in keeping with the overall ethos of the studio process for the album – in one take. The intention at that initial session was for songs to be rehearsed, but after running through 'Biker' for 15 minutes or so, the band decided it was going so well they should record it. And that was it – when they listened back to the take a couple of weeks later, they all agreed it was worth keeping just as it was.

In the notes for the souvenir programme to the New World Tour, Paul outlined how the song came about. He and Linda had been talking about cameras, and she said "I like a Leica" which became "I like a Nikon" and from that Paul cooked up the story of the biker whose girlfriend loved him "like an icon".

From there it was a small step to a string of similarly trite devices – "biker" and "like her", "persisted" and "twisted", "permission" and "ambition", and of course, "biker like an icon". For him, the wordplay was reminiscent of his songwriting days in The Beatles, when silly rhymes and puns were all important: "I remember when John and me would always look at the new titles in the American charts and get intrigued by things like 'Quarter To Three' by US Bonds – what could that be about? It was very important to us to get a title that had that buzz."

Released in November 1993, 'Biker Like an Icon' failed to sell particularly well, despite a strong sepia-tinted video featuring a leather-clad blonde woman seeking her elusive biker. It fared best in Germany, where it reached just #62 in the national chart.

"A few weeks later we listened back to it, looked at one another and thought, 'Are we going to spend a day trying to better this?' No point. The magic is there."

Hamish Stuart, guitarist

Opposite Paul in one of his old schoolrooms, during a visit to the Liverpool Institute High School for Boys, Liverpool 1991.

Above Paul and Linda, photographed promoting their 1993 single from *Off the Ground*, 'Biker Like an Icon'.

FLAMING

PIE

THE SONG WE WERE SINGING

THE WORLD TONIGHT

IF YOU WANNA

SOMEDAYS

YOUNG BOY

CALICO SKIES

FLAMING PIE

HEAVEN ON A SUNDAY

USED TO BE BAD
(STEVE MILLER, PAUL MCCARTNEY)

SOUVENIR

LITTLE WILLOW

REALLY LOVE YOU
(PAUL MCCARTNEY, RICHARD STARKEY)

BEAUTIFUL NIGHT

GREAT DAY

(All songs written by Paul McCartney, except where indicated)

Paul McCartney (vocals, guitars, bass guitar, double bass, harmonium, drums, piano, percussion, Hammond organ, keyboards, harpsichord, vibraphone), Jeff Lynne (vocals, guitars, keyboards, spinette, harpsichord), Steve Miller (vocals, guitars), Linda McCartney (vocals), James McCartney (vocals), Chris Davis (saxophone), Dave Bishop (saxophone), Kevin Robinson (trumpet), Ringo Starr (drums, percussion, vocals), Michael Thompson (French horn), Richard Bissill (French horn), Richard Watkins (French horn), John Pigneguy (French horn), plus orchestral musicians on 'Somedays' and 'Beautiful Night'

FLAMING PIE

RECORDED: SEPTEMBER 3, 1992; FEBRUARY 22–MAY 11, 1995; NOVEMBER 1, 1995–FEBRUARY 14, 1997 // **STUDIOS:** HOG HILL MILL, ICKLESHAM, SUSSEX; ABBEY ROAD STUDIOS, LONDON; AIR STUDIOS, LONDON; STEVE MILLER STUDIO, SUN VALLEY, IDAHO
PRODUCERS: PAUL MCCARTNEY, JEFF LYNNE, GEORGE MARTIN // **RELEASED:** MAY 5, 1997

Appearing in May 1997, *Flaming Pie* was Paul McCartney's tenth studio album, and his first to be released in over four years. In the interim, Paul had been spending a lot of time – along with his fellow ex-Beatles George Harrison and Ringo Starr – putting together the huge *The Beatles Anthology* project, a TV documentary series on the history of the band, accompanied by a set of three double-album CDs released over two years. *The Beatles Anthology* was first broadcast in November 1995, and it was only after the work on the project was completed earlier in that year that Paul began working on the bulk of *Flaming Pie*.

Because of the two-year release schedule for the *Anthology*, EMI Records made it clear that they didn't want McCartney to release a solo set in the interim. As first he felt it was an imposition, but quickly came to realize it was pointless competing against himself as one of The Beatles: "So I fell in with the idea and thought, 'Great, I don't even have to think about an album,'" he told *Q* magazine in 1996, "Which won't be released until 1997 because of *Anthology*, which suits me fine. I'm enjoying just making music without all the farting. I'm working to my own deadlines."

Undoubtedly inspired by the attention he had been paying to The Beatles' archive throughout the work on *Anthology*, Paul's title for the album came from an article John Lennon had written for the first edition of the local Liverpool music paper *Mersey Beat*, back in 1961. Called (by Bill Harry, the paper's founder and editor, as Lennon hadn't supplied a title) "Being A Short Diversion

On The Dubious Origins Of Beatles (Translated From The John Lennon)", it was a nonsense-language "biography" of the band, who were just starting to take off locally. "Many people ask, 'What are Beatles?'" Lennon wrote. "Why Beatles? Ugh, Beatles, how did the name arrive? So we will tell you. It came in a vision – a man appeared on a flaming pie and said unto them, 'From this day on you are Beatles with an 'A'. Thank you, mister man, they said, thanking him."

The opening track of *Flaming Pie*, 'The Song We Were Singing', harks back to those early days of The Beatles, a waltz-time delight recalling the nights he and John would spend at the McCartney family home and elsewhere, drinking wine, smoking, putting the world to rights (and writing songs, of course). Paul plays the double bass that once belonged to Bill Black, the legendary Memphis musician on Elvis Presley's

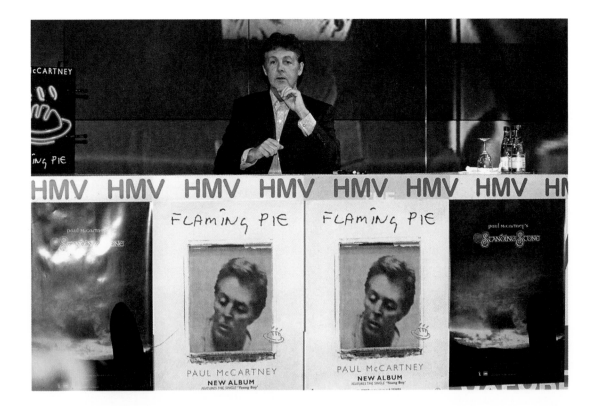

earliest recordings. The only other instrumentalist is Jeff Lynne, who features throughout the album.

Lynne was an established name in his own right. As well as making big-selling records with his Electric Light Orchestra (ELO), he'd been part of the late-1980s supergroup the Travelling Wilburys, alongside George Harrison, Bob Dylan, Roy Orbison and Tom Petty. On 'The World Tonight', a loping, gentle rocker on which Paul reflects on a life of fame, Lynne is again his only accomplice. And it's another two-hander on 'If You Wanna', but this time Paul's partner is the American blues-rock star Steve Miller. A lightly-coloured road trip of a song, the West Coast sound perfectly conjured up in East Sussex, England.

Written in March 1994, when Paul was giving Linda a lift to a photoshoot for one of her cookery books, 'Somedays' is another love song to his wife. Delicately recorded on acoustic guitar, any instrumental addition might have seemed unnecessary, but George Martin's orchestral overdubs are nothing short of a sheer delight. It's one of McCartney's most finely crafted songs, and arguably the stand-out track on a memorable album.

Previous to recording 'If You Wanna' in May 1995, McCartney and Steve Miller had already teamed up a few months earlier at Miller's home studio in Sun Valley, Idaho. There they cut 'Young Boy', an up-tempo celebration of young love… or at least the search for it! According to Paul, the lyrics were written "against the clock" when he was waiting while Linda cooked a lunch for a feature in the *New York Times*. He started with "Poor Boy", but realized that had been the title of an old Elvis song (featured in Presley's debut movie, *Love Me Tender*), so changed it to "Young Boy".

In the booklet accompanying *Flaming Pie*, McCartney describes how 'Calico Skies' was written in August 1991 when the McCartneys were staying in Long Island, and Hurricane Bob caused a total blackout. The song he came up with that night was eventually taped as a solo acoustic track at Hog Hill studios a year later, and became the earliest recorded track on the album.

The title track, 'Flaming Pie' is a simple duet with Jeff Lynne, recorded, on Paul's suggestion, in a matter of hours – as was the way with The Beatles' early albums. It's a straight-ahead rock number, with some rollicking piano from Paul, and nonsensical lyrics that fit the genealogy of the title. 'Heaven on a Sunday', by contrast, is a languid love ballad which Paul wrote while on holiday in August 1996, in a boat off the American coast. It features his son James, then 19 years old, on guitar. The two trade licks, McCartney Senior on acoustic, Junior on electric.

The session that produced 'If YouWanna' included another collaboration with Steve Miller, this time with the American blues-rocker as co-author of 'Used to be Bad'. Miller said he wanted to hear Paul singing some real "Texas blues", and provided a bedrock of riffs over which the two joyously jammed. It's the nearest thing to a basic low-down blues in the McCartney catalogue, with Paul on drums and bass, his guest on an incisive electric guitar.

A laid-back slice of soul music is how Paul and Jeff Lynne envisioned 'Souvenir', the voice backed with a three-piece horn

Previous page and above Paul at the album launch for *Flaming Pie* at the HMV shop in Oxford Street, London, 1997.

Opposite ELO star Jeff Lynne and producer George Martin, who both worked on *Flaming Pie*, at the launch party for the Beatles *Anthology* series, November 1995.

BEAUTIFUL NIGHT

RECORDED: MAY 13, 1996
STUDIOS: HOG HILL MILL, ICKLESHAM, SUSSEX;
ABBEY ROAD STUDIOS, LONDON
PRODUCERS: PAUL MCCARTNEY, JEFF LYNNE
COMPOSER: PAUL MCCARTNEY
RELEASED: MAY 5, 1997, DECEMBER 15, 1997 (SINGLE)

section echoing the 'Stax' sound of Memphis in its mid-1960s heyday. And it's just McCartney and Lynne on a multitude of instruments for 'Little Willow', a poignant tribute to the memory of Maureen Cox, the ex-wife of Ringo Starr whose death from cancer in December 1994 prompted the composition. In the album liner notes, Paul dedicates the song to Maureen and her children.

The following track, 'Really Love You', brings in Ringo himself on drums, for a rare co-composition with McCartney. A funky number in the R&B style of the day, over a straight blues structure that owes more to its traditional rhythm and blues antecedents – it's just Paul, Jeff and Ringo having fun. And recorded immediately before 'Really Love You' at the same session, 'Beautiful Night' features Ringo on lead vocals shared with his old colleague.

Flaming Pie concludes with 'Great Day', another spectacular solo work, with just Linda sharing the vocals. The song had been in Paul's head, and his off-the-cuff unrecorded repertoire, for a quarter of a century, since the days of *RAM*. A short but highly effective end to the album.

Released on May 5, 1997 in the UK, and two weeks later in the US, the collection earned McCartney his best reviews since *Tug of War* in 1982. Carol Clerk, in *Uncut* magazine, called it, "The most relaxed album he's made in years," continuing, "Macca doesn't have to try to change the world because he's done that once already." And in *Uncut*'s UK rival *Mojo*, an otherwise sceptical Chris Ingham was effusive about Paul's actual vocal talents: "It must be noted that the man's singing is a marvel. The grey-around-the-edges folk-balladeering of 'Calico Skies', the falsetto blues-croon of 'Heaven On A Sunday', the deliriously uninhibited rock-shriek of 'Really Love You' re-confirm that McCartney's vocal style range is without equal in pop."

Flaming Pie made it to #2 in the album charts and earned gold discs on both sides of the Atlantic. In fact, in the US, it was his first Top 10 entry since *Tug of War*, and it went on to enter the Top 20 in over a dozen other countries around the world.

The first of three collaborations with Ringo Starr in the *Flaming Pie* sessions (only two of which appeared on the original album), 'Beautiful Night' was first recorded by McCartney in New York City in August 1986. Paul was recording with Phil Ramone, although much of their work never saw the light of day. He made another attempt at the song in 1987, in collaboration with George Martin, but that too remained unreleased.

Then, when Ringo was recruited to do some recording for *Flaming Pie*, Paul resurrected the number. "I unearthed this old song for when Ringo was coming, changed a few lyrics and it was really like the old days," he recalled. "I realized that we hadn't done this for so long, but it was very comfortable. And it was still there."

The dramatic love story at the core of the song was brought to life by strong performances from McCartney, Jeff Lynne and Starr, and further enhanced by a full orchestral backing overdubbed at Abbey Road by George Martin. The intense saga described in the lyrics was enhanced by a very impressive, largely black-and-white video, shot on the waterfront backstreets of Liverpool by director Julien Temple.

Ringo appeared in the video, as did Linda (on backing vocals on the record) on her last-ever appearance in a music video. The film, which was first shown on *The Oprah Winfrey Show*, had to be edited slightly because of a brief glimpse of a naked woman skinny-dipping! Released in the UK in December 1997, 'Beautiful Night' was the third and final single to be taken from *Flaming Pie*, making it to #25 in the British chart.

Above Nam Cover collage artwork for the Beatles' *Anthology* set of CDs, released in November 1995.

Opposite Ringo Starr, who appeared on two tracks of the original *Flaming Pie* release, pictured here in May 1998.

"It was really good to see that Ringo and I locked in, The Beatles' rhythm section, drum and bass, we just locked in. It would have been kind of disappointing if we'd lost it, but we hadn't."

Paul McCartney

RUN

DEVIL RUN

BLUE JEAN BOP
(GENE VINCENT, HAL LEVY)

SHE SAID YEAH
(RODDY JACKSON, DON CHRISTY)

ALL SHOOK UP
(OTIS BLACKWELL, ELVIS PRESLEY)

RUN DEVIL RUN
(PAUL MCCARTNEY)

NO OTHER BABY
(DICKIE BISHOP, BOB WATSON)

LONESOME TOWN
(BAKER KNIGHT)

TRY NOT TO CRY
(PAUL MCCARTNEY)

MOVIE MAGG
(CARL PERKINS)

BROWN EYED HANDSOME MAN
(CHUCK BERRY)

WHAT IT IS
(PAUL MCCARTNEY)

COQUETTE
(JOHNNY GREEN, CARMEN LOMBARDO, GUS KAHN)

I GOT STUNG
(DAVID HILL, AARON SCHROEDER)

HONEY HUSH
(JOE TURNER)

SHAKE A HAND
(JOE MORRIS)

PARTY
(JESSIE MAE ROBINSON)

Paul McCartney (vocals, bass, guitars, percussion), David Gilmour (guitars, vocals), Mick Green
(guitar), Ian Paice (drums, percussion), Pete Wingfield (keyboards, piano, Hammond organ),
Dave Mattacks (drums, percussion), Geraint Watkins (piano), Chris Hall (accordion)

RUN DEVIL RUN

RECORDED: MARCH 1–5 AND MAY 4–5, 1999 // **STUDIOS:** ABBEY ROAD STUDIOS, LONDON
PRODUCER: PAUL MCCARTNEY, CHRIS THOMAS // **RELEASED:** OCTOBER 4, 1999 (UK), OCTOBER 5, 1999 (US)

After *Flaming Pie*, Paul McCartney's next venture to be released was *Rushes* in 1998. It featured ambient techno music credited to The Fireman, the soubriquet for Paul and producer Youth (Martin Glover), under which the duo had already worked on *Strawberries Oceans Ships Forests* in 1993.

A similar collection to his 'Russian' album from 1988, *Run Devil Run* was McCartney harking back to the sounds and musical influences of his teenage years. He'd been coming to terms with the death of Linda for almost a year, when in March 1999 he put together a line-up specifically to record a collection of old rock 'n' roll numbers. He and Linda had been talking about such an exercise; now, he felt the time was right to pursue it, partly as a tribute to her memory.

Taking his cue from the work dynamic of *Flaming Pie*, laying down the tracks as quickly and efficiently as possible, he arrived at Abbey Road Studio 2 with a manila envelope full of lyrics for the songs he wanted to try out. "I'd say to the guys, 'Anybody know 'She Said Yeah'?' They'd say no, because they were slightly obscure choices, I'd say okay, this is how it goes. We'd take five or 10 minutes – and that's how we did it in The Beatles – because how many times can you go through a song without everyone getting bored?"

The album opens with the Gene Vincent classic 'Blue Jean Bop', which was the opening title track on Vincent's debut LP in 1956. With Paul on bass and some atmospheric echo on his vocals, the twin lead guitars of David Gilmour and Mick Green tear things up in time-honoured style. Pete Wingfield adds some piano to the proceedings on the second track, 'She Said Yeah', a lesser-known song originally recorded by the great Larry Williams. Williams was a firm favourite of The Beatles, who covered three of his songs: 'Bad Boy', 'Slow Down' and 'Dizzy Miss Lizzie'.

According to the liner notes for *Run Devil Run*, 'All Shook Up' was Elvis' first UK #1, in June 1957 – the same week Paul McCartney celebrated his 15th birthday! The title track, the first of three McCartney originals on the album, is named after a range of bath salts in a "herbal medicine" shop specializing in "hoodoo" remedies that Paul came across in downtown Atlanta, Georgia. It became a story song, in real Chuck Berry style.

'No Other Baby' is the most obscure song on the album, but in many ways the most evocative. Paul released it as the only single from the album, with 'Brown Eyed Handsome Man' on the flipside. Another slowie, 'Lonesome Town', was a hit for Ricky Nelson in 1958, a relaxed ballad with lyrics along the lines of 'Heartbreak Hotel' – broken hearts and broken dreams, concluding with "Maybe down in Lonesome Town, I can learn to forget".

The second original by Paul, 'Try Not to Cry' is a mid-tempo rocker, the hard driving beat contrasting the emotions behind the lyrics, reflecting on Paul's anguish after the loss of Linda in April 1998. From the master of the genre, Carl Perkins, 'Movie Magg' is a rockabilly song dating back to 1955. It was the first song that Perkins wrote, telling how he took his girlfriend Maggie to the local cinema on the back of his horse. Paul relates the true tale with a mellow croon, befitting of the band's light touch all round.

'Brown Eyed Handsome Man', powerfully delivered, was a Chuck Berry song that Buddy Holly scored with in a posthumous single release in 1963. Paul decided to add some accordion, courtesy of Chris Hall, to get more of a Tex-Mex/Cajun feel.

'What It Is' is a strong slice of blues-rock, and a direct tribute by Paul to his late wife. "I was playing bluesy riffs on the piano and this song started to come out," he explained on the album sleeve notes. "Linda was there and I enjoyed it just for that, for the little feedback she gave. So I thought I'll do that as sort of my little tribute to Linda." Another musical tribute to one of his rock 'n' roll heroes, the six-to-the-bar piano vamping that kicks off 'Coquette' tells us we're in Fats Domino territory, and Paul delivers a vocal in true 'Fat Man' style.

'I Got Stung' was one of Elvis Presley's lesser-applauded rockers, but a chart-topper all the same, which McCartney renders with appropriate verve. He does the same on 'Honey Hush', a rock 'n' roll stand-by from rhythm and bluesman Joe Turner. But it was Johnny Burnette's 1956 version of the track that caught Paul's ear back in the early days of The Beatles.

McCartney again delves back into the lesser-known gems of the rock pioneers, with 'Shake a Hand'. The tried and trusted songs from Little Richard's catalogue, like 'Lucille', 'Tutti Frutti' and 'Good Golly Miss Molly', were familiar to any fan of vintage rock 'n' roll, but 'Shake a Hand' was not as obvious a choice. With some fitting piano from Pete Wingfield and great guitar breaks from Mick Green and David Gilmour, Paul's "Little Richard" voice was never better applied.

The Elvis Presley 1957 hit 'Party' rounds off the album in an appropriately raucous manner, a free-for-all jam that captures the spontaneous nature of the whole collection, and a "false ending" that evokes its culmination at a live gig.

Run Devil Run was released on October 4, 1999, enjoying mostly positive reviews and peaking at #12 in the UK charts and #27 in America – a good showing for what was essentially an album of cover versions. To promote the album, Paul performed with the line-up for several key TV appearances in the UK, including *Later with Jules Holland*, *The Tube* and *Parkinson*. And on December 14 they played an historic performance at the Cavern Club in Liverpool, which was shown live on the Internet, with a reported 50 million people trying to connect worldwide.

Previous page Paul – almost incognito – in linen suit and shades, on a Paris street in 1999.

Right Paul playing at the "Concert for Linda" memorial benefit, held at London's Royal Albert Hall on April 10, 1999.

Below Paul receiving his knighthood at Buckingham Palace, March 11, 1997.

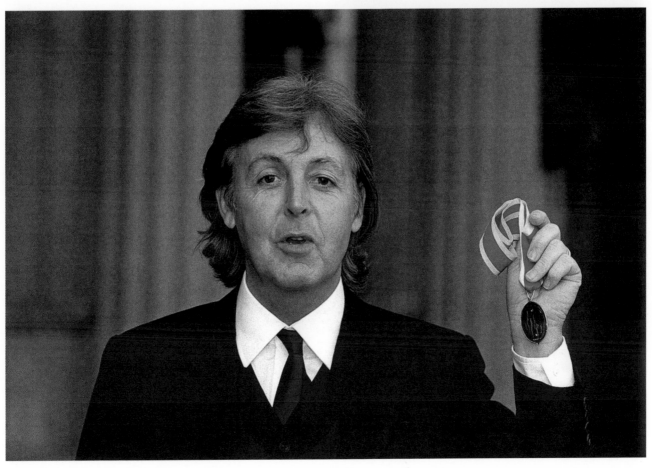

RUN DEVIL RUN [SONG]

RECORDED: MARCH 3, 1999
STUDIO: ABBEY ROAD STUDIOS, LONDON
PRODUCERS: PAUL MCCARTNEY, CHRIS THOMAS
COMPOSER: PAUL MCCARTNEY
RELEASED: OCTOBER 4, 1999 (UK), OCTOBER 5, 1999 (US)

The name of the title track for *Run Devil Run* came from a visit to Atlanta, Georgia, which Paul had made with his son James. They were wandering around what he described as the "funky side of town" when they came across Miller's Rexall Drugs, a well-known pharmacy specializing in "hoodoo" medicines and remedies. There McCartney spied a bottle of bath salts in the window called "Run Devil Run"; intrigued by the name, he bought a bottle, and later made it the basis for a song.

Paul used a picture of the "voodoo" drug store on the cover of the album, the banner over the shop front altered to read as the record title. In a press interview before the release of *Run Devil Run*, he would be trying out the bath salts, "Not that I have got many demons to get rid of…".

Written in the narrative style of many of Chuck Berry's compositions, the lyrics came easily to McCartney, a parable of a "holy roller" in deepest Alabama with the power to drive out the devil.

"At the early recordings of the Beatles we worked in a very specific way – recording two songs in the morning and two more after lunch. I have a professional nostalgia for that way of recording, and I wanted to see if we could do that with this album."

Paul McCartney, Press Release for *Run Devil Run*, October 1999

For the album, Paul had assembled an all-star line-up including Pete Wingfield on piano, Mick Green and David Gilmour (Pink Floyd) on guitars, and Ian Paice (Deep Purple) on drums. One of the most dynamic tracks on a powerful album, 'Run Devil Run' absolutely crackles with raw energy. The soaring guitar breaks from Green and Gilmour, and Pete Wingfield's piano fills, make a rock 'n' roll sound as authentic as any that McCartney ever committed to disc. Surprisingly, it was never released as a single.

NO OTHER BABY

RECORDED: MARCH 5, 1999
STUDIO: ABBEY ROAD STUDIOS, LONDON
PRODUCERS: PAUL MCCARTNEY, CHRIS THOMAS
COMPOSERS: DICKIE BISHOP, BOB WATSON
RELEASED: OCTOBER 4, 1999 (UK) (ALBUM), OCTOBER 5, 1999
(US) (ALBUM), OCTOBER 24, 1999

The only single released from *Run Devil Run*, 'No Other Baby' was originally recorded in 1957 by Dickie Bishop and The Sidekicks. Dickie "Cisco" Bishop was a UK folk singer-guitarist, who had recorded with the "King of Skiffle", Lonnie Donegan in 1955, but 'No Other Baby' was better known by the cover version cut by The Vipers skiffle group in 1958.

Although the song went on to be covered by pop singer Bobby Helms in 1959, and the duo Paul and Paula in 1964, it was The Vipers' version that captivated the teenage Paul McCartney around the time he was starting to play with John Lennon and The Quarrymen. And although he later forgot who was on the record, the song stayed in his head: "I didn't have a record of it. I didn't know who'd recorded it or who'd written it. But I knew I loved the song from the late '50s."

When he decided he might record it for the forthcoming sessions, Paul dug a little deeper and discovered it was The Vipers' record he'd remembered all those years ago. And when he mentioned the song to George Martin, McCartney realized it was Martin who had worked with The Vipers at the time. So the song that had lodged in his head for decades had been produced by George Martin, long before anyone had heard of The Beatles.

With a hypnotically simple guitar and bass riff, the track is a stripped-down classic. Even the short guitar breaks are a no-frills affair. The only embellishment comes from a hint of harmonies buried in the mix before the fade-out – a perfect ending to a minimalist classic.

Released with a double B-side of 'Brown Eyed Handsome Man' from the album, and Charlie Gracie's 'Fabulous' (which wasn't on the original track list), the single reached just a modest #42 on the UK chart.

Opposite Rock 'n' roll legend Chuck Berry, a huge influence on Paul McCartney, and who featured on the album *Run Devil Run*.

Below Paul with his *Run Devil Run* band before playing a gig at the Cavern Club in Liverpool, December 14, 1999.

DRIVING

RAIN

(All songs written by Paul McCartney, except where indicated)

Paul McCartney (vocals, bass, guitars, drums, electric piano, piano, percussion), Abe Laboriel Jr (tambourine, electronic percussions, drums, vocals, accordion), Rusty Anderson (guitars, bass guitar, vocals, percussion, tanpura), Gabe Dixon (keyboards, piano, vocals), David Kahne (keyboard, guitar, synthesizer), James McCartney (guitar, percussion), Ralph Morrison (violin), David Campbell (viola), Matt Funes (viola), Joel Derouin (violin), Larry Corbett (cello), Eric Clapton (guitar), Ringo Starr (drums)

DRIVING RAIN

RECORDED: FEBRUARY AND JUNE 2001 // **STUDIOS:** HENSON RECORDING STUDIOS, LOS ANGELES
PRODUCER: DAVID KAHNE // **RELEASED:** NOVEMBER 12, 2001

After *Run Devil Run*, Paul McCartney ventured into different sounds before returning to the studio for a regular album of new songs. In November 1999 he released *Working Classical*, his third album of original classical music (after 1991's *Liverpool Oratorio*, and *Standing Stone* in 1997), followed by an experimental set, *Liverpool Sound Collage* in 2000.

He'd also already ventured into ambient techno and electronic music with *Strawberries Oceans Ships Forests* in 1993, and *Rushes* in 1998, both with producer Youth (Martin Glover) under the soubriquet, The Fireman. And although it also involved Youth (co-credited alongside The Beatles and Super Furry Animals), *Liverpool Sound Collage* was an altogether more avant-garde proposition, literally a collage of sounds using snippets of music, street interviews, and general background sounds. In 2001, it went on to be nominated for a Grammy Award as the Best Alternative Music Album.

So when Paul decided to work on a new, more conventional project, he adopted a similar approach to *Run Devil Run*, aiming for an album that could be recorded in a matter of days rather than months. He considered various producers, including a list of possibles drawn up by Bill Porricelli from the McCartney New York office, which Paul whittled down to David Kahne, a young producer with an impressive track record in post-punk and New Wave music.

Similarly, the key personnel at the Los Angeles sessions were all new to Paul. Again, he went down the *Run Devil Run* route, only presenting the musicians with material when they were about to record, with no prior knowledge of the songs – a case of "no homework", as Paul put it.

The opening track on *Driving Rain*, 'Lonely Road', was written while Paul was on holiday in Goa, India, in January 2001. It was the first time he had been to India since the 1960s, and he was accompanied by his new girlfriend, Heather Mills. A loping, mid-tempo love song, it's a middle-of-the-road number that sounds effortless in the hands of McCartney. As with many of his songs, the lyrics came partly by accident, driven by the need for a rhyme, as he readily admitted: "So it's half imagination, half reality. If I'm looking for a rhyme for 'old', and 'pot of gold' comes into my mind, then I don't resist."

'From A Lover to A Friend' is a delicate ballad, which some critics read as his coming to terms with the death of Linda. It would be the first of two singles released from the album. 'She's Given Up Talking', something of an experimental track by the

general standards of the collection, echoes the reverse tape tricks pioneered by The Beatles in 1966–67. It tells the true story of a friend's daughter who refused to speak while at school.

The title track, 'Driving Rain', was written after Paul had driven up the Pacific Coast Highway out of Los Angeles to Malibu, for lunch. Apparently, the song had started life as a ballad, which he decided to speed up, turning it into a catchy song and one of the most instantly likeable tracks on the album. Surprisingly, although it was the title track, it was never released as a spin-off single.

As more than one commentator has said of 'I Do', it's not clear whether the elegant love song is primarily dedicated to Linda or Heather, as they both had a place in Paul's emotions. His vocal performance takes us from a deep, simply-backed expression of love to a more strident, emotional delivery supported by some light orchestral sampling, courtesy of producer Kahne. And 'Tiny Bubble' is a straightforward pop song – well, as straightforward as McCartney chooses to make it. It features a cool melody, a universal lyrical message that could be applied to all sorts of circumstances, and a modern-soul texture that hints at the blues roots of much of Paul's music.

A languid recollection of a pivotal moment in Paul's life, 'Magic' recalls, without metaphor or ambiguity, the moment he first met Linda in 1967, at the London nightclub Bag O' Nails. An unrelated ride-out on synthesized strings adds some obtuse humour to an otherwise very straightforward storyline. Then 'Your Way', a lightly-brushed slice of country pie, has McCartney receiving some fine vocal backing support from the rest of the band.

Paul penned 'Spinning on an Axis' while relaxing with his son, James, in New Hampshire, watching the sun go down. James had started jamming on a keyboard, while Paul did what he recalled as a "parody rap". The repetitive guitar riff was used as a basis when they played the song in the studio with the rest of the band.

The first song recorded at Henson Studios sessions in Los Angeles, 'About You', is a straightforward dedication to Heather. Written when the couple were on holiday in Goa, India, the lyrics were partly assembled from a copy of *The India Times*.

"I do draw on things that seem important at that time. But it's like you have a dream: the minute you start analyzing it all this extra significance comes out. It's one of the reasons I love doing it: there's a mystery to it. And I've been involved in this amazing succession of mysteries."

Paul McCartney

And Heather was certainly the subject of the next eponymously titled track, a mainly instrumental number with Paul playing bass, guitars and piano, the others supplying backing vocals and drums, as well as some string sampling and violin.

James McCartney was on hand for 'Back in the Sunshine Again', a song he and his father had written five years earlier, on holiday in Arizona. The laid-back ballad has the feel of a minor blues, a relaxed, confident treatment with James making the only guest appearance on the studio sessions.

Premiering the song on British TV in December 1999, Paul recalled how 'Your Loving Flame' was written after he was booked into the Carlyle, a hotel in New York City. His 36th-floor room had a plate glass window overlooking Central Park, and there was a baby grand piano to hand. What else could a songwriter do but write a song? He later said it was the first song he had written for Heather.

Once again recalling the heyday of Beatle experimentation, 'Riding into Jaipur' is an atmospheric piece of Indian escapism. Paul had written the melody while on holiday in the Maldives with Linda, and the words in January 2001 on an overnight train journey to the "Pink City" of Jaipur. The suitably minimalistic lyrics are supported by acoustic guitars, various "exotic" electronic effects, and the authentic Indian drone of Rusty Anderson's tanpura.

McCartney explained that 'Rinse the Raindrops' was one of the few songs – citing The Beatles' 'All My Loving' as another example – where he wrote the lyrics first. The track is in fact a condensed version, courtesy of David Kahne, of a marathon 30-minute jam. The producer worked into the early hours editing it down, keeping what he felt were the best bits, and had to declare it completed at a still-mammoth 10 minutes.

'Rinse the Raindrops' would have been the final song on *Driving Rain*, before 'Freedom' was tacked onto the end (after the original album artwork had already been printed) as a "hidden" track, in response to the 9/11 attacks on New York City.

Driving Rain was released in November 2001, and although the last-minute inclusion of 'Freedom' gave it an emotive edge, it failed to make the impression expected. The added track came too late in many ways, with the bulk of the album already leaked to the media weeks earlier. Reviews were mainly favourable, but the album only made it to #46 in the UK charts, and #26 in the USA. It did however spawn the Driving USA Tour the following spring, which saw Paul McCartney on the road for the first time in nearly 10 years.

Previous page Recording 'From a Lover to a Friend' in February 2001. All proceeds were donated to the firefighters fund in the aftermath of 9/11.

Above Paul and his famous Hofner bass guitar, silhouetted behind a screen at the opening of his performance at Philips Arena in Atlanta, Georgia on May 12, 2002.

FROM A LOVER TO A FRIEND

RECORDED: FEBRUARY 20, 2001
STUDIO: HENSON RECORDING STUDIOS, LOS ANGELES
PRODUCER: DAVID KAHN
COMPOSER: PAUL MCCARTNEY
RELEASED: OCTOBER 29, 2001 (SINGLE),
NOVEMBER 12, 2001 (ALBUM)

The first of two singles to be released in quick succession from *Driving Rain*, 'From a Lover to a Friend' has been often interpreted as Paul reflecting on the death of Linda. There's no direct reference to that trauma in the lyrics but McCartney called it his favourite track on the album.

A stand-out track, and possibly the nearest thing to a classic on *Driving Rain*, the song was a collage of bits and pieces that Paul had recorded as a demo at his home studio. Not all the pieces fitted instantly, and he was the first to admit that there was an element of late-night chaos in the crude recordings that he presented to guitarist Rusty Anderson, pianist Gabe Dixon and drummer Abe Laboriel Jr at the session. McCartney said, "I had some words on this demo that didn't make any sense.... Who says words have to make sense? Certainly not poets. There is this thing called surrealism and many of us love it. I seriously have no idea what that's about. Written very late at night, a rather drunken demo..." And there was an intimate, almost scarred quality to his late-night voice that he was anxious to retain, giving the song a closeness that matched the tender quality of the lyrics.

The song was released as a single, prior to the album, at the end of October 2001. It spent just two weeks in the UK chart, peaking at #45. In America, it appeared as the B-side to 'Freedom', released just a week later, which made it to #24 on the *Billboard* Adult Contemporary chart.

> "To me it's a 'We Shall Overcome'.
> That's sort of how I wrote it."

Paul McCartney

Opposite above Paul performing 'Vanilla Sky', his Oscar-nominated song from the movie *Vanilla Sky*, at the Academy Awards in Hollywood, March 24, 2002.

Opposite below Paul holding up the hand of a New York police officer at the finale of "The Concert for New York City", Madison Square Garden, October 20, 2001.

FREEDOM

RECORDED: OCTOBER 20, 2001
STUDIOS: MADISON SQUARE GARDEN, NEW YORK (LIVE RECORDING); QUAD RECORDING STUDIOS, NEW YORK
PRODUCER: DAVID KAHN
COMPOSER: PAUL MCCARTNEY
RELEASED: NOVEMBER 5, 2001 (SINGLE),
NOVEMBER 12, 2001 (ALBUM)

On September 11, 2001, when terrorist attacks destroyed the Twin Towers of the World Trade Center in New York City, Paul McCartney and Heather Mills were on board an aircraft at John F. Kennedy airport, about to take off. They could see the catastrophe clearly from the tarmac, where the plane was held for hours without allowing the passengers to disembark.

The tragedy prompted Paul to write 'Freedom' the day after the attack, and he went on to organize a benefit concert to raise funds for the families of victims. 'The Concert for New York City' was held at New York's Madison Square Garden on October 20, where Paul would premier the song. As well as raising funds, the concert aimed to honour the members of the New York Fire Department and New York Police Department, many of whom had died on September 11. Among the many star names from the UK taking part were The Who, Elton John, David Bowie, Eric Clapton, Mick Jagger and Keith Richards, while a host of American performers included Bon Jovi, James Taylor, Destiny's Child and Billy Joel.

The recording of 'Freedom' – with re-recorded vocals dubbed in the studio – was rush-released to radio the following week, with a disc release on November 5. It starts with the sound of the concert audience clapping in unison, an anthemic song which Paul delivers with a passion, aided by Eric Clapton on lead guitar, plus a quartet of his touring musicians. With the lyrics talking of freedom being a right, its certainly the most universally relevant "message song" Paul created, with a theme that has resonated down the years.

With the only-just released 'From a Lover to a Friend' as its companion track, 'Freedom' appeared as a CD single. And Paul decided to add the song to *Driving Rain* just days before the album's release, classing it as a "hidden" track, given that it was too late for it to be listed on the label or cover artwork. The single made it to #97 in the *Billboard* Hot 100, and #20 in their Adult Contemporary chart, and profits went to the Robin Hood Foundation, set up to aid dependants of New York fireman and police.

CHAOS AND CREATION IN THE BACKYARD

FINE LINE

HOW KIND OF YOU

JENNY WREN

AT THE MERCY

FRIENDS TO GO

ENGLISH TEA

TOO MUCH RAIN

A CERTAIN SOFTNESS

RIDING TO VANITY FAIR

FOLLOW ME

PROMISE TO YOU GIRL

THIS NEVER HAPPENED BEFORE

ANYWAY

(All songs written by Paul McCartney)

Paul McCartney (vocals, piano, keyboards, bass, guitars, drums, violin, maracas, tambourine, flugelhorn, guiro, cello, melodica, recorder, tubular bells, autoharp, gong, triangle, toy glockenspiel, percussion, Moog synthesizer), Millennia Ensemble (strings, brass), Nigel Godrich (piano, Epiphone guitar loops), Pedro Eustache (duduk), Jason Falkner (guitars), James Gadson (drums), Joey Waronker (percussion), Los Angeles Music Players (strings), Rusty Anderson (guitar), Brian Ray (guitar), Abe Laboriel Jr (percussion, tambourine)

CHAOS AND CREATION
IN THE BACKYARD

RECORDED: SEPTEMBER 2003–APRIL 2005 // **STUDIOS:** RAK STUDIOS, LONDON; AIR STUDIOS, LONDON; OCEAN WAY RECORDING, LOS ANGELES // **PRODUCER:** NIGEL GODRICH // **RELEASED:** SEPTEMBER 12, 2005

Released in September 2005, *Chaos and Creation in the Backyard* was Paul McCartney's first studio album after 2001's *Driving Rain*. In the interim there had been two live sets – *Back in the US* (2002) and *Back in the World* (2003) – and, in early 2005, the oddity *Twin Freaks*, which featured re-workings of various items from the McCartney back catalogue in collaboration with DJ and producer Roy "Freelance Hellraiser" Kerr.

On George Martin's recommendation, Paul invited Nigel Godrich to be the producer. Godrich had made a name for himself working with Radiohead, and admitted that he approached the project tentatively. Nevertheless, the sessions, which lasted on and off for 18 months from September 2003, were highly productive, with the two cementing a firm creative relationship. Godrich's positive input was key in his collaboration with McCartney, who played most of the instruments on the album, and the result was welcomed by fans and critics alike as a positive change in direction.

The album opens with 'Fine Line', a classy – some would say classic – pop song, that was chosen as the first of two singles to be released. And 'How Kind of You', like the opening track, has Paul playing all the instruments himself, apart from some tape loop support from Godrich. This solo involvement, encouraged by the producer, characterized much of the album. A somewhat sombre song, Paul said the lyrics were influenced by a fascination with the English language, where "posh" folk actually use a different vocabulary, as in the name of the track.

'Jenny Wren', which became the other track selected as a single release, was a classic example of Paul's acoustic fingerpicking. 'At the Mercy' was a result of some direct inspiration from Godrich, with lyrics that are pessimistic by McCartney standards. Paul's roster of instruments include the cello, assisted by James Gadson on drums, Jason Falkner on guitar, and the Millennia Ensemble.

A self-confessed tribute to George Harrison, Paul's delivery of 'Friends to Go' actually sounds like an outtake from his late colleague's post-Beatle years. Like 'How Kind of You', 'English Tea' displays a fascination with the English language and the mannerisms of a bygone age, referencing hollyhocks and roses, games of croquet, and distant church bells, moving one writer to call it "one of the prettiest watercolours ever composed by McCartney".

Previous page On stage at the Bradley Center, Milwaukee, Wisconsin, October 23, 2005.

Above Nam Performing at the Super Bowl XXXIX half-time show; Jacksonville, Florida, February 6, 2005.

Above Paul playing a ukulele intro to 'Something', at the "Concert for George", at London's Royal Albert Hall on November 29, 2002.

"I'd bring songs in and Nigel would say, 'No, I don't like that. That's a bit ordinary, can you think of a new tune for it?' 'Whaaaat?!!' He didn't always get away with it, but working with a producer, you've got to at least listen to his opinion."

Paul McCartney

Paul later admitted that the inspiration for 'Too Much Rain' was the sentimental ballad 'Smile' written by Charlie Chaplin (initially as an instrumental for his 1936 movie *Modern Times*), and a hit for Nat King Cole in 1954. In the song, McCartney pleads that sadness has to be balanced by optimism. It is one of the outstanding tracks on the album. Overtly romantic, 'A Certain Softness' is classic McCartney, a relaxed love song with bongo drums and shakers adding a Latin tinge to the overall laid-back atmosphere.

An unusually acerbic mood comes through in the lyrics of 'Riding to Vanity Fair' – McCartney was not usually one to scold others in public. But here he vents his bitterness at a betrayal of trust in a powerful track that leaves the listener wondering who, if anyone in particular, it was aimed at. "I don't write many songs like that," he told *Rolling Stone*, "I thought it might be good to tell some people you can't stand them."

A straightforward piece of McCartney magic, 'Follow Me' is an acoustic song that came out of the earliest sessions with Nigel Godrich, at RAK Studios in September 2003. The lyrics have a semi-religious quality, but who they are actually addressed to is never revealed. And layered with innumerable harmony overdubs, all from Paul, 'Promise to You Girl' is a totally solo enterprise. A jaunty, hugely enjoyable track, it progresses from a slow, considered intro to a full-blown celebration of the art of the recording studio.

Again, on 'This Never Happened Before', its (almost) Paul alone, with just the strings of the Millennia Ensemble adding a lush backdrop to a heartfelt love ballad. And closing the collection, 'Anyway' strikes a fittingly reflective note, an emotional plea for a phone call that never comes. But that's not quite all. There follows a "hidden" track, a three-minute instrumental appropriately called 'I've Only Got Two Hands', on which everything is played by McCartney.

The album, with its black-and-white cover picture of a teenage Paul strumming a guitar in his home backyard, taken by his brother Mike, was greeted favourably all round. It made #6 on the *Billboard* chart, #10 in the UK, and the Top Five in several countries around the world. By March 2006, just six months after its release, it had sold 1.3 million copies worldwide.

A BBC review concluded: "*Chaos and Creation in the Backyard* is a better album than anyone could reasonably expect from a 63-year-old who helped remould not just world popular music, but world popular culture, as well. He's Paul bloody McCartney, after all."

Right Nigel Godrich, renowned producer for Radiohead among others, who Paul engaged to work on *Chaos and Creation in the Backyard*.

Opposite Pedro Eustache, who appeared on 'Jenny Wren' playing the duduk, here in action at a concert in Glasgow in 2019.

FINE LINE

RECORDED: SEPTEMBER 2004
STUDIOS: AIR STUDIOS, LONDON
PRODUCER: NIGEL GODRICH
COMPOSER: PAUL MCCARTNEY
RELEASED: AUGUST 29, 2005 (SINGLE),
SEPTEMBER 12, 2005 (ALBUM)

The first of two songs to be released as a single from *Chaos and Creation in the Backyard*, 'Fine Line' pre-empted the album by six weeks. It's one of a number of tracks in which Paul played virtually a solo role, backed only by the Millennia Ensemble.

Counted in with a "one-two", the insistent piano chording takes us into some perfect pop. Referencing the album title, McCartney muses throughout the lyrics on the fine line between extremes, as he explained: "I just kind of followed on from that idea that you've got to choose which of the two you're going to do, you know, be reckless or courageous, so that was lyrically based on that."

Nigel Godrich's input was crucial, as with most of the album. Apparently, the producer advised that at least one "wrong note" should be kept (against Paul's instinct), a rare third-party input that McCartney would immediately appreciate. "I realized I needed someone who would give me a definite opinion and not beat around the bush," he later admitted.

'Fine Line' is a near-definitive example of the kind of song that catches the ear instantly. There's a tight, highly arranged dynamic, which nevertheless has the infectious feel of an uninhibited, piano-driven jam – an automatic choice as a single to prelude an upcoming album.

Despite the timing and attendant promotion, the release didn't do as well as anticipated, and although it was well received by most of the music press it failed to chart significantly, just scraping into the UK Top 20 at #20, and peaking at #31 in *Billboard*'s Adult Contemporary category. It was, however, nominated for Best Male Pop Vocal Performance at the 2006 Grammy Awards.

JENNY WREN

RECORDED: OCTOBER, 2004
STUDIOS: OCEAN WAY RECORDING, LOS ANGELES
PRODUCER: NIGEL GODRICH
COMPOSER: PAUL MCCARTNEY
RELEASED: SEPTEMBER 12, 2005 (SINGLE),
NOVEMBER 21, 2005 (ALBUM)

One of the many memorable tracks on *Chaos and Creation in the Backyard*, 'Jenny Wren' is a fine example of Paul at his most lyrical. With its simple acoustic guitar accompaniment, 'Jenny Wren' is clearly in the mould of The Beatles' 'Blackbird' and 'Mother Nature's Son', or McCartney's more recent 'Calico Skies' from 1997's *Flaming Pie*.

McCartney wrote the song while in Los Angeles. He felt like getting away from it all, so made his way to one of the canyons, a lone nature spot where he strummed his guitar and came up with the outline of the song. After returning to where the family were staying, he "just sat around with the girls and sang it and made it up".

Paul related the little British bird, the wren – one of his favourites in the English countryside – to a fictitious woman. He said: "It's the smallest English bird and I always feel very privileged to see a wren because they're very shy…" The girl in the song is another of McCartney's "lonely people" who, unlike the little bird, cannot sing because of a broken heart. Paul was later reminded that there was a character in the Charles Dickens novel *Our Mutual Friend* called Jenny Wren. An avid reader of Dickens, he realized that the name of the girl in the song must have come to him subconsciously, although he had assumed it just came into his head when thinking about the delicate little bird and the sad subject of his song.

After recording the basic song, an evocative solo was overdubbed at a later session using an ancient Armenian woodwind instrument, the duduk. It was performed by Pedro Eustache, a Venezuelan virtuoso specializing in folk wind instruments.

The song never appeared as a single in the United States, and in Europe it fared best in Denmark where it peaked at #17, and the UK at #22. It also earned a nomination for the 2007 Grammy Award for Best Male Pop Vocal Performance.

MEMORY ALMOST FULL

DANCE TONIGHT
EVER PRESENT PAST
SEE YOUR SUNSHINE
ONLY MAMA KNOWS
YOU TELL ME
MR BELLAMY
GRATITUDE
VINTAGE CLOTHES *
THAT WAS ME *
FEET IN THE CLOUDS *
HOUSE OF WAX *
THE END OF THE END *
NOD YOUR HEAD
(* FIVE-SONG MEDLEY)

(All songs written by Paul McCartney)

Paul McCartney (vocals, bass, guitars, harpsichord, keyboards, Mellotron, drums, clavioline, synthesizer, tambourine, xylophone, mandolin, autoharp, vocoder, spinetta, flugelhorn), Paul Wickens (keyboards), Rusty Anderson (guitar), Brian Ray (bass), Abe Laboriel Jr (drums)

MEMORY ALMOST FULL

RECORDED: OCTOBER 2003, FEBRUARY 2004, MARCH 2006–FEBRUARY 2007 // **STUDIOS:** ABBEY ROAD STUDIOS, LONDON; AIR STUDIOS, LONDON; RAK STUDIOS, LONDON; HENSON RECORDING STUDIOS, LOS ANGELES; HOG HILL MILL, ICKLESHAM, SUSSEX
PRODUCER: DAVID KAHNE // **RELEASED:** JUNE 4, 2007

After their successful collaboration for *Driving Rain*, Paul arranged another block of sessions with producer David Kahne, starting in October 2003. Eight numbers were recorded at Abbey Road, but then the whole project was put on hold when McCartney started working on *Chaos and Creation in the Backyard* with Nigel Godrich.

Once the new album was done and dusted, and released in September 2005, it struck Paul that he had another unfinished album still to work on. The material came from a scattering of sessions that had taken place since the first in 2003, concluding in earnest between March 2006 and February 2007. As Paul put it, "I was just finishing up everything concerned with *Chaos* and had just got the Grammy nominations." Released in June 2007, *Memory Almost Full* is, as Paul would admit at the time of its release, in many ways retrospective. And while some of the songs hark back to childhood memories, others address more recent loves and losses.

The opening song, 'Dance Tonight', was released in the UK as a download single on June 18, 2007 – Paul's 65th birthday. It was a modest hit in its own right, a singalong, sticks-in-your-head delight. 'Ever Present Past' is definitely one of the retrospective tracks that McCartney acknowledged, a catchy song talking about past times, which fly by "in a flash". As *Rolling Stone* commented, he "tapped into the restless energy of a man half his age." Almost

certainly not deliberate, the opening notes of the melody are identical to the old Duke Ellington song 'Don't Get Around Much Anymore', which Paul had covered on his 1988 retro "Russian" collection, *Choba B CCCP.*

Paul was the first to admit that 'See Your Sunshine' was written as a love song to Heather Mills. He explained that much of the album was written before, during and following their separation, and this was penned while they were still happily together: "That one was written during a good time with Heather. I'm not a great grudge-holder. It's just unfortunate it didn't work out."

After a sweeping string intro, 'Only Mama Knows' crashes into a dramatic narrative about a woman stranded in an airport transit lounge. As Paul would point out, the subject is as fictional as 'Eleanor Rigby', but makes for a powerful lyric delivered over a suitably strident backing. Like 'Only Mama Knows', the basic recording of 'You Tell Me' dates from early 2004. It's a tender, melancholy, love song remembering his times with Linda.

"I wouldn't use the word 'nostalgia', I would use the word 'memory'...
if you're using your imagination, you tend to look into the past."

Paul McCartney

Another powerful "story" song, 'Mr Bellamy' focuses on a man sitting on a skyscraper ledge, contemplating suicide. Paul's talent for adopting different voices is exploited to the full here, with the eponymous Bellamy, passers-by, and the rescue team all represented in first-person lines. There was a controversy among McCartney fans regarding the song, some of whom claimed it was about his recent divorce – even citing the title as an anagram of "Mills betray me" – but he denied anything of the sort.

'Gratitude', on the other hand, was one song that definitely referenced his often bitter divorce proceedings, lacing the lyrics with a sarcastic irony not usually exhibited even in his most personal writing.

A medley of five songs follows, each one fading into the other, linked only by the fact that they are all about personal memories. It's a link that could be said to extend to the album as a whole, as Paul later described it: "A lot of it is retrospective, drawing from memory, like memories from being a kid, from Liverpool and from summers gone." 'Vintage Clothes' uses the fact that Paul kept many of his clothes from the 1960s as a cipher for looking back at his past life. Similarly, 'That Was Me' is a series of snapshots of his personal recollections, evoked in the context of a straight-ahead rock song. 'Feet in the Clouds' is more specifically about McCartney's schooldays at the Liverpool Institute High School for Boys (the premises of which became the Liverpool Institute for Performing Arts, co-founded by Paul in 1996). The peculiarities of life as a celebrity are addressed in the surreal

language of 'House of Wax', while the finality of death is dealt with in an almost optimistic, reflective manner in 'The End of the End'.

'Nod Your Head', which closes the album, was something of an afterthought, an intended instrumental that Paul overdubbed with his 'Little Richard' wild-man voice. The original plan was to end the collection with the finality (in more ways than one!) of 'The End of the End'.

Memory Almost Full was the first record by Paul McCartney to be released on Starbucks' 'Hear Music' label – McCartney's 45-year-old contract with EMI (and Capitol in the USA) had expired in March of the previous year. It was, in fact, the first album to be released by the coffee giant's label. It was also McCartney's first album to be made available as a digital download.

Promotion via Starbucks was worldwide, with a global "listening party" involving 10,000 stores on release day. That way, an estimated six million got to hear the album right away. In America, the album entered the *Billboard* 200 chart at #3, McCartney's best performance since *Flaming Pie* in 1997, with nearly half those sales via Starbucks' coffee shops. And even though coffee shop sales were not counted on the chart system in the UK, it still managed a healthy #5 in Great Britain.

Previous page An exclusive gig at the Electric Ballroom, Camden, London, promoting *Memory Almost Full*; June 7, 2007.

Opposite In-store display for *Memory Almost Full* in Starbucks, who released the album as the first on its record label, available in over 10,000 shops in 29 countries.

Above Rehearsing for the 2008 BRIT Awards, Earl's Court, London.

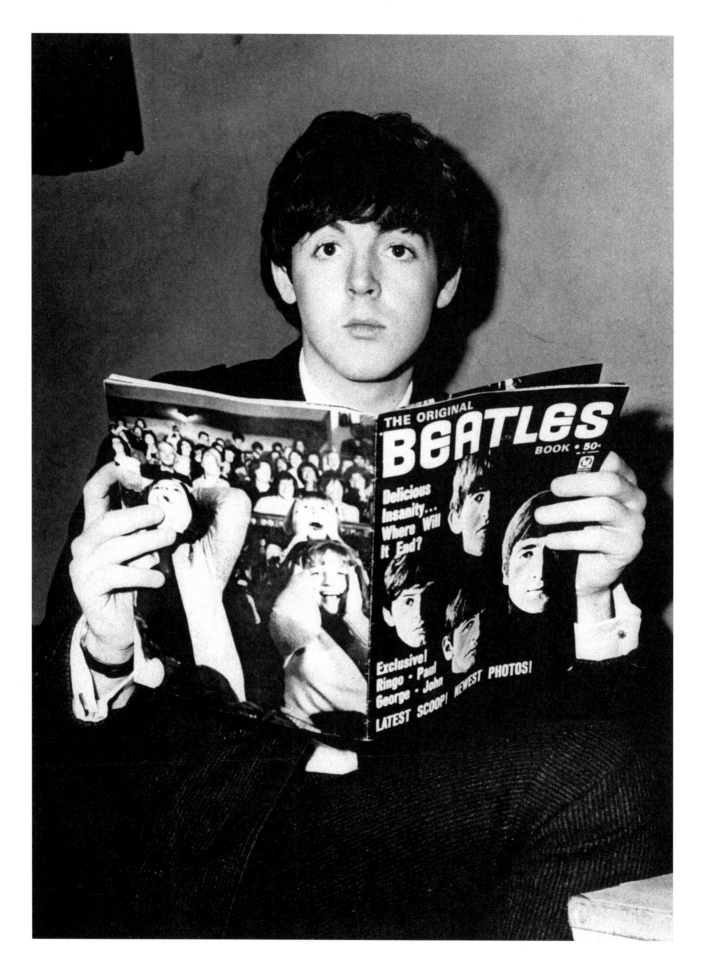

DANCE TONIGHT

RECORDED: JANUARY–FEBRUARY, 2007
STUDIOS: RAK STUDIOS, LONDON
PRODUCER: DAVID KAHNE
COMPOSER: PAUL MCCARTNEY
RELEASED: JUNE 4, 2007 (ALBUM), JUNE 18, 2007 (SINGLE)

A completely solo effort by McCartney, 'Dance Tonight' was released as a single on his 65th birthday – June 18, 2007. As the opening track on *Memory Almost Full*, it kicks off the album as a catchy singalong number, with an earworm chorus that's hard to shake off once heard. From the opening mandolin chords, and the insistent thumping rhythm, it's a totally infectious piece of dance-pop that urges you to do just what it says on the label.

The song originated after Paul, on his way to his office in London's Soho, called into a guitar shop he often visited. The salesman told him he had a left-handed mandolin that might be of interest, and Paul tried it out. He bought the instrument, knowing he would have to learn to play it afresh as it was tuned like a violin, and he didn't even know where to start with the chords. "I had to figure it out for myself," he recalled, "I found one chord, then another one, then a real strange chord, very simple shape, but an odd chord, I still don't know what it is but it sounded great."

It was Christmas 2006 and he'd brought the mandolin home, strumming away in the kitchen, a half-formed song in his head. As he started improvising, singing "everybody gonna dance tonight", his three-year-old daughter Beatrice joined in, dancing around. Paul said: "I was hitting the floor, singing, and she came running in, dancing around. I went, 'Whoa, there's my proof.' After that, the song kind of wrote itself."

A week after its release, the song hit the UK singles chart at #34, peaking at #26. The sales were supported by a bizarre video directed by Michael Gondry and starring Natalie Portman and Mackenzie Crook. Crook is a postman, delivering a left-handed mandolin to Paul. When McCartney starts playing the song, out of the mandolin case leaps a spirit played by Portman. A chase around the house ensues, then as the music fades, Paul (now a spirit himself) is dragged into the case, where a party is in full swing. As with many promotional videos, the link between the visuals and the actual music seems tenuous, and little to do with the mood or lyrics of the song.

Opposite Paul holding a Beatles fanzine in 1964. Forty years later, he would recall the era nostalgically in the song 'That Was Me'.

THAT WAS ME

RECORDED: FEBRUARY, 2004
STUDIOS: ABBEY ROAD STUDIOS, LONDON
PRODUCER: DAVID KAHNE
COMPOSER: PAUL MCCARTNEY
RELEASED: JUNE 4, 2007

The second song on the five-part medley in *Memory Almost Full*, 'That Was Me' presents a succession of images from Paul's early life, as seen though the prism of his own memories. Some are almost universal to British childhoods of the post-war era – a bucket and spade on a seaside holiday, taking part in the school play, at camp with the Boy Scouts, playing conkers – while others are more personal, like the woods he played in, where he recalled that in the spring the ground was carpeted with bluebells.

This blues-based rockabilly song, with Paul almost talking though the verses, also focuses on the formative days of The Beatles. The "Royal Iris" was an actual ferry across the Mersey that would host "riverboat shuffles" featuring all the local Merseybeat bands. "Sweating cobwebs" derives from the Liverpudlian expression "sweating cobs", which they certainly did when playing in the Cavern cellar club, the group's famous launch-pad referenced obliquely in the song.

In an interview in *The New Yorker*, it was suggested to Paul that the song expressed amazement at the life he had led. "That's exactly it, and I am amazed," he replied, "How could I not be? Unless I just totally blocked it off. There were four people in the Beatles, and I was one of them. There were two people in the Lennon–McCartney songwriting team, and I was one of them. I mean, right there, that's enough for anyone's life."

"People often say they can remember more from their childhood than they can from a month ago. I think that is a fact of life – I don't know why. So all I had to do for this song was to think back."

Paul McCartney

ELECTRIC ARGUMENTS

NOTHING TOO MUCH JUST OUT OF SIGHT
TWO MAGPIES
SING THE CHANGES
TRAVELLING LIGHT
HIGHWAY
LIGHT FROM YOUR LIGHTHOUSE
SUN IS SHINING
DANCE 'TIL WE'RE HIGH
LIFELONG PASSION
IS THIS LOVE?
LOVERS IN A DREAM
UNIVERSAL HERE, EVERLASTING NOW
DON'T STOP RUNNING
ROAD TRIP

(All songs written by Paul McCartney)

Paul McCartney (vocals, guitars, bass, double bass, drums, keyboards, piano,
Mellotron, percussion, flute, harmonica, mandolin, tambourine, harmonium,
tubular bells, synthesizer, clavioline, vibraphone, cello, harpsichord)

ELECTRIC ARGUMENTS

RECORDED: DECEMBER 2007–JUNE 2008 // **STUDIO:** HOG HILL MILL, ICKLESHAM, SUSSEX
PRODUCER: THE FIREMAN (PAUL MCCARTNEY, YOUTH) // **RELEASED:** NOVEMBER 24, 2008

Unlike Paul's previous albums under The Fireman banner – 1993's
Strawberries Oceans Ships Forests, and *Rushes* in 1998, both of which were
largely instrumental – *Electric Arguments* includes more conventional songs
and prominent vocals, hence its inclusion in this book.

The earlier albums had consisted of predominantly ambient techno, created in collaboration with the Killing Joke bass player and producer Martin Glover, under his pseudonym, Youth. *Electric Arguments* was actually the pair's fourth project together since Youth was also involved in the *Liverpool Sound Collage* remix album, credited only to Paul McCartney, in 2000.

Recording at his Hog Hill studio, Paul laid down the 13 basic tracks over a period of six months, each taking just a day, starting in December 2007. There had been no mention of the names of the two contributors on the earlier Fireman albums, but here both were named on the cover artwork. The album's title came from a 1966 poem *Kansas City to St Louis* (in which Lennon and McCartney are mentioned by name) by the influential poet Allen Ginsberg, with Paul explaining that Ginsberg was seeking the power of word combinations rather than their literal meaning. With that in mind, he approached the songs with an improvisational spirit, likening some of the lyrics to the "cut-up" technique pioneered by Ginsberg's fellow "Beat" writer, William Burroughs.

The opening track, 'Nothing Too Much Just Out of Sight', has Paul in full roaring voice, an angry-sounding vocal enhanced with some heavy metal bass and drums. The song opens with a hint of a wailing harmonica, adding to the hypnotic trance-like quality of the dangerous, raging one-chord blues. Paul's voice is much lighter on 'Two Magpies', a finger-picking "bird" song in the McCartney 'Blackbird' mode, with quotes from the nursery rhyme *One for Sorrow* – with toddler Beatrice heard giggling at the end.

The most overtly commercial track on *Electric Arguments*, 'Sing the Changes', was also the only one Paul decided to release as a single. A straightforward pop song complete with a singalong chorus chant, the accompanying video undoubtedly helped the overall sales of the album. 'Travelling Light' has a folky, medieval feel to it and Paul's voice is deep and serious on this waltz-time ballad, his self-accompaniment including piano, guitar and flute.

With its up-tempo "road song" narrative, 'Highway' hints at a Chuck Berry-style slice of rock 'n' roll, another mainly

conventional song on an ostensibly more experimental album. And 'Light from Your Lighthouse', with its reworking of a well-known gospel song from America's past, is as instantly effective as its pedigree deserves.

Another song that goes against the grain of what would be expected from a Fireman album, 'Sun Is Shining' is an effectively joyous song in the vein of the Beatles' 'Good Day Sunshine'. For what is basically a one-man recording, this is a highly sophisticated, layered production. "Macca permits himself to burst out of the groove and into full-throated song," commented writer Mat Snow in a *Finest 50 Tracks of the Year* round-up, "With results that gloriously flash back to his summer '67–summer '68 peak." And 'Dance 'Til We're High', with its sound of bells and sweeping arrangements, sounds like a Christmas song – it's certainly a ballad of celebration.

"The first two Fireman albums were instrumental. Youth suggested to me, 'How about a bit of vocal?' and I said, 'Well, I haven't got any songs, I've got no idea.' And because it's The Fireman and anything goes, I said 'Yeah sure.' So I just ad-libbed it, and eventually a song came out of it."

Paul McCartney

An Indian-flavoured track, reflecting a taste for the music of the sub-continent that Paul had shared with his fellow Beatles (George Harrison in particular) since *Rubber Soul*, 'Lifelong Passion' uses a harmonium to achieve the essential droning effect. In June 2008, five months before the release of the album, a sneak preview of the song was offered to those donating $25 (£18) to the Adopt-A-Minefield charity, part of a "Virtual Night of a Thousand Dinners Party" online charity event which Paul hosted, with a menu set by TV chef Jamie Oliver.

Blending McCartney's natural melodic leanings with the ambient Fireman concept, 'Is This Love?' is a highly atmospheric piece, with repetitive lyrics delivered via multi-layered vocal tracks. Much nearer to the anticipated electro explorations of the album, 'Lovers in A Dream' is a claustrophobic incantation set against a repetitive musical backdrop.

'Universal Here, Everlasting Now' is the most avant-garde piece on the album. Almost completely instrumental – plus an assorted collage of sound effects – it's carried along by electronic drum beats and distorted guitars, ending where it began with a sole, melancholy piano. And in keeping with much of the ethic of *Electric Arguments*, 'Don't Stop Running' is clearly an improvised

piece, the lyrics arrived at like a vocal jam. It was the final song on the track listing on the original album, but there's an added "hidden" number, 'Road Trip', a long chord played on synthesizer and assorted keyboards, on top of which McCartney dubs further spacey effects and even some backwards vocal parts.

The album was the first appearance of a Fireman release in the UK charts, debuting at #79, while it peaked in the US at #67. Critical response was generally favourable. In the UK, the *Sunday Times* called it "The most exciting McCartney album since *Band on the Run*," while the *Daily Telegraph* enthused, "Embracing raw blues, delicate folk, gospel, country and dubby psychedelia, it's like a solo *White Album* and confirms the ex-Beatle's resurgence." And in America, the influential *Wall Street Journal* called it "A seriously good piece of modern rock."

Previous page Paul on stage in Tel Aviv, Israel, during the Friendship First concert, September 2008.

Opposite Paul at a promotional event at the HMV store in Oxford Street, London, where he signed copies of *Electric Arguments*, December 21, 2008.

Above At the 2008 Brit Awards, having just been presented with the Outstanding Contribution to Music award.

LIGHT FROM YOUR LIGHTHOUSE

RECORDED: DECEMBER 2007–JUNE 2008
STUDIO: HOG HILL MILL, ICKLESHAM, SUSSEX
PRODUCERS: THE FIREMAN (PAUL MCCARTNEY, YOUTH)
COMPOSER: PAUL MCCARTNEY
RELEASED: NOVEMBER 24, 2008

Paul was the first to admit, amid accusations of plagiarism, that 'Light From Your Lighthouse' was indeed based on an old traditional gospel song, 'Let Your Light Shine on Me', name-checking the blues/gospel singer Blind Willie Johnson as his inspiration in the *Electric Arguments* liner notes.

In fact, the lineage of the song goes back further than Johnson's emotive version from 1929. It first appeared on record in 1923, performed by The Wiseman Quartet, under its original title. The old-time country musician and gospel singer Ernest Phipps covered it in 1928 as 'Shine on Me', then the blind itinerant Johnson released it, reverting to 'Let Your Light Shine on Me'.

There have been many recordings since, under its original title or variously as 'Shine On Me', 'Let It Shine on Me', 'Light from the Lighthouse' and 'Light from Your Lighthouse'. Among the most celebrated versions among folk-blues aficionados were by the great Lead Belly, who recorded it at least three times. But as well as the Willie Johnson recording, Paul McCartney was highly likely to have come across it when it appeared on Lonnie Donegan's second album, *Lonnie*, in 1958.

With a deep voice reminiscent of the gravelly delivery of Willie Johnson, Paul launches into a lively up-tempo rendition, with a predominantly mandolin-led accompaniment. It's very much a jam in line with the general improvised mood of the album, although its folk and skiffle roots would seem at odds with the electronic outings of The Fireman.

Many reviews of *Electric Arguments* enjoyed the element of spontaneous fun evident on the track, but others were dubious about it appearing as part of a Fireman collection. While *Uncut* magazine conceded "There's meat on these musical bones, pushed along by a lugubrious boom-thump and a chorus that comes with its own ready-made campfire glow", Julian Marszalek of *The Quietus* disparagingly commented: "This being Macca, the album occasionally dips into the lowest common denominator; it's as if he can't resist, as if it's built into his DNA," deriding the track as an "electro hoe-down".

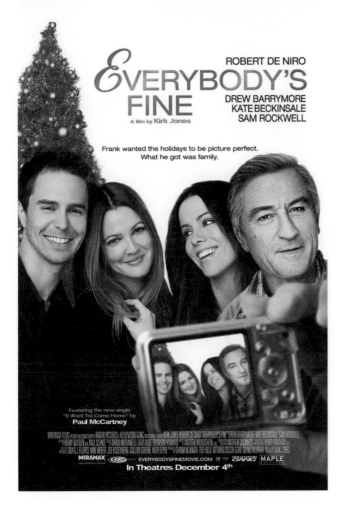

(I WANT TO) COME HOME [SINGLE]

RECORDED: JUNE, 2009
STUDIO: HOG HILL MILL, ICKLESHAM, SUSSEX
PRODUCER: PAUL MCCARTNEY
COMPOSER: PAUL MCCARTNEY
RELEASED: MARCH 1, 2010

One of Paul McCartney's relatively hidden gems, '(I Want To) Come Home' was written in response to an invitation in the spring of 2009 from the film director Kirk Jones to write a song for a new movie, *Everybody's Fine*, starring Robert De Niro, Drew Barrymore and Kate Beckinsale. Paul accepted immediately, and was invited to a small viewing theatre not far from his office in London's Soho. He loved the film, which centred on De Niro's character, a widower who embarks on a road trip to reconnect with his grown-up children, and get them together for a family gathering at Christmas.

McCartney empathized with the story, recognizing the man who has lost his wife and has adult kids who have their own lives to lead. "When your kids grow up and have families of their own and inevitably turn to you and say, 'Do you mind? We'd like to have our own little family Christmas,' it's a difficult thing. It's a big turning point. Like in the movie, you work around it."

When Paul was watching the film for the first time, however, director Jones had inserted Aretha Franklin's version of 'Let It Be' as a placeholder, to mark where he wanted a new song to go. This threw McCartney for a moment: "I thought, 'Holy cow, I can't do this.' Sure, write another 'Let It Be'? I was thinking of ringing him the next day and saying, 'I'm sorry, it's too big a task.'" But he thought about it overnight, started playing with some ideas and the next day sent a demo of the song to Jones.

The director liked what he heard, with one proviso – that Paul insert an instrumental introduction to the piece, rather than what he felt was an abrupt start. So there's a 17-second piano intro that sets the scene perfectly for a moving vocal. Paul augmented the arrangement by collaborating with the composer of the film's main score, Dario Marianelli, bringing in an orchestral build-up that evokes the restrained passion underlying the emotion of the storyline.

'(I Want to) Come Home' was released as an online-only single on March 1, 2010, following the movie's release in December 2009. And although it failed to chart, the song was nominated for a Golden Globe Award for Best Original Song, and in 2012 was covered by Tom Jones on his album *Spirit in the Room*.

Opposite Paul accompanying the poet Allen Ginsberg reading 'Ballad of the Skeletons' at the Royal Albert Hall, London, October 19, 1995.

Above The legendary blues and gospel singer Blind Willie Johnson, a prime source for Paul's version of 'Let Your Light Shine on Me'.

Left Poster for the 2009 movie *Everybody's Fine,* for which Paul penned '(I Want To) Come Home'

KISSES ON THE BOTTOM

I'M GONNA SIT RIGHT DOWN AND WRITE MYSELF A LETTER
(FRED E. AHLERT, JOE YOUNG)

HOME (WHEN SHADOWS FALL)
(PETER VAN STEEDEN, JEFF CLARKSON, HARRY CLARKSON)

IT'S ONLY A PAPER MOON
(HAROLD ARLEN, E.Y. HARBURG, BILLY ROSE)

MORE I CANNOT WISH YOU
(FRANK LOESSER)

THE GLORY OF LOVE
(BILLY HILL)

WE THREE (MY ECHO, MY SHADOW, AND ME)
(SAMMY MYSELS, DICK ROBERTSON, NELSON COGANE)

AC-CENT-TCHU-ATE THE POSITIVE
(HAROLD ARLEN, JOHNNY MERCER)

MY VALENTINE
(PAUL MCCARTNEY)

ALWAYS
(IRVING BERLIN)

MY VERY GOOD FRIEND THE MILKMAN
(HAROLD SPINA, JOHNNY BURKE)

BYE BYE BLACKBIRD
(RAY HENDERSON, MORT DIXON)

GET YOURSELF ANOTHER FOOL
(HAYWOOD HENRY, MONROE TUCKER)

THE INCH WORM
(FRANK LOESSER)

ONLY OUR HEARTS
(PAUL MCCARTNEY)

Paul McCartney (vocals, guitar), Diana Krall (piano), Tamir Hendelman (piano), Stevie Wonder (harmonica), John Pizzarelli (guitar), Anthony Wilson (guitar), Eric Clapton (guitar), Bucky Pizzarelli (guitar), John Chiodini (guitar), Robert Hurst (double bass), John Clayton (double bass), Christian McBride (double bass), Chuck Berghofer (double bass), Vinnie Colaiuta (drums), Karriem Riggins (drums), Jeff Hamilton (drums), Mike Mainieri (vibraphone), Andy Stein (violin), Ira Nepus (trombone), London Symphony Orchestra, children's choir

KISSES ON THE BOTTOM

RECORDED: APRIL–MAY 2011 // **STUDIOS:** CAPITOL STUDIOS, LOS ANGELES; AVATAR STUDIOS, NEW YORK
PRODUCER: TOMMY LIPUMA // **RELEASED:** FEBRUARY 6, 2012 (UK), FEBRUARY 7, 2012 (US)

In 2011, Paul decided to fulfill an ambition he'd nurtured for some years:
to record an album of standards, drawn from the so-called "great American
songbook" of classic popular songs, mainly written in the inter-war years of
the 1920s and 1930s. Among them would be songs of his parents' generation,
songs he remembered from his childhood in the 1940s, and songs that were
sung at family gatherings, busked on the piano by his father, Jim.

He had postponed the project for some years, partly because others – including Ringo Starr in 1970, Harry Nilsson in 1973, and Rod Stewart (no fewer than five times between 2002 and 2010) – had already released albums of similar material. In 2010, McCartney was introduced to producer Tommy LiPuma, who had worked with musicians and vocalists as varied as Miles Davis, Randy Newman, and – crucially as it turned out – the Canadian jazz singer and pianist, Diana Krall.

LiPuma visited Paul at his home in 2010 and they ran through the kind of songs that might be suitable. Then in the spring of 2011, the producer booked the legendary Capitol Studios in Los Angeles for the recording, organized the sessions musicians, and contacted Diana Krall with a view to her taking part. Paul was delighted, having played at Krall's wedding to his old friend Elvis Costello in 2003. In the event, they used Diana's road-band members Robert Hurst on bass and Karriem Riggins on drums on all but four of the tracks.

Paul later admitted that at first he felt slightly intimidated, not least because he was singing through a microphone used by Nat 'King' Cole and Frank Sinatra. And working with seasoned jazz players at first seemed a challenge, but he soon realized all he had to do was come in with the songs, talk through 'head arrangements' and take it from there. "There's such a high level of musicianship on there," he recalled, "And the nice thing for me was, other than going in to do the vocals, I didn't feel like I had to do much hard work. The players did all the hard work, and I was just in the booth, singing."

With its brushed snare drum, piano and bass intro, the opening track 'I'm Gonna Sit Right Down and Write Myself a Letter' promises an exercise closer to "cool" jazz than McCartney had ever attempted before. The song, which Paul delivers in a soft crooning style, was a huge hit for Fats Waller in 1935, with the line in the the first verse – 'A lotta kisses on the bottom' – providing the album's title. It's one of several tracks recorded after the Capitol sessions, at Avatar Studios in New York City.

With some rich overdubbed strings, a "lounge jazz" feel dominates 'Home (When Shadows Fall)'. Paul remembered the song from strumming it in his earliest days on the guitar, even before the formation of the Beatles. A hit for its composer Peter van Steeden in 1931, McCartney was amazed when Diana Krall revealed that she too was familiar with the number.

'It's Only a Paper Moon' was written by Harold Arlen for a 1932 Broadway play that flopped, *The Great Magoo*. The song became a standard, however, after hugely successful versions were sung by Ella Fitzgerald and Nat 'King' Cole, among others. On the album, the track was another singalong arrangement, with Andy Stein adding flourishes of jazz violin. From another musical, *Guys and Dolls*, the languid 'More I Cannot Wish You' was the song that convinced McCartney and Tommy LiPuma that they were on the right track, as the producer explained: "We all went in with a bit of trepidation as to whether or not it was going to work out, and 'More I Cannot Wish You' was probably the breakthrough. That, I think, was the song that gave Paul a sense as to how he should approach this material."

More familiar sounding than some of the tracks, 'The Glory of Love' was a #1 pop hit for 'King of Swing' Benny Goodman back in 1939, but R&B fans would be more likely to remember the 1951 version by The Five Keys. And 'We Three (My Echo, My Shadow and Me)' is another relaxed gem of pop song composition, a 1940 hit for The Ink Spots and Frank Sinatra, both of whom made #3 in the *Billboard* chart.

With a full-bodied piano break from Diana Krall, 'Ac-Cent-Tchu-Ate the Positive' is a great example of novelty wordplay by Harold Arlen and lyricist Johnny Mercer. It's followed by the first of two originals on the album, both in the general style and mood of the rest of the collection, with Eric Clapton guesting on acoustic guitar. 'My Valentine' is the elegant tribute to Nancy Shevell, who Paul married in October 2011.

Possibly the most familiar of all the songs on the collection, 'Always' was penned by the great Irving Berlin in 1925. It has been covered by virtually everyone who was part of the pre-rock mainstream, including Sinatra, Peggy Lee and Bing Crosby, and more recently Harry Nilsson, Phil Collins and Leonard Cohen. Here Paul sings it absolutely straight, phrase by phrase, to stunning effect.

Alongside the album opener, 'My Very Good Friend the Milkman' was another song popularized by Fats Waller, who made it a hit in 1935. There's a mellow trombone break by Ira Nepus, and some laid-back whistling from Paul. And 'Bye Bye Blackbird' is notable for being the nearest Paul gets to real jazz phrasing, holding a word here, extending a lyric there – it's simply one of his best vocal interpretations on the album.

Paul makes a rare instrumental appearance on the album with 'Get Yourself Another Fool', on which he plays some effective acoustic guitar alongside Eric Clapton, on the 1949 song written by Frank Heywood and Monroe Tucker. 'The Inchworm', also known simply as 'Inchworm', is familiar to anyone old enough to remember the Danny Kaye version from his 1952 film *Hans Christian Anderson* – which is probably how Paul McCartney first heard it. It also appeared on the Beatles' Apple label, as a track on the 1969 Mary Hopkin album *Post Card*, produced by McCartney.

The final track on *Kisses on the Bottom*, 'Only Our Hearts', is the second of the two originals. It features the first involvement of Stevie Wonder on a Paul McCartney album since *Tug of War* in 1981, and like 'My Valentine' is a knowing evocation of a bygone era of songwriting, for which Paul clearly displays a great affection.

The critics were welcoming in the main, but usually with some reservations. Patrick Humphries, for one, had it in perspective in a review for the BBC: "This, after all, is an album from a man whose band effectively blew this style of popular music right out of the water half a century ago," Humphries wrote, "But Paul's music-loving dad Jim would have known these songs, and while thrashing through Hamburg all-nighters or lunchtimes at the Cavern, The Beatles often found room for songs from this showbiz pantheon."

The album made it to #3 in the UK, and #5 in the US *Billboard* chart. It also topped the Jazz Albums list in *Billboard*, and won the award for Best Traditional Pop Vocal Album at the 2013 Grammy Awards.

Previous page Paul playing a newly renovated 1877 Steinway piano, at a Steinway Hall, New York, charity event for the Motown Museum; September12, 2012.

Opposite left The great Irving Berlin, composer of 'Always', among many other memorable popular songs.

Opposite right The highly acclaimed Canadian jazz singer and pianist Diana Krall, a key collaborator on *Kisses on the Bottom*.

MY VALENTINE

RECORDED: MAY AND OCTOBER 5–6, 2011
STUDIO: AVATAR STUDIOS, NEW YORK, ABBEY ROAD
STUDIOS, LONDON
PRODUCER: TOMMY LIPUMA
COMPOSER: PAUL MCCARTNEY
RELEASED: DECEMBER 20, 2011 (SINGLE),
FEBRUARY 6, 2012 (ALBUM)

When it came to putting the album of standards *Kisses on the Bottom* together, producer Tommy LiPuma felt that Paul should include a couple of his own compositions, but obviously they would need to fit in with the overall character of the rest of the material. 'My Valentine', with its title an echo of the Rodgers and Hart 1937 classic 'My Funny Valentine', was a perfect inclusion.

One of the purest of love songs that Paul McCartney has ever recorded, he had written the beautiful ballad on a rainy afternoon while on holiday in Morocco with Nancy Shevell. Paul recalled that as they sheltered at their hotel, an Irish guest sat at the piano and sang old sentimental songs like 'Beautiful Dreamer', 'If You Were The Only Girl In The World' and other material from his father's era. It inspired him to write something along those lines, and the timing was perfect: it was actually Valentine's Day.

Paul first performed it for Nancy at their wedding on October 9, 2011. As the late broadcaster David Frost, a guest at the celebration, recalled: "Paul performed a special song late in the evening. He had written it especially for 'his lovely' Nancy for this day. It was lovely. She was truly touched and looked as though she shed a tear."

After the original recording of the song in May 2011 in New York, the overdubs were conducted at Abbey Road in October (just days before the wedding) and Paul and Tommy LiPuma brought in Eric Clapton to help add some finishing touches. His acoustic guitar part fitted perfectly, as did the added strings of the London Symphony Orchestra.

Released as a single in December 2011, six weeks before the album, 'My Valentine' climbed to #20 in the *Billboard* Adult Contemporary chart. And Paul would perform the song at the 54th Grammy Awards in 2012, with Diana Krall and Joe Walsh of The Eagles.

Opposite Paul joins Bruce Springsteen and the E Street Band during the "Hard Rock Calling" concert in London's Hyde Park, July 14, 2012.

ONLY OUR HEARTS

RECORDED: APRIL–MAY, 2011
STUDIO: CAPITOL STUDIOS, LOS ANGELES
PRODUCER: TOMMY LIPUMA
COMPOSER: PAUL MCCARTNEY
RELEASED: FEBRUARY 6, 2012 (UK ALBUM), FEBRUARY 7, 2012
(US ALBUM), FEBRUARY 7, 2012 (US SINGLE)

The second McCartney original, and closing track, from *Kisses on the Bottom*, 'Only Our Hearts' had a completely different line-up to the rest of the album, but was recorded during the same sessions at Capitol Studios in LA. With its lush orchestral backing, it sounds from the start like it was tailored to fit into the back catalogue of the legendary studio, where Nelson Riddle's studio orchestra would once have backed the likes of Sinatra, Nat Cole and Peggy Lee.

Paul had played the song to producer Tommy LiPuma when the two first got together in March 2010 at Paul's home studio. "He played me this song and I loved it, I thought it was great," LiPuma recalled. It's not clear whether the recording at Capitol took place before the rest of the *Kisses on the Bottom* sessions with Diana Krall and assorted session players, but for 'Only Our Hearts' LiPuma engaged the services of the great Johnny Mandel to take care of the orchestrations. Mandel's track record at the jazz end of mainstream popular music was impeccable, having worked with Count Basie, Frank Sinatra, Barbra Streisand, Tony Bennett and many others over the years. In 1999 he'd arranged and conducted the orchestrations for Diana Krall's award-winning album *When I Look In Your Eyes*.

When they were putting the track together, LiPuma and McCartney realized there was space for a solo that had yet to be filled. Tommy suggested Stevie Wonder, and Paul agreed it was a great idea. The last time the two had worked together was 30 years earlier, on *Ebony and Ivory*. Paul rang Stevie and he came over to the studio just before they had started mixing. "Well, talk about a giant set of ears," LiPuma enthused, "Stevie just listened to the track a couple of times and within 15 to 20 minutes we had the take." The result was the icing on the cake for a magnificent recording.

Released as a single in February 2012, 'Only Our Hearts' made little impression on the charts, despite a promotional tie-in with Tiffany & Co, which offered a limited number of free downloads ahead of the album.

NEW

SAVE US
(PAUL MCCARTNEY AND PAUL EPWORTH)

ALLIGATOR

ON MY WAY TO WORK

QUEENIE EYE
(PAUL MCCARTNEY AND PAUL EPWORTH)

EARLY DAYS

NEW

APPRECIATE

EVERYBODY OUT THERE

HOSANNA

I CAN BET

LOOKING AT HER

(All songs written by Paul McCartney, except where indicated)

Paul McCartney (vocals, guitars, bass, percussion, synthesizer, celeste, glockenspiel, piano, drums, Mellotron, double bass, harmonium, harpsichord, keyboards, bouzouki, tubular bells, ngoni, washboard), Rusty Anderson (guitars, bouzouki, vocals), Brian Ray (guitars, dulcimer, congas, vocals), Steve Sidwell (trumpet), Paul Wickens (keyboards, guitars, piano, accordion, Hammond organ, vocals), Abe Laboriel Jr (drums, vocals, djembe), Jamie Talbot (tenor saxophone), Toby Pitman (keyboards), Ethan Jones (drums, percussion, guitar), Paul Epworth (drums), Eliza Marshall (flute), Anna Noakes (flute), Dave Bishop (baritone saxophone), Cathy Thompson (violin), Laura Melhuish (violin), Patrick Kiernan (violin), Nina Foster (violin), Peter Lale (viola), Rachel Robsin (viola), Caroline Dale (cello), Katherine Jenkinson (cello), Chris Worsey (cello), Richard Pryce (double bass), Steve McManus (double bass)

NEW

RECORDED: JANUARY 2012–MARCH 2013 // **STUDIOS:** HENSON RECORDING STUDIOS, LOS ANGELES; AVATAR STUDIOS, NEW YORK; ABBEY ROAD STUDIOS, LONDON; AIR STUDIOS, LONDON; WOLF TONE STUDIOS, LONDON; HOG HILL MILL, ICKLESHAM, SUSSEX
PRODUCER: GILES MARTIN, PAUL EPWORTH, MARK RONSON, ETHAN JONES // **RELEASED:** OCTOBER 11, 2013

After the generic approach on his most recent albums, including 2008's *Electric Arguments* and the "standards" collection *Kisses on the Bottom*, in late 2011 Paul decided to try out some young producers whose work he liked. Initially he planned to select the one he preferred for his next album, but eventually settled on working with all four, each collaborating on a number of tracks.

With each producer bringing a different angle to the project, the end result was a multi-faceted collection that was deemed McCartney's most successful album of new original material in some years. Acting as overall executive producer was Giles Martin, son of George Martin, who also produced five of the final selection of tracks. Glyn Johns' son Ethan was recruited, as was Amy Winehouse producer Mark Ronson, and Paul Epworth, whose credits at the time included working with Adele, and Florence and the Machine.

The first of the quartet to work on the 20-plus songs that McCartney had in hand was Paul Hepworth. The pair convened at Hepworth's small Wolf Tone Studio in London in January 2012, where instead of trying one of the pre-written numbers they started to jam, out of which came the opening track on the album, 'Save Us'. Two more tracks with Hepworth were created at Paul's Hog Hill Mill studios, and AIR Studios in London.

Second up was Mark Ronson, whose two-song contribution comprised the title track 'New', as well as 'Alligator', which Paul said was the oldest song he'd written for the album. Ethan Johns

also ended up responsible for two tracks, including 'Hosanna' – which like 'Save Us' wasn't on the pre-recorded CD of demos that Paul had prepared, but was something new that he wanted to try out there and then.

Of the four production men, Giles Martin certainly had most experience of working in Paul McCartney's orbit. That included the reworking of Beatles' material for the 2006 Cirque du Soleil theatrical production *Love*, and on Martin Scorsese's George Harrison documentary, *Living in the Material World*, in 2011. As well as his executive role, Martin contributed six tracks to the album, including the "hidden" track 'Scared'.

Opening the album, the frantic 'Save Us' (the result of the jam with producer Hepworth), had Paul coming up with lyrics more or less as the session was under way. A great guitar-driven power-pop starter, it was released as a single in March 2014, six months after the album. Mark Ronson's first listed track, 'Alligator', was recorded on the original four-track recorder that Paul had used on his post-Beatles debut, *McCartney*. Embellished with a voice synthesizer – at the time what Ronson described as "cutting edge" technology – it's a jaunty, lighthearted slice of classic McCartney, with the tempo changes and shifts of texture that characterize many of his trademark songs.

The opening lines of 'On My Way to Work' tell us this is going to be an "autobiographical" song in the best McCartney tradition, based on real life situations from his own history. He explained this was a daily bus journey he made to a short-lived job as a teenager (as the second man on a delivery lorry) recalled as a collection of first-person snapshots illustrated with intimate detail. And 'Queenie Eye', produced by Paul Epworth, was another song drawing on McCartney's recollections of his early life, the second single to be released from the album.

Similarly, with 'Early Days', recorded with Ethan Johns in the producer's chair, the clue is in the title. The lyrics, Paul told *Rolling Stone* in 2014, are "based on my reminiscences of formative times with John before The Beatles, when we were first starting out. I can see every minute of John and I writing together, playing together, recording together. I still have very vivid memories of all of that. It's not like it fades." The track is a simple folky ballad with Johns on drums, embellished for more of a country feel with the addition of double bass and harmonium (both played by Paul), and Brian Ray's mountain-music dulcimer.

The title track, 'New', is the most accessible song on the album, almost a jolly singalong. With an insistent clapping on the offbeat, it was an obvious choice for the lead single release. With its tape loops and spliced-together sections, 'Appreciate' is, in many ways, more challenging than most tracks on the album. It had started with Giles Martin and Paul fooling around with a collage of bits and pieces, then they found a chorus intended for a previous song that was never used. "We spliced that together and it all just worked," recalled Martin.

'Everybody Out There' has the shape and feel of a straightforward McCartney song, even down to the fact that it came to the studio "oven ready". Martin recalled that he had little to do to it and they finished the track in six hours. It's one of those anthemic songs that invites the listener to join in.

Ethan Johns was stunned when he first heard 'Hosanna', a love song that likewise needed little work on it. "We threw up a couple of microphones and within four hours we had this great

Previous page Paul making a signing appearance at HMV in London's Oxford Street, for his album *New*, October 18, 2013.

Opposite left Guitarist and drummer Ethan Jones, who appeared on *New*.

Opposite right George Martin and son Giles with Grammy awards for their work on The Beatles' *Love* album. Both worked on *New*.

Below Paul McCartney and group after a free concert in Covent Garden marking the release of *New*, October 18, 2013.

track," he told *Rolling Stone.* "It had an incredible feel – a really evocative piece of music." Giles Martin was at the helm for 'I Can Bet', another fairly straightforward pop song – recorded at AIR and Hog Hill, and overdubbed in Los Angeles – which some compared to vintage Wings recordings.

'Looking at Her' is an interesting ballad that isolates Paul's voice in a gentle groove until, with a burst of Moog effects, he announces he's losing his mind. Which takes us into the final track, 'Road'. With Paul playing a variety of backing instruments, including xylophone, harmonica and Moog synthesizer, 'Road' was another track that came out of a jamming session with Paul Epworth. In many ways it's an ominous, almost fatalistic track that talks of being lost in the darkness. But it leads to a glint of light, as the finality of 'Road' segues into the "hidden" track 'Scared'. An elegant ballad, accompanied by Paul's piano, this is a confession of frailty and self-doubt that nevertheless confirms love. It makes a remarkable end to the album.

New was greeted favourably in most parts of the media, with positive praise from the music press including *Rolling Stone*, *Mojo*, and online magazines such as *PopMatters*. And mainstream sources embraced the album, too. It was selected as the "Record of the Week" on BBC Radio 2, while Helen Brown in the *Daily Telegraph* observed, regarding Paul's delving back into the past, "He needn't be so defensive, or so concerned about detractors – this album proves his talent is timeless." At the end of the year, *Rolling Stone* rated it as the fourth-best album of 2013.

Sales-wise, it was equally well-received, placing at #3 in both the US *Billboard* chart and the *Billboard* Canadian listing. Other territories where it did well included Norway, where it topped the charts, and Denmark and Japan, where it made second place, and the UK at #3.

Above Producer Mark Ronson during an interview on *Sunday Today* with Willie Geist, June 13, 2019.

Opposite Ex-Beatles Paul McCartney and Ringo Starr at the 2014 Grammy Awards ceremony.

NEW

RECORDED: JANUARY 2012
STUDIO: HOG HILL MILL, ICKLESHAM, SUSSEX
PRODUCER: MARK RONSON
COMPOSER: PAUL MCCARTNEY
RELEASED: SEPTEMBER 2, 2013 (SINGLE), OCTOBER 11, 2013 (ALBUM)

The first single to be released from *New*, the title track is a perfect piece of McCartney musical optimism. When he began the album sessions with Mark Ronson, he encouraged Paul to come up with some consciously commercial tracks, and this fitted the bill perfectly. As McCartney often described it when songs were composed more or less spontaneously, it just "wrote itself", while he was busking away on his piano at home.

Although a relatively short track, the song is rich in the kind of hooks and chorus lines that make for instantly classic pop music. Instrumentally, the track is driven by Paul on various keyboards – including piano, harpsichord and a Wurlitzer electric piano – plus some chugging, solid guitars. With the horn section of two saxes and a trumpet, and the band providing backing vocals, a spirited a cappella style ride-out concludes the track in an open-ended fashion with a warm harmonic glow.

The song has been compared variously to the Beatles' 'Got To Get You Into My Life' and 'With A Little Help From My Friends'. In the album's press release, Paul enthused, "It's a happy, positive, summer love song. It makes me think of driving across America in a Cadillac."

As the lead "trailer" track for the album, the song was initially made available to download from the iTunes Store from August 28, 2013, followed by the official single release on September 2. With some strong airplay, the single became a #4 hit in Japan, while BBC Radio 2 named it (along with the album) their "Record of the Week". It was also featured in the opening and closing credits for the 2013 animated film *Cloudy with a Chance of Meatballs 2*. As a Sony Pictures executive enthused: "We're thrilled and honoured to have Paul's infectious and inspiring song in the film."

QUEENIE EYE

RECORDED: JANUARY 2012
STUDIO: HOG HILL MILL, ICKLESHAM, SUSSEX
PRODUCER: PAUL EPWORTH
COMPOSERS: PAUL MCCARTNEY, PAUL EPWORTH
RELEASED: OCTOBER 11, 2013 (ALBUM),
OCTOBER 24, 2013

For the relentlessly upbeat 'Queenie Eye', the second single to be released from *New*, Paul McCartney once again drew on the memories of his childhood in 1940s Liverpool. Queenie Eye (also known as "Queenio") was the name of a children's street game, back in the days when there wasn't too much traffic in suburban streets.

In the game, one person (the Queenie Eye) would turn their back on the rest and throw a ball over his/her head, not knowing who would catch it. The kids would chant, "Queenie Eye, Queenie Eye, who's got the ball? I haven't got it, it isn't in my pocket, O-U-T spells out." Then Queenie Eye would turn to the children and try to guess who had the ball.

Paul Epworth recalled how the track was very primitive to start with, just the two of them in the Hog Hill studio with two amplifiers, he on drums and McCartney on assorted keyboards. Paul later overdubbed all the other instruments, including bass, various guitars, and synthesizers. The resulting track is a strident, tough anthem echoing the street chant that inspired it, heavy on bass and drums, interrupted by a reflective middle section that soon reverts to the frantic kids' playtime.

In an ambitious video to promote the single – directed by his son-in-law Simon Aboud (married to Mary McCartney) – Paul drew on a crowd of famous friends to simulate an impromptu party in the Abbey Road studios. The cast list for the four-minute film was impressive. It included actors Johnny Depp, Sean Penn, Meryl Streep, George Ezra, Jeremy Irons, Jude Law and Alive Eve; the actor-comedians James Corden and Tracey Ullman; models Kate Moss, Lily Cole and Laura Bailey; singers Gary Barlow and Jack Savoretti; and the artist Peter Blake.

In 2014, Paul performed 'Queenie Eye' at the 56th Annual Grammy Awards, with Ringo Starr (who probably recalled the street game from his own Liverpool childhood) on drums.

> "'Queenie Eye' has more twists and turns than you would have thought possible to cram in to a mere three minutes and 40 seconds."
>
> Paul McCartney

EGYPT STATION

OPENING STATION
I DON'T KNOW
COME ON TO ME
HAPPY WITH YOU
WHO CARES
FUH YOU
(PAUL MCCARTNEY, RYAN TEDDER)
CONFIDANTE
PEOPLE WANT PEACE
HAND IN HAND
DOMINOES
BACK IN BRAZIL
DO IT NOW
CAESAR ROCK
DESPITE REPEATED WARNINGS
STATION II
HUNT YOU DOWN/NAKED/C-LINK

(All songs written by Paul McCartney, except where indicated)

Paul McCartney (vocals, guitars, keyboards, bass, percussion, drums, harmonica), Greg Kurstin (guitar, keyboards, Mellotron, marimba, vibraphone, vocals), Rob Millett (cimbalom), Paul "Wix" Wickens (keyboards), Abe Laboriel Jr, drums, percussion, tack piano, vocals), Rusty Anderson (guitars, vocals), Brian Ray (guitars, bass, vocals), Tim Loo (cello), Greg Phillinganes (piano), Pedro Eustache (flute, duduk), Ryan Tedder (vocals), Vanessa Freebairn-Smith (cello), Jodi Burnett (cello), Inara George (vocals), Alex Pasco (vocals), Matt Tuggle (vocals), Collin Kadlec (vocals), Caroline Le'gene (vocals), Roy Bennett (vocals), Julian Burg (vocals), plus session musicians, orchestra and choir

EGYPT STATION

RECORDED: JANUARY 2016–FEBRUARY 2018 // **STUDIOS:** EMMANUEL PRESBYTERIAN CHURCH, LOS ANGELES; HENSON RECORDING STUDIOS, LOS ANGELES; HOG HILL MILL, ICKLESHAM, SUSSEX; ABBEY ROAD STUDIOS, LONDON; PATRIOT STUDIOS, LOS ANGELES; KLB STUDIOS, SAO PAULO, BRAZIL // **PRODUCERS:** GREG KURSTIN, PAUL MCCARTNEY, RYAN TEDDER, ZACH SKELTON // **RELEASED:** SEPTEMBER 12, 2018

It would be almost five years between the release of *New* in October 2013 and Paul's next studio album, *Egypt Station*. Appearing in September 2018, the collection was the result of over two years' collaboration with producer Greg Kurstin, who had a solid reputation as producer and songwriter from his work with Adele, Beck and Ellie Goulding, among many others.

Conscious of the time gap between this and the previous album, and the speculation about when there would be another collection, Paul announced the forthcoming release in June 2018. He explained that the title – based on a painting of the same name that he had done in 1988 – related to the project being something of a concept album, each song linked by some common theme, a device The Beatles had pioneered with *Sgt Pepper's Lonely Hearts Club Band* in 1967. In this case, the link was the railway station of the title, with the music taking the listener on a journey, each of the 14 songs being a different "station" on the way.

The album opens with 'Opening Station', a relaxed 40-second ambient noise instrumental (preceded by some station location effects), which takes us into the first song, 'I Don't Know'. A mournful ballad, the song was released as a double A-side single

along with the next track, the up-tempo 'Come On to Me', three months prior to the album's release.

The gently acoustic confessional, 'Happy With You', celebrates a contented McCartney, happy in his present situation, while 'Who Cares' – released as a promotional track ahead of the album – adopts a loping, modern jump-band sound, somewhat at odds with the serious message of the lyrics, which were devised to inspire young people to stand up to bullying. The supporting video had the Oscar-winning actress Emma Stone visiting a psychiatrist, played by Paul. The two are tormented by symbolic figures before escaping in a car. On his website, McCartney said that kids listening to the song, or watching the video, would hopefully realize that bullying was often something they could stand up to.

'Fuh You', unlike most of the album, was not produced by Greg Kurstin, but by the singer-songwriter and producer Ryan Tedder. Paul recalled when he contacted Tedder about the gig: "I liked Ryan, rung him up and we chatted. He said, 'What do you hope to get [out of this]?' I was like, 'Oh, I don't know.' And then I thought, 'Come on Paul, don't be so shy.' So I said, 'A hit?' And he was like, 'Yeah! Now you're talking my language!'"

Another confessional of sorts, 'Confidante' is a lilting dedication to the Martin D28 acoustic guitar that Paul had been using for about 30 years. Gazing at it one day, it reminded him of his earliest days strumming a guitar, when it was the "special friend" he returned to, confiding musically, again and again.

'People Want Peace' is an anthemic message song, simple and effective. It stemmed partly from Paul's decision in 2008 to do a gig in Tel Aviv, Israel. He was advised against it, but went anyway, supporting the One Voice initiative which sought a peaceful two-nation resolution to the Palestinian–Israeli conflict. And on an altogether more personal level, 'Hand in Hand' is a straightforward love song to his future wife Nancy, with some evocative accompaniment from two cello players, Vanessa Freebairn-Smith and Jodi Burnett.

'Dominoes', is a light, melodic song that – as with many of McCartney compositions – has a far more serious lyric than the seemingly trite orchestration might suggest. 'Back in Brazil' is a genuine travelogue number in keeping with the supposed theme of the album, and tells the story of a Brazilian couple much in love. It has a promotional video that involves the girl going to a McCartney concert and ending up on stage dancing with Paul!

Based on a saying that his father was fond of, 'Do It Now' is a gentle piece of Paul's personal philosophy – if you intend to do something don't put it off till later. Producer Greg Kurstin was in no doubt, declaring, "A song like 'Do It Now' knocked me out."

Paul's voice is a lot tougher on 'Caesar Rock' than on the rest of the album, a result of recording it through Auto-Tune. With a bizarre set of lyrics that became more surreal as the recording developed in the studio – "Caesar rock" was originally "she's a rock", for instance – the track is a piece of modern-day psychedelic blues of the highest order.

Although some listeners thought the epic closing song, 'Despite Repeated Warnings', might be about Brexit, Paul assured

Previous page Paul taking part in the March for Our Lives rally in New York on March 24, 2018, calling for legislative action to address school safety and gun violence.

Opposite Paul leaving Abbey Road Studios, where he played a secret gig on July 23, 2018, attended by (among others) Kylie Minogue and Johnny Depp.

Above On arrival at Tokyo airport, Paul signs copies of *Egypt Station*, ahead of his "Freshen up Japan tour, 2018" with concerts in Tokyo, Ryogoku and Nagoya.

us that it was in fact addressing climate change denial, and more specifically those in power who encouraged it. Without naming names in the song, he would concede that the "Captain", who was sailing his boat into disaster, was a veiled reverence to Donald Trump. *"I don't want to be an activist particularly, but if I feel there's an injustice I want to make myself heard,"* he told Mojo magazine. *"It's so insane. I know who the captain is, I think most people get it."*

The lead-out 'Station II' takes us back to the station where we began, a continuation of the soundscape collage that opened the album, but this isn't the end. The apparently final track also serves as an intro to a further trio of linked songs, 'Hunt You Down', 'Naked' and 'C-Link'. The first two songs connect with an abrupt change of tempo from straight 4/4 time into a waltzing 3/4 for 'Naked', while the 'C-Link' section that finally brings an amazing album to an end is just Paul, in his own words "totally indulging myself in wanting to play guitar".

The promotion campaign for the album was extensive. After announcing the forthcoming release on his 76th birthday, June 18, 2018, a two-track double A-side single was released as a trailer. That same week, one of the songs, 'Come On to Me', had been previewed during Paul's "Carpool Karaoke" segment of the *Late*

Late Show with James Corden, when Paul staged a surprise gig at the Philharmonic Dining Rooms, an historic pub in Liverpool. Then a month later, he staged three more secret UK concerts for fans – one at the Abbey Road Studios on July 19, one a few days later at the Liverpool Institute for Performing Arts (where he also held a talk called "Casual Conversation", moderated by Jarvis Cocker), and one the next day at the Cavern Club in Liverpool. And he made a similar secret appearance at New York's Grand Central Station (live streamed on You Tube) on September 7, 2018, when again he previewed songs from the album, just days before its release.

Reviews of the album were congratulatory. Giving it a four out of five rating in the often-critical *NME*, Dan Stubbs welcomed "a record that's going to delight McCartney's fans and – importantly – Beatles fans who might sniff at some of his solo work," adding, "It's an album of upbeat and winsome notes, and it's simple and honest, as if one of the most famous people in the world has left his diary open for us to read."

It was certainly the best-selling McCartney album for some time, in fact his first US #1 since *Tug of War* in 1982, 36 years earlier. It also topped the charts in Germany and Japan, while hitting the #3 position in the UK.

I DON'T KNOW

RECORDED: 2017–2018
STUDIO: HENSON RECORDING STUDIOS, LOS ANGELES; HOG HILL MILL, ICKLESHAM, SUSSEX; ABBEY ROAD STUDIOS, LONDON
PRODUCERS: GREG KURSTIN, PAUL MCCARTNEY
COMPOSER: PAUL MCCARTNEY
RELEASED: JUNE 20, 2018 (SINGLE),
SEPTEMBER 12, 2018 (ALBUM)

'I Don't Know' was released as a double A-side single along with 'Come On to Me', the second and third songs on *Egypt Station*, predating the album's release by nearly three months.

A languid, bluesy ballad, the track was described as "soul-soothing" on the Paul McCartney website. Paul reflected that he wrote the song after going through a personal difficult period and songwriting was a sort of therapy – it was easier to voice a problem in a song than talk about it face-to-face with a therapist or counsellor.

Asked whether the confessional constituted a ballad in the classic blues tradition, Paul agreed that to some extent it shared that feeling. He said, "Ma woman left me!" It wasn't that, but it was that sort of feeling. I didn't really know what to do about it, other than write a song. So I wrote the song and then felt I had more of an idea what to do. You write out your demons. It felt good to just say, 'I don't know what to do!' It's like owning up."

Paul accompanies himself on a variety of guitars, keyboards and percussion, with producer Greg Kurstin on guitar and keyboards, and Rob Millett on an Eastern European stringed instrument, the cimbalom. It's a sparse musical landscape for a song that's at times bleak, but ultimately optimistic.

Opposite On stage during the last tour stop for his "Freshen Up Tour" at Dodger Stadium, Los Angeles, on July 13, 2019.

Above Paul and wife Nancy after an Investiture ceremony, at which McCartney was made a Companion of Honour, at Buckingham Palace on May 4, 2018.

"'I Don't Know' shows his extraordinary melodic facility is completely intact – the tune is impossibly sumptuous – and taps into a strain of darkness in his writing that is often disregarded."

The Guardian, September 6, 2018

COME ON TO ME

RECORDED: 2017–2018
STUDIO: HENSON RECORDING STUDIOS, LOS ANGELES; HOG HILL MILL, ICKLESHAM, SUSSEX; ABBEY ROAD STUDIOS, LONDON
PRODUCERS: GREG KURSTIN, PAUL MCCARTNEY
COMPOSER: PAUL MCCARTNEY
RELEASED: JUNE 20, 2018 (SINGLE), SEPTEMBER 12, 2018 (ALBUM)

In complete contrast to 'I Don't Know', the other "top side" of the double A-side taken from *Egypt Station* is a straight-ahead up-tempo rocker or, in the words of the official press release, "a raucous stomper".

As Paul related it, it's a "pick-up song" where two people are attracted to each other but who makes the first move – would you come on to me, or am I going to come on to you? And as with some of McCartney's most memorable tracks, there's a catchy chorus line that provides a singalong fade out, ideal for live performances when the audience becomes part of the musical action.

In fact, the song (and by implication, the album) was previewed in a series of unique live appearances that Paul put together in the spring and summer of 2018, that later became known among fans and McCartney chroniclers as the "Secret Gigs Tour". The first date was on June 9, as the culmination to his appearance on James Corden's "Carpool Karaoke" during the *Late Late Show*, when he and the band appeared before an invited audience of about 50 fans at the Philharmonic Dining Rooms. Known locally as "The Phil", this is an iconic Art Nouveau pub just down the road from the Liverpool College of Art, and undoubtedly known to the Beatles in their early days.

GET ENOUGH [SINGLE]

RECORDED: SUMMER 2017 AND MARCH 2018
STUDIO: HOG HILL MILL, ICKLESHAM, SUSSEX; PATRIOT STUDIOS, LOS ANGELES
PRODUCERS: PAUL MCCARTNEY, RYAN TEDDER, ZACH SKELTON
COMPOSERS: PAUL MCCARTNEY, RYAN TEDDER
RELEASED: JANUARY 1, 2019 (STREAMING), MAY 10–17, 2019 (CD)

When McCartney collaborated with Ryan Tedder on *Egypt Station*, they recorded three tracks, with only 'Fuh You' included on the original album. 'Nothing for Free' would subsequently be included as a bonus track on various other editions of the collection, while 'Get Enough' suddenly appeared as a surprise release – with no promotion by Paul or the record company – on New Year's Day, 2019.

The song begins as a fairly conventional piano-led ballad, a plea to a former lost love, a meditation on past memories. Even at the outset, the familiar rounded quality of McCartney's voice is appropriately more weary-sounding than usual, slightly ragged at the edges with a hint of latter-day Bob Dylan at his most poignant. And as the song progresses, the production shifts into a more complex gear, with a dramatic heightening of mood and change of pace. A hardly discernible spoken word passage (is that his former lover we can hear?) is briefly engulfed in a swirl of electronic effects, before Paul returns with the outgoing chorus repeated.

The song features a heavy use of Auto-Tune, distorting Paul's voice in varying degrees throughout. While McCartney was recorded on bass, piano, guitars, harpsichord, synthesizer and synth-bass, Tedder and fellow producer Zach Skelton took care of programming and editing. The result was a skilled use of vocal processing which McCartney had initially resisted but then realized that the Beatles would have made use of, as he told *GQ* magazine: "You know what? If we'd had this in the Beatles, we'd have been – John, particularly – so all over it."

When it was released as a surprise single, 'Get Enough' was just available on YouTube and other streaming services, and only appeared in CD form on later deluxe and box-set editions of *Egypt Station*. Despite its relative lack of exposure or conventional promotion, the track stands as a minor classic in the McCartney songbook.

> "I'm really excited about the Paul McCartney stuff. Beyond happy, it's probably my favourite session ever. I'd go as far as saying my favourite week in my life was working with Paul McCartney."
>
> Ryan Tedder

HOME TONIGHT [SINGLE]

RECORDED: LATE 2017 AND FEBRUARY 2018
STUDIO: HENSON RECORDING STUDIOS, LOS ANGELES; HOG
HILL MILL, ICKLESHAM, SUSSEX; ABBEY ROAD STUDIOS, LONDON;
PRODUCER: GREG KURSTIN
COMPOSER: PAUL MCCARTNEY
RELEASED: NOVEMBER 22, 2019

An out-take from the *Egypt Station* sessions with producer Greg Kurstin, 'Home Tonight' was released in late November 2019, over a year after the album appeared. Backing Paul is a horn section of three saxes, trumpet and trombone, creating a lilting anthem in the McCartney tradition of up-tempo optimism.

There were a number of songs that Kurstin held back during the album sessions because they weren't developing as planned, some of which they returned to at a later date. Sometimes it was a case of Kurstin making a suggestion that McCartney seemingly ignored, but then came back to later: "A couple of times where I might have suggested something that might have been challenging... I remember him just sort of carrying on, and I'm wondering, 'Did he hear me?' Then maybe half an hour would go by and I'd say, 'Hey, Paul, what about that idea I mentioned a little while ago?' He said, 'Oh, I heard you. I was just pretending to ignore you...' Then sometimes two days later he'd try the idea."

'Home Tonight' was released as a double A-side single with 'In A Hurry' (also from the Kurstin sessions) on November 22, 2019. The date was deliberately chosen to coincide with Black Friday shopping day, marked in the United States on the Friday after Thanksgiving.

A week later, the release took advantage of another marketing opportunity when a limited edition vinyl picture disc was exclusively created for Record Store Day, with a design based on the Exquisite Corpse (or Consequences) ancient parlour game. The design, the work of the London-based graphics team of Ferry Gouw and Gary Card, involved animated images that moved as the record spun on the turntable, based on a painting by Paul.

Opposite Producer Ryan Tedder, photographed at the Pre-Grammy Gala in New York City on January 27, 2018.

Below Broadcaster Sharyn Alfonsi, preparing for an interview with Paul McCartney for *60 Minutes* on CBS TV, aired on September 30, 2018.

MCCARTNEY III

(All songs written by Paul McCartney)

Paul McCartney (vocals, guitars, bass, double bass, piano, harpsichord, Mellotron, harmonium, Fender Rhodes, synthesizers, Wurlitzer electric piano, drums, percussion, recorder), Rusty Anderson (guitar), Abe Laboriel Jr (drums)

MCCARTNEY III

RECORDED: SEPTEMBER 3, 1992; APRIL–JUNE 2020 // **STUDIOS:** HOG HILL MILL, ICKLESHAM, SUSSEX
PRODUCER: PAUL MCCARTNEY // **RELEASED:** DECEMBER 18, 2020

When the global Covid-19 pandemic struck early in 2020, Paul was forced into lockdown like everyone else, having to "work from home". But in his case, home was very close to his Hog Hill studio so he was able to put the time in isolation ("rockdown", as he called it) to good use.

He hadn't planned to release an album in 2020, but after spending a couple of months working on some bits and pieces for songs that were lying around, and creating some new ones in the process, he realized he had a new collection on his hands. "I had some stuff I'd worked on over the years but sometimes time would run out and it would be left half-finished so I started thinking about what I had," he explained in the press release for the album. "Each day I'd start recording with the instrument I wrote the song on and then gradually layer it all up, it was a lot of fun."

As it happened, 2020 marked the 50th anniversary of Paul's first solo album, the self-titled *McCartney,* in 1970. Then 10 years later, after his seventh album with Wings, his second solo collection, *McCartney II* appeared. So *McCartney III*, 40 years later, was certainly aptly titled. The album was a home-grown DIY project that evolved out of unforeseen circumstances.

The opening track, 'Long Tailed Winter Bird', was also the first track Paul worked on for the album. It's an energetic instrumental (apart from some doo-wop vocal interruptions), dominated by acoustic guitar and crisp percussion, which originated in a 1992 unreleased track produced by George Martin, 'When Winter Comes'– and which in turn would spawn the final track for *McCartney III.*

'Find My Way' was also written at the beginning of the pandemic. Despite the gloom, the bouncy guitar-dominated song projects an optimistic feel and message – a reassurance for people, as Paul put it, "who worry more than I do." With an insistent guitar riff running through it, 'Pretty Boys' is the slice of observational narrative we've come to expect from McCartney. It's a rather uneasy look at the world of male photographic models, and the way they can often be exploited and used, drawing a disturbing analogy with the lines of hire bikes seen on the streets of New York and London.

Written while Paul was reading a book about the great folk-blues singer Huddie "Lead Belly" Ledbetter, 'Women and Wives' is a solemn, earnest song, accompanied by some

Previous page A pensive-looking Paul, backstage at Stella McCartney's Spring-Summer 2020 show at Paris Fashion Week; September 30, 2019.

Above Paul appearing in an interview on *The Tonight Show Starring Jimmy Fallon,* talking about *McCartney III*, December 18, 2020.

Opposite Paul at a news conference introducing him as the winner of the Gershwin Prize for Popular Song at the Library of Congress in Washington, June 1, 2010.

equally serious piano – and a double bass, we're told, that originally belonged to Bill Black, when he backed Elvis Presley on his iconic early records.

Although it sounds like it might be written as a humorous song, with its thumping bass and genuine early rock sound from a 1954 Telecaster guitar, 'Lavatory Lil' is, in fact, a barbed diatribe against a real person who had crossed Paul in the past. Drawing a comparison with John Lennon's 'Polythene Pam' (who was taken from a real-life character in The Beatles' days in Liverpool), he explained he wrote the song about someone who had caused him trouble, creating the fictional character of Lavatory Lil rather than naming names.

What Paul agreed could be called indulgent, 'Deep Deep Feeling' is an eight-minute epic jam: "I was thinking of editing it down to a shorter, more reasonable length, but when I listened through it I liked it so much... that I kept it [at] eight minutes," he told *NME* magazine. With layers of sound in the mix, 'Slidin'' uses a near-metal slice of heavyweight, distorted guitar. The riff originated at a sound check in Dusseldorf, Germany, in May 2016. Paul planned to develop it into a song

"Hang on, what if I do a fourth?
I'm not planning on shutting the door just yet."

Paul McCartney

at the *Egypt Station* sessions, but nothing came of it, until he resurrected it for *McCartney III*.

A lighter-touch McCartney surfaces on 'Kiss of Venus', an acoustic love song telling the story of lovers circling each other like the planets in an astrology book he'd recently read. 'Seize the Day', on the other hand, was (consciously or not) written as a response to the pandemic. An enjoiner to recognize the good things in life when they occur, it's a Beatle-flavoured song about embracing the positive.

Another song that came out of a jam, 'Deep Down' is highly orchestrated with an insistent snare drum keeping everything tight. There's a big Moog-synthesized bass, although the whole effect is somewhat repetitive. As Paul told the *NME*: "Some songs you know you don't quite know where you're going. You've just got half an idea and it's really just that you're enjoying the groove and that one was one of those, I just thought of ideas as I went along."

For the final track of *McCartney III*, the short instrumental 'Winter Bird' takes the acoustic motif from the album's opening 'Long Tailed Winter Bird' as a lead-in to 'When Winter Comes'. Originally recorded in 1992 with George Martin, it makes for a delicate acoustic treasure in the best McCartney tradition, and a fitting end to an album born out of an unplanned solitude.

Promotion for the album was the most extensive for any Paul McCartney record in a long time, with numerous editions in a variety of formats, including CD, vinyl and digital. The vinyl pressing came in various colours, including black, red, yellow, pink, violet and more, with the colours being allotted to specific outlets and retailers in limited quantities. The cover art and typography was designed by Ed Ruscha, a major name in the 1960s pop art movement.

Reviews were universally positive and resulted in strong sales around the world. It topped the chart in the UK in its first week of entry, on Christmas Day 2020, and was Paul's first solo #1 since *Flowers in the Dirt* in 1989. In America, it debuted at #2 in the *Billboard* 200, and #1 in *Billboard*'s Top Rock Albums list. Elsewhere, it topped the chart in Germany and Holland, and appeared in the top five in Austria, Belgium, Finland, Japan, Portugal, Sweden and Switzerland.

It was a remarkable success for what was initially an unplanned album. As he confirmed on BBC TV during an hour-long conversation with the actor Idris Elba, "I didn't know I was making an album. Somebody said to me the other day, you know why did everyone in lockdown do all this stuff they'd be meaning to get around to? And so that was my equivalent. I wasn't trying to make an album."

Right Playing headline at the Austin City Limits event, Austin, Texas, on October 5, 2018.

FIND MY WAY

RECORDED: APRIL–JUNE, 2020
STUDIO: HOG HILL MILL, ICKLESHAM, SUSSEX
PRODUCER: PAUL MCCARTNEY
COMPOSER: PAUL MCCARTNEY
RELEASED: DECEMBER 18, 2020

Written during the early stages of the pandemic lockdown, 'Find My Way' was the only track on *McCartney III* to be released as a single. "It was a very scary time," Paul recalled, "Other scares we've had – SARS, avian flu – they seemed to happen to other people. But this was happening to everyone, people you knew, everyone in the world."

Although there was no official single release, the track – which appeared on the same day as the album – was flagged with stickers reading "Featuring 'Find My Way'" on the CD and vinyl LPs. There was also a promotional video directed by Roman Coppola.

Recording at Hog Hill, Paul had laid down two different drum tracks, then added two separate bass tracks, and went on to record several guitar parts at different tape speeds. It was a perfect illustration of how a simple song could benefit from seemingly complex technical solutions, without sounding overtly tech-based.

As he said to the actor Idris Elba during an interview for BBC TV, 'Find My Way' was one of those songs that had gone through various stages of correction, deletion and replacement before he arrived at a result he was happy with. Having established what he called a positive "I can do it" type of verse, he said, "I had some rubbish stuff about going on holiday with someone and it didn't work out. And she left and it was like… it was terrible. And so I came back and wiped all that bit, and put another middle into it, which is better."

Born out of the pandemic that was sweeping the world, 'Find My Way' represented Paul's natural optimism, though tested to the limit, through which he hoped to reassure others, most of whom were carrying a far bigger burden of worry than himself.

WHEN WINTER COMES

RECORDED: SEPTEMBER 3, 1992; APRIL–JUNE 2020
STUDIO: HOG HILL MILL, ICKLESHAM, SUSSEX
PRODUCER: PAUL MCCARTNEY
COMPOSER: PAUL MCCARTNEY
RELEASED: DECEMBER 18, 2020

The whole process of *McCartney III* could be said to have been triggered by 'When Winter Comes'. Paul had originally recorded the song with George Martin in September 1992, along with 'Calico Skies' and 'Great Day', both of which appeared on *Flaming Pie* in 1997. Paul was digging through some old recordings, and when he came across the track, decided to make a short, animated film based on the lyrics. It was when he was recording the short introductory music for the film that the world went into lockdown.

Even back in 1992, the song was already something of a nostalgic recollection of the idyllic days Paul spent on his farm in Scotland in the early 1970s where he would "paint the roof, fix the drains, fix the fence." At that time, the "good life" of rural self-sufficiency was a respite from the pressures of his post-Beatles situation. Now he sees a parallel with a lot of people – himself included – finding similar relief in the context of the current world, particularly in light of the Covid-19 crisis.

The song was originally mooted as a bonus extra track for a reissue of *Flaming Pie*, but Paul had second thoughts about it and it languished on a studio shelf for almost 30 years before being resurrected, albeit inadvertently, at a very appropriate time.

Opposite: Meeting school pupils at a London launch event for his children's book *Hey Grandude*, September 6, 2019.

"We finished the album with it because it was the reason for doing the whole thing, because me and my mate Geoff Dunbar, who's an animation director, were talking about making an animated film to that song. So that's where the opening and closing tracks come from, which got me into the studio in the first place."

Paul McCartney

DISCOGRAPHY

ALBUMS

STUDIO

(all credited to Paul McCartney, except where indicated)

McCartney	1970	
Ram	1971	Paul and Linda McCartney
Wild Life	1971	Wings
Red Rose Speedway	1973	Paul McCartney and Wings
Band on the Run	1973	Paul McCartney and Wings
Venus and Mars	1975	Wings
Wings at the Speed of Sound	1976	Wings
The Family Way (soundtrack)	1967	
Thrillington	1977	Percy 'Thrills' Thrillington
London Town	1978	Wings
Back to the Egg	1979	Wings
McCartney II	1980	
Tug of War	1982	
Pipes of Peace	1983	
Give My Regards to Broad Street (soundtrack)	1984	

Press to Play	1986	
Choba B CCCP	1988	
Flowers in the Dirt	1989	
Off the Ground	1993	
Strawberries Oceans Ships Forests	1993	The Fireman
Flaming Pie	1997	
Rushes	1998	The Fireman
Run Devil Run	1999	
Liverpool Sound Collage	2000	Paul McCartney, The Beatles, Super Furry Animals, Youth
Driving Rain	2001	
Twin Freaks	2005	with DJ The Freelance Hellraiser
Chaos and Creation in the Backyard	2005	
Memory Almost Full	2007	
Electric Arguments	2008	The Fireman
Kisses on the Bottom	2012	
New	2013	
Egypt Station	2018	
McCartney III	2020	

LIVE

Wings Over America	1976	Wings
Tripping the Live Fantastic	1990	
Unplugged	1991	
Paul Is Live	1993	
Back in the US	2002	
Back in the World Live	2003	
Good Evening New York City	2009	
Amoeba Gig	2019	

CLASSICAL

Liverpool Oratorio	1991
Standing Stone	1997
Working Classical	1999
Ecce Cor Meum	2006
Ocean's Kingdom	2011

COMPILATIONS

Wings Greatest	1978	Wings
All the Best!	1987	
Wingspan: Hits and History	2001	
Pure McCartney	2016	

SINGLES

Another Day	1971	
Uncle Albert/Admiral Halsey	1971	Paul and Linda McCartney
The Back Seat of My Car	1971	Paul and Linda McCartney
Eat at Home	1971	Paul and Linda McCartney
Give Ireland Back to the Irish	1972	Wings
Mary Had a Little Lamb	1972	Wings
Hi, Hi, Hi	1972	Wings
My Love (live)	1973	Paul McCartney and Wings
Live and Let Die	1973	Paul McCartney and Wings
Helen Wheels	1973	Paul McCartney and Wings
Jet	1973	Paul McCartney and Wings
Mrs Vandebilt	1973	Paul McCartney and Wings
Band on the Run	1974	Paul McCartney and Wings
Junior's Farm	1974	Paul McCartney and Wings
Walking in the Park with Eloise	1974	The Country Hams
Listen to What the Man Said	1975	Wings
Letting Go	1975	Wings
Venus and Mars/Rock Show	1975	Wings
Silly Love Songs	1976	Wings
Let 'Em In	1976	Wings
Maybe I'm Amazed (live)	1977	Wings
Seaside Woman	1977	Wings
Mull of Kintyre	1977	Wings
With a Little Luck	1978	Wings
I've Had Enough	1978	Wings
London Town	1978	Wings
Goodnight Tonight	1979	Wings
Old Siam Sir	1979	Wings
Getting Closer	1979	Wings
Wonderful Christmastime	1979	
Coming Up	1980	
Waterfalls	1980	
Temporary Secretary	1980	
Ebony and Ivory	1982	Paul McCartney and Stevie Wonder
Take It Away	1982	
Tug of War	1982	
The Girl is Mine	1982	Michael Jackson and Paul McCartney
Say Say Say	1983	Paul McCartney and Michael Jackson
Pipes of Peace	1983	
No More Lonely Nights	1984	
We All Stand Together	1984	Paul McCartney and the Frog Chorus
Spies Like Us	1985	
Press	1986	
Pretty Little Head	1986	
Only Love Remains	1986	
Once Upon a Long Ago	1987	
My Brave Face	1989	
This One	1989	
Figure of Eight	1989	
Put It There	1990	
Hope of Deliverance	1992	
C'Mon People	1993	
Off the Ground	1993	
Biker Like and Icon	1993	
A Leaf	1995	(featuring Anya Alexeyev)
Young Boy	1997	
The World Tonight	1997	
Beautiful Night	1997	
Wide Prairie	1998	Wings
The Light Comes from Within	1999	(with Linda and James McCartney)
No Other Baby	1999	
Voice	1999	(with Heather Mills)
From a Lover to a Friend	2001	
Freedom	2001	
Tropic Island Hum	2004	(with Linda McCartney)
Fine Line	2005	
Jenny Wren	2005	
Dance Tonight	2007	
Ever Present Past	2007	
My Valentine	2011	
Only Our Hearts	2012	(featuring Stevie Wonder)
New	2013	
Queenie Eye	2013	
Hope for the Future	2014	
Only One	2014	Kanye West featuring Paul McCartney
FourFiveSeconds	2015	Rihanna, Kanye West and Paul McCartney
All Day	2015	(with Kanye West, Theophilus London and Allan Kingdom)
1985 (remix)	2016	Paul McCartney and Wings
I Don't Know	2018	
Fuh You	2018	
Get Enough	2019	
Home Tonight	2019	
Find My Way	2020	

Opposite McCartney in the studio, filming *The South Bank Show* for ITV. It was first broadcast in the UK on January 14, 1978.

QUOTE CREDITS

MCCARTNEY

'We decided we didn't want to tell anyone…' Paul McCartney talking to *Rolling Stone*, 1970, quoted in Barry Miles *Many Years From Now*, Secker & Warburg, 1997

'I found that I was enjoying…' Paul McCartney quoted in Barry Miles *Many Years From Now*, Secker & Warburg, 1997

'Who does Paul McCartney think he is?' Paul McCartney, letter to Mailbag, *Melody Maker*, May 2 1970

'We had a lot of fun…' Paul McCartney in *Rolling Stone*, 1970

MAYBE I'M AMAZED

'Boastfully casual' The *Guardian*

'It was an easy album to do…' PM quoted in Pete Jones, *Record Mirror* 18.4.70

'At the time we thought "Maybe I'm Amazed" was a good track…' PM

ANOTHER DAY

'Eleanor Rigby in New York City…' Denny Seiwell in *Paul McCartney: A Life*, Peter Ames Carlin, Touchstone Books, 2009.

'We were sitting in Studio A2 one day…' Dixon Van Winkle, in Gary Eskow, Classic Tracks: Paul McCartney's "Uncle Albert/ Admiral Halsey", www.mixonline.com January 8, 2004

'Great song. I remember doing many tracks…' David Spinozza, www.urblremedy.com quoted in www.beatlesbible.com

'He'd strap on a guitar or piano…' Denny Seiwell

'I found this New York drummer named Denny…' PM quoted in Alan Smith, *New Musical Express*, 22/5/71

RAM

'We went to New York…' Paul McCartney quoted in The Paul McCartney Project (the-paulmccartney-project.com) from paulmccartney.com

'Slaughtered at birth ….' Chris Roberts, BBC online review, May 21, 2012

'I'd been serious long enough…' Paul McCartney, interview by Ryan Dombal, Pitchfork (pitchfork.com), June 7, 2012

HEART OF THE COUNTRY

'Linda said "we could do this place up…' Paul McCartney in *Many Years From Now*, Barry Miles, Secker & Warburg, 1997

'I liked its isolation…' ibid.

'To me it was the first feeling I'd ever had…' ibid.

WILD LIFE

'The early albums…' Paul McCartney, quoted in paulmccartney.com

'Just hope they don't ask…' Paul McCartney quoted in *Conversations With McCartney*, Paul Du Noyer, Hodder & Stoughton, 2015

'Just me and Linda's…' ibid

'Vacuous, flaccid…' John Mendelsohn, *Rolling Stone* review, January 20, 1972

'I quite enjoyed it…' John Lennon on *The Mike Douglas Show*, February 5, 1972

'We were not trying to follow…'

Denny Laine, interviewed by Mark Hinson, *Tallahassee Democrat*, 2017

DEAR FRIEND

'The track was recorded at Armin Steiner's…' Denny Seiwell in *Paul McCartney Recording Sessions*, Luca Perasi, L.I.L.Y., 2013

'"Dear Friend" was written about John…' Paul McCartney in *Club Sandwich*, Winter 1994

'This was me reaching out…' Paul McCartney, paulmccartney.com, October 29, 2018

HI HI HI

'A bit of a dirty song…' Paul McCartney in *The Beatles: The Dream is Over*, Keith Badman, Omnibus, 2000

'That was a very difficult…' Henry McCullogh in *Eight Arms to Hold You: The Solo Beatles Compendium*, Chip Madinger and Mark Easter, 44 1 Productions, 2001

'It was like "Ooh, what does Dylan mean?' Paul McCartney in *Man On the Run: Paul McCartney in the 1970s*, Tom Doyle, Polygon, 2013

'It took a few days…' John Leckie in *Paul McCartney Recording Sessions*, Luca Perasi, L.I.L.Y., 2013

'I thought the "Hi Hi Hi" thing…' PM talking to Paul Gambaccini, *Rolling Stone*, January 31, 1974

C MOON

'I thought of the idea…' Paul McCartney in *Band on the Run: A History of Paul McCartney and Wings*, Garry McGee, Taylor Trade Publishing, 2003

RED ROSE SPEEDWAY

'I wasn't happy about the song…' Denny Laine quoted in Spencer Leigh 'Paul McCartney and Wings', *Record Collector*, February 1993

'Quite possibly the worst album…' *Christgau's Record Guide; Rock Albums of the 70s*, Robert Christgau, Ticknor & Fields, 1981

'I for one am bloody pleased…' Tony Tyler in *New Musical Express*, quoted in Hunt, Chris (ed.) *NME Originals: Beatles – The Solo Years 1970–1980*, IPC Ignite!, 2005

MY LOVE

'I can't remember…; Henry McCullough interview, quoted in songfacts.com, August 23, 2011

'I'd sort of written the solo…' Paul McCartney, quoted in Nick Levine, Henry McCullough obituary, *New Musical Express*, June 15, 2016

'among his seemingly…' Chris Welch, singles reviews, *Melody Maker*, April 7, 1973

'"My Love" was my definitive one for Linda…' Paul McCartney interview in *Billboard*, 2001

HELEN WHEELS

'Helen Wheels is our Land Rover….' *Paul McCartney: In His Own Words*, Paul McCartney, Omnibus (1976)

BAND ON THE RUN

'At that particular time…' Howie Casey talking to Mike Evans, January 30, 2021

'It's even more amazing…' *Here, There and Everywhere: My Life Recording the Music of the Beatles*, Geoff Emerick, Gotham Books, 2006

'Writing with [Paul] wasn't a chore…' Denny Laine, interview with Eoghan Lyng for Culture Sonar (culturesonar.com). December 24, 2018

'And with this album…' Chris Welch review, *Melody Maker*, December 1, 1973

'Band On The Run is a great album…' Charles Shaar Murray review, *New Musical Express*, January 19, 1974

'"Let Me Roll It" was a riff…' Paul McCartney interview 'Paul McCartney On His Not-So-Silly Lovesongs', *Billboard*, March 16, 2001

BAND ON THE RUN

'The whole world decided to run along with him…' 'Paul McCartney's Greatest Solo Songs', *Rolling Stone*, September 2017

'We'd started off as kids really…' Paul McCartney talking to Simon Harper, *Clash*, October 2010

'The song not only anchors…' Michael Gallucci, 'Top 10 Paul McCartney Songs', Ultimate Classic Rock (ultimateclassicrock.com), June 18, 2013

'Band on the Run was pretty significant…' Denny Laine, quoted by Keith Valcourt, *The Washington Times*, January 19, 2017

JET

'I make up so much stuff up…' *Paul McCartney: In His Own Words*, Paul McCartney, Omnibus, 1976

"He wanted that one to be totally mad…" Linda McCartney in 1976, quoted in songfacts.com

LIVE AND LET DIE

'We were at AIR studios…' Denny Seiwell in *Paul McCartney Recording Sessions*, Luca Perasi, L.I.L.Y., 2013

'They had a sixty-three-piece orchestra…'Mark Berry quoted in theamgroup.com

'After the record had finished…'Paul McCartney quoted in The Beatles Bible (beatlesbible.com)

'"Live and Let Die" shows…' BMI President Del Bryant, *BMI News*, Oct 16, 2012

'I read the *Live and Let Die* book…'Paul McCartney in *The Beatles: The Dream is Over*, Keith Badman, Omnibus, 2000

'I remember a thing in *Rolling Stone*…'PM talking to Paul Gambaccini, *Rolling Stone*, January 31 1974

JUNIOR'S FARM

'I wasn't trying to say anything…' Paul McCartney in *The Beatles: The Dream is Over*, Keith Badman, Omnibus, 2000

'He wasn't supposed to be recording…' Buddy Killen talking to Bill DeMain, in 2002, quoted in Bill DeMain 'Wings Over Nashville!' *Nashville Lifestyles*, March 2008

'As a vocalist, he was a true artist…' Ernie Winfrey quoted in Bill DeMain, 'Wings Over Nashville!' *Nashville Lifestyles*, March 2008

'I rather fancy the place…' Paul McCartney talking to *Nashville Banner*, 1974

SALLY G

'That was the whole point about "Sally G"…' Paul McCartney talking to Chris Welch, 'Paul McCartney: Abbey Road Revisited', *Melody Maker*, May 31, 1975

VENUS AND MARS

'I was rehearsing with Bonnie Bramlett…' Joe English, interview with uncredited writer 'Wings Take Off With New Member', *Beat Instrumental*, July 1975

'So he pulled in local musicians…' Howie Casey talking to Mike Evans, January 30, 2021

'We just wanted to record in America…' Paul MCartney talking to Chris Welch 'Abbey Road Revisited', *Melody Maker*, May 31, 1975

LISTEN TO WHAT THE MAN SAID

'We thought it would be great to have…' *Paul McCartney: In His Own Words*, Paul McCartney, Omnibus, 1976

'It wasn't quite "The Hustle"…' 'Paul McCartney's Greatest Solo Songs', *Rolling Stone*, September 2017

'My stuff is never "a comment from within"…' Paul McCartney, *Club Sandwich*, Spring 1988

WINGS AT THE SPEED OF SOUND

'You know Paul, bless him…' Howie Casey talking to Mike Evans, January 30, 2021

'They had these pots…' Paul McCartney in *The Beatles After the Break-Up, 1970–2000*, Keith Badman, Omnibus, 1999

'Much good music…' Chris Welch, *Melody Maker* review, March 27, 1976

'Family man?…' Linda McCartney to Barbara Charone, *Sounds*, April 3, 1976

LET 'EM IN

'Well, as it happens, it is our actual doorbell….' Paul McCartney talking to Chris Welch, 'Paul McCartney: Pressure Cooking', *Melody Maker*, March 27, 1976

SILLY LOVE SONGS

'Originally I wrote this song…' Paul McCartney in *Give My Regards to Broad Street*, Pavilion Books, 1984

'A clever retort…' Stephen Holden, Wings at the Speed of Sound review, *Rolling Stone*, May 20, 1976

'Hate all you want…' Michael Gallucci, 'Top 10 Paul McCartney Songs', Ultimate Classic Rock (ultimateclassicrock.com), June 18, 2013

'After years of doing his best…' 'Paul McCartney's Greatest Solo Songs', *Rolling Stone*, September 2017

'I was getting slagged off…' Paul McCartney, *Club Sandwich*, Spring 1988

MULL OF KINTYRE

'Paul and I were very into folk music…' Denny Laine, interviewed in Culture Sonar (culturesonar.com), December 24, 2018

'It took an hour to record…' Ian McKerrals in 'The Paul McCartney Story', *The Scottish Daily*, August 6, 2002, quoted in Paul McCartney Recording Sessions, Luca Perasi, L.I.L.Y., 2013

'A bagpipe-assisted pub singalong…' 'Paul McCartney's Greatest Solo Songs', *Rolling Stone*, September 2017

SEASIDE WOMAN

'"Seaside Woman" is very reggae inspired…' Linda McCartney quoted in *Band on the Run: A History of Paul McCartney and Wings*, Garry McGee, Taylor Trade Publishing, 2003

'I was so in love with reggae…' Linda McCartney quoted in *Linda McCartney: The Biography*, Danny Fields, Little, Brown & Company, 2000

'When we were in Jamaica…' Linda McCartney quoted in Adrian Ernesto Cepeda, Don't Forget the Songs 365 (dontforgetthesongs365.wordpress.com) 2012

'We went in to do a B-side for it…' Paul McCartney talking to Paul Gambaccini, *Rolling Stone*, January 31, 1974

LONDON TOWN

'We recorded London Town…' Paul McCartney in *Club Sandwich*, Spring 1988

'A distinctly European flavour…' Stephen Thomas Erlewine, review in AllMusic (allmusic.com)

LONDON TOWN

'Linda and I were sitting…' Paul McCartney, interview with Paul Gambaccini, BBC Radio 1, 1978, quoted in *Paul McCartney Recording Sessions*, L.I.L.Y., Luca Perasi, 2013

'A melodic, atmospheric ballad…' *Billboard* 'Top Single Picks', August 26, 1978

GOODNIGHT TONIGHT

'I'm making records…' Paul McCartney quoted in Paul McGuiness' 'Best Paul McCartney Songs: 20 Essential Post-Beatles Macca Tracks', U Discover Music (udiscovermusic.com) June 18, 2020

'We scrapped the whole thing…' Paul McCartney in 'Paul McCartney's Greatest Solo Songs', *Rolling Stone*, September 2017

'That was all based round some rhythm…' Paul McCartney in *Club Sandwich*, spring 1988

'I had just spent some time…' Steve Holley, interviewed September 19, 2012, in *Paul McCartney Recording Sessions*, Luca Perasi, L.I.L.Y., 2013

BACK TO THE EGG

'I don't know why Jimmy…' Howie Casey talking to Mike Evans, January 30, 2021

'It's too bad *Back to the Egg* …' Beverly Paterson, Something Else!, (somethingelsereviews.com), June 8, 2015

'We knew from the get-go…' Laurence Juber, *Daytrippin' Beatles Magazine*, August 9, 2010

GETTING CLOSER

'There is some dandy material…' Mitchell Cohen, *Back to the Egg* album review, *Creem*, September 1979

MCCARTNEY II

'I wasn't trying to do an album…' Paul McCartney quoted in *Paul McCartney Recording Sessions*, Luca Perasi, L.I.L.Y., 2013

'The song seemed right…' Paul McCartney in *The Beatles – The Dream is Over: Off the Record 2*, Keith Badman, Omnibus, 2009

'An album of aural doodles…' Stephen Holden, *Rolling Stone* review, June 24, 1980

'I got into all sorts of tricks…' Paul McCartney talking to Paul Gambaccini, 'Paul McCartney's one-man band' *Rolling Stone*, June 26, 1980

COMING UP

'I went into the studio each day…' ibid.

WATERFALLS

'I decided to do a song…' Paul McCartney in *The Beatles: The Dream is Over*, Keith Badman, Omnibus, 2000

'"Waterfalls" is basically saying…' Paul McCartney from *McCartney II* Archive Collection, 2011 quoted in The Paul McCartney Project (www.the-paulmccartney-project.com) May 21, 2020

'McCartney's second single…' Review, 'Top Single Picks' *Billboard*, August 2, 1980

'Overall the thing is…' Phil Sutcliffe, *McCartney II* album review *Sounds*, May 17, 1980

TUG OF WAR

'I wanted to work…' Paul McCartney, quoted in *The Beatles Bible*, Monday 15 August 2011 www.beatlesbible.com

'John was killed…' Paul McCartney, interview in *Newsweek*, May 1982

'Anyone who was a legend…' Paul McCartney talking to Tom Mulhern in *Guitar Player*, July 1990

'McCartney at last appears…' Nick Kent, *New Musical Express*, May 1, 1982

'The masterpiece everyone…'
Stephen Holden, *Rolling Stone*, May 27, 1982

'With George Martin, it was…' Paul McCartney in *The Beatles: The Dream is Over*, Keith Badman, Omnibus, 2000

TUG OF WAR

'I wanted to do the whole album…' Paul McCartney quoted in Jim Millar 'Paul

McCartney Looks Back', *Newsweek*, May 3, 1983

'The title track…' Nick Kent, *Tug of War* album review, *New Musical Express*, May 1, 1982

EBONY AND IVORY

'Although some considered…' Craig Werner in *Goldmine*, October 8, 1999

'It was nevertheless…' Carol Cooper, *The Face*, June 1984

'I listened to the song…' Stevie Wonder talking to Dick Clark, *National Music Survey*, (album release by Mutual Broadcasting System) April 10, 1982

PIPES OF PEACE

Pipes of Peace 'an awful sense…' Paul McCartney Recording Sessions, Luca Perasi, L.I.L.Y., 2013

'Just when you thought…' J. D. Considine, review in *Musician*, January 1984

PIPES OF PEACE

'He used his hands on my drums…' James Kippen, interviewed October 23, 2011, in *Paul McCartney Recording Sessions*, Luca Perasi, L.I.L.Y., 2013

'I recall that AIR…' James Kippen quoted in Caludio Dirani 'The Stunning Percussion on Pipes of Peace', posted July 27, 2011; That Would Be Something: The Paul McCartney Blog (thatwouldbe something.com)

LIVE AND LET DIE

"I remember a thing in *Rolling Stone*…" PM talking to Paul Gambaccini, *Rolling Stone*, January 31 1974

SAY SAY SAY

'But when it got to Paul…' Nathan Watts interviewed by Rick Suchow, 'Nathan Watts: The Groove of Wonder', *Bass Player*, 2011

'Amiable though vapid…' Parke Puterbaugh, *Pipes of Peace* review, *Rolling Stone*, January 19, 1984

'Michael came over…' Paul McCartney in Paul McCartney World Tour booklet, quoted in *Paul McCartney Recording Sessions*, Luca Perasi, L.I.L.Y., 2013

NO MORE LONELY NIGHTS

'I had been messing around…' Paul McCartney quoted in The Paul McCartney Project (www.the-paulmccartney-project.com), March 31, 2020

'It's a nice track…' Paul McCartney quoted in 1984 interview My Gold Music (www.mygoldmusic.co.uk)

'I found it quite amazing…' David Gilmour, *Q* magazine, 1986

PRESS TO PLAY

"'Oklahoma was never like this"…' Paul McCartney interview, *Sound On Sound* magazine, October 1986

'Britain's attitude towards apartheid…' Paul McCartney, *Rolling Stone*, September, 1986

'It did suggest the epic finale…' Paul McCartney interview, *Sound On Sound* magazine, October 1986

'McCartney's most rocking…' Lynne Van Matre, 'No Silly Love Songs on Press to Play' *Chicago Tribune*, September 12, 1986

STRANGLEHOLD

'The song sounded great…' Eric Stewart from Ken Sharp 'A Conversation with Eric Stewart', *Beatlefan* #140

'…a great song…' Eric Stewart in *FarOut* magazine, 2017

'Wait a minute…' Paul McCartney talking to Chris Salewicz, *Q* magazine, October 1986

CHOBA B CCCP

'Paul McCartney has released an album…' *New York Times*, January 12, 1989

ONCE UPON A LONG AGO

'I remember that Paul…' Stan Sulzmann in *Paul McCartney Recording Sessions*, Luca Perasi, L.I.L.Y., 2013

FLOWERS IN THE DIRT

'his best work since…' Mark Cooper review, *Q* magazine, July 1989

'We enjoy each other…' Paul McCartney quoted in Nicholas Jennings 'Paul Gets Back', *Maclean's*, October 2, 1989

MY BRAVE FACE

'Well it seemed like it could be a hit…' Mitchell Froom quoted in 'In Their Own Words: The Producers discuss McCartney's Flowers in the Dirt', Super DeLuxe Edition blog (www.superdeluxeedition.com)

"We got these songs…' Paul McCartney quoted in *Conversations With McCartney*, Paul Du Noyer, Hodder & Stoughton, 2015

YOU WANT HER TOO

'another stand-out, a rancorous dialogue…' David Silverman in 'Paul Is Back – Well, Almost', *Chicago Tribune*, June 11, 1989

'As Elvis and Paul…' Mark Cooper, Flowers in the Dirt review, *Q* magazine, July 1989

'That's a good old trick…' Paul McCartney quoted in Jordan Runtagh 'Behind the Songs: Paul McCartney Shares Intimate Memories of Recording Flowers in the Dirt', People (www.people.com) March 24, 2017

OFF THE GROUND

'I didn't do serious demos…' Paul McCartney in The New World Tour souvenir programme, 1993

'One of the great vocal performances…' Elvis Costello, *Mojo*, August 2011

'Vibrant new tunes…' Jon Young, Docklands Arena, London, concert review, *Musician*, April 1993

HOPE OF DELIVERANCE

'An international message…' Paul McCartney quoted in 'Paul McCartney's Greatest Solo Songs', *Rolling Stone*, September 2017

'A soft, acoustic-anchored…' Larry Flick, 'Single Reviews' *Billboard*, February 6, 1993

BIKER LIKE AN ICON

'I remember when John…' Paul McCartney in The New World Tour souvenir programme, 1993

'A few weeks later …' Hamish Stuart, ibid.

FLAMING PIE

'So I fell in with the idea…' Paul McCartney quoted in Thom Duffy's 'McCartney Let Loose on Capitol's Flaming Pie Set', *Billboard*, April 12, 1997

'I'm working on a new album…' Paul McCartney, interviewed in *Q* magazine, October 1996

'Many people ask…' John Lennon, 'Being A Short Diversion On The Dubious Origins Of Beatles', Bill Harry, *Mersey Beat*, July 6, 1961

'Against the clock…' Paul McCartney in liner notes for *Flaming Pie*

BEAUTIFUL NIGHT

'I unearthed this old song…' ibid.

'It was really good to see…' Paul McCartney quoted in Paul McGuinness' 'Best Paul McCartney Songs: 20 Essential Post-Beatles Macca Tracks', U Discover Music (www.udiscovermusic.com), June 18, 2020

RUN DEVIL RUN

'At the early recordings…' Paul McCartney, Press release for *Run Devil Run*, October 1999

'Chuck Berry-style' Paul McCartney, liner notes for *Run Devil Run*, October 1999

'Maybe down in Lonesome Town…' Lyrics 'Lonesome Town' by Baker Knight, ©1958 Matragun Music Inc

RUN DEVIL RUN

'Not that I have got many…' Paul McCartney, *Run Devil Run* press release interview, October 1999

'Chris Thomas thought…' Paul McCartney to Jim Irvin, *Mojo*, October 1999

NO OTHER BABY

'I didn't have a record of it…' Paul McCartney, promotional interview with Laura Gross for *Run Devil Run*, October 1999

DRIVING RAIN

'No homework…' Paul McCartney, interview for *Driving Rain*, November 2001

'So it's half imagination…' Paul McCartney quoted in *Conversations With McCartney*, Paul Du Noyer, Hodder & Stoughton, 2015

'I do draw on things…' Paul McCartney interviewed by Gavin Martin, *The Independent*, November 15, 2001

FROM A LOVER TO A FRIEND

'I had some words…' Paul McCartney quoted in *Conversations With McCartney*, Paul Du Noyer, Hodder & Stoughton, 2015

FREEDOM

"To me it's a 'We Shall Overcome'…" Paul McCartney quoted in The Paul McCartney Project (www.the-paulmccartney-project.com) February 22, 2014

CHAOS AND CREATION IN THE BACKYARD

'One of the prettiest…' *Paul McCartney Recording Sessions*, Luca Perasi, L.I.L.Y., 2013

'I don't write many songs like that…' Paul McCartney talking to *Rolling Stone*, quoted in 'Paul McCartney's Greatest Solo Songs', *Rolling Stone*, September 2017

'I'd bring songs in and Nigel would say…' Paul McCartney interviewed by Graeme Thomson, *The Word*, October 2005

'*Chaos and Creation in the Backyard* is a better album…' BBC review by Daryl Easlea, November 20, 2005

FINE LINE

'I just kind of followed on…' Paul McCartney interview with Gary Crowley, *Chaos and Confusion* EMI promotional CD, AIR Studios July 2005

'I realized I needed…' Paul McCartney interviewed by Graeme Thomson, *The Word*, October 2005

JENNY WREN

'Just sat around with the girls…' Paul McCartney interview with Gary Crowley, *Chaos and Confusion* EMI promotional CD, AIR Studios July 2005

'It's the smallest English bird…' ibid.

MEMORY ALMOST FULL

'I was just finishing up…' Paul McCartney in *Memory Almost Full* website, September 4, 2007

'Tapped into the restless energy…' 'Paul McCartney's Greatest Solo Songs', *Rolling Stone*, September 2017

'That one was written…' Paul McCartney quoted in Jason Gregory, Gigwise, June 22, 2007

'Truly a work of…' *Paul McCartney Recording Sessions*, Luca Perasi, L.I.L.Y., 2013

'A lot of it is retrospective…' Paul McCartney in *Memory Almost Full* website, September 4, 2007

'I wouldn't use the word "nostalgia"….' Paul McCartney quoted in 'Paul McCartney's Greatest Solo Songs', *Rolling Stone*, September 2017

DANCE TONIGHT

'I had to figure it out for myself…' Paul McCartney in *Memory Almost Full* website, September 4, 2007

'I was hitting the floor…' Paul McCartney, *Rolling Stone*, November 7, 2013

THAT WAS ME

'That's exactly it…' Paul McCartney interviewed by John Colapinto, 'When I'm Sixty-four: Paul McCartney then and now', *The New Yorker*, May 28, 2007

'People often say…' Paul McCartney interview, *The Mail on Sunday*, May 12, 2008

ELECTRIC ARGUMENTS

'Macca permits himself…' Mat Snow, 'Finest 50 Tracks of the Year', Rock's Backpages, December 2008

'The most exciting McCartney album…' Album review, *The Sunday Times Culture*, November 2008, quoted in paulmccartney.com, November 28, 2008

'Embracing raw blues…' Album review, *Daily Telegraph*, November 2008, quoted in paulmccartney.com, November 28, 2008

'A seriously good piece…' Album review, *Wall Street Journal*, November 2008, quoted in paulmccartney.com, November 28, 2008

'The first two Fireman albums…' Paul McCartney, *Electric Arguments* press release, quoted in paulmccartney.com, November 28, 2008

LIGHT FROM YOUR LIGHTHOUSE

'There's meat on these…' Peter Paphides, *Uncut*, November 12, 2008

'This being Macca…' Julian Marszalek, *The Quietus* (thequietus.com), November 20, 2008

(I WANT TO) COME HOME

'When your kids grow up…' Paul McCartney quoted in Edna Gundersen, 'McCartney pens original song for film *Everybody's Fine*', *USA Today*, December 10, 2009

'I thought, "Holy cow…' ibid.

KISSES ON THE BOTTOM

'There's such a high level of musicianship on there…' Paul McCartney interviewed by Paul Du Noyer, *Kisses on the Bottom* liner notes, 2011

'A lotta kisses on the bottom…' From "I'm Gonna Sit Right Down and Write Myself a Letter", lyrics by Joe Young, music by Fred Ahlert © 1935 Rytvoc Inc./ Pencil Mark Music / Azure Pearl Music / Beeping Good Music Publishing / David Ahlert Music

'We all went in…' Tommy LiPuma interviewed by Richard Buskin, *Sound on Sound*, May 2012

'This, after all…' Patrick Humphries, BBC Review, February, 2012

MY VALENTINE

'Paul performed a special song…' Sir David Frost, quoted in The Paul McCartney Project (the-paulmccarteny-project.com)

'Like "Beautiful Dreamer"…' Paul McCartney interviewed by Paul Du Noyer, *Kisses on the Bottom* liner notes, 2011

ONLY OUR HEARTS

'He played me this song…' Tommy LiPuma interviewed by Howie Edelson, 'Q&A: Tommy LiPuma, Making McCartney's Kisses Album', Beatlefan, May-June 2012

NEW

'Based on my reminiscences…' Paul McCartney, liner notes to *New*, October 2013

'I can see every minute of John…' Paul McCartney, to Simon Vozick-Levinson, 'Paul McCartney The Long And Winding Q&A', *Rolling Stone*, July 17, 2014

'We spliced that together…' Giles Martin, press release for *New*, October 2013

'We threw up a couple of microphones…' Ethan Johns talking to Simon Vozick-Levinson, *Rolling Stone*, August 29, 2013

'He needn't be …' Helen Brown, album review, *Daily Telegraph* October 10, 2013

NEW

'It's a happy, positive…' Paul McCartney, press release for *New*, October 2013

'We're thrilled and honoured…' Lia Vollack, Sony Pictures Animation, September 10, 2013

QUEENIE EYE

'Queenie Eye, Queenie Eye…' Traditional childrens' street song

'Queenie Eye' has more twists…' Press release for *New*

EGYPT STATION

'I liked Ryan…' Paul McCartney, interview with Lisa Wright, DIY, June 20, 2018

'A song like "Do It Now"…' Greg Kurstin, quoted in The Paul McCartney Project

'I don't want to be an activist…' Paul McCartney, interview in *Mojo*, October, 2018

'Just me totally indulging myself…' Paul McCartney talking on 'Words Between The Tracks', YouTube, 2018

'A record that's going…' Dan Stubbs album review, *NME*, September 7, 2018

I DON'T KNOW

'"Ma woman left me!"… Paul McCartney, interviewed in *Mojo*, October, 2018

'"I Don't Know' shows…' Alexis Petridis Egypt Station review, *The Guardian*, September 6, 2018

COME ON TO ME

'Would you come on to me….' Paul McCartney talking on 'Words Between The Tracks', YouTube, 2018

'That was sort of how it happened…' PaulMcCartney interview for Sodajerker podcast (sodajerker.com), 2018

GET ENOUGH

'You know what?…' Paul McCartney interviewed by Chris Heath, 'The Untold Stories of Paul McCartney', *GQ*, September 11, 2018

'I'm really excited about…' Ryan Tedder, *Schön!* magazine, (schonmagazine.com) August 8, 2017

HOME TONIGHT

'A couple of times…' Greg Kurstin, quoted by Martin Kelty, *Ultimate Classic Rock*, November 22, 2019

MCCARTNEY III

'I had some stuff…' Paul McCartney, *McCartney III* press release

'who worry more than I do…' Paul McCartney interview, The Adam Buxton Podcast, December 11, 2020

'I was thinking of editing…' Paul McCartney in *NME*, December 23, 2020

'I didn't know I was making an album…' Paul McCartney talking to Idris Elba, BBC TV, December 19, 2020

'Hang on, what if I do a fourth…' Paul McCartney talking to Jonathan Dean, 'A Great Gift from Rockdown', *Sunday Times*, December 6, 2020

FIND MY WAY

'It was a very scary time…' Paul McCartney, *Uncut*, January 2021

WHEN WINTER COMES

'Paint the roof…' ibid.

'We finished the album with it…' Paul McCartney, interview with Stuart Stubbs, *Loud and Quiet*, October 2020

INDEX OF SONGS

INDEX

BIBLIOGRAPHY

Keith Badman, *The Beatles: The Dream is Over*, Omnibus (2000)

Peter Ames Carlin, *Paul McCartney: A Life*, Touchstone Books (2009)

Robert Christgau, *Christgau's Record Guide; Rock Albums of the 70s*, Ticknor & Fields (1981)

Tom Doyle, *Man On the Run: Paul McCartney in the 1970s*, Polygon (2013)

Paul Du Noyer, *Conversations With McCartney*, Hodder & Stoughton (2015)

Geoff Emerick, *Here, There and Everywhere: My Life Recording the Music of the Beatles*, Gotham Books (2006)

Mike Evans, *The Art of the Beatles*, Anthony Blond (1984)

Mike Evans (ed.), *The Beatles Literary Anthology*, Plexus (2004)

Danny Fields, *Linda McCartney: The Biography*, Little, Brown & Company (2000)

Paul Gambaccini *Paul McCartney: In His Own Words*, Omnibus (1976)

Clinton Heylin (ed.), *The Penguin Book of Rock & Roll Writing*, Viking (1992)

Patrick Humphries, *Lonnie Donegan and the Birth of British Rock & Roll*, Robson Press (2012)

Chris Hunt (ed.) *Beatles – The Solo Years 1970–1980*, IPC Ignite! (2005)

Paul McCartney, *Give My Regards to Broad Street*, Pavilion Books (1984)

Garry McGee, *Band on the Run: A History of Paul McCartney and Wings*, Taylor Trade Publishing (2003)

Barry Miles, *Many Years From Now*, Secker & Warburg (1997)

Luca Perasi, *Paul McCartney Recording Sessions*, L.I.L.Y. (2013)

Other reference sources

Periodicals:

Bass Player, Beat Instrumental, Beatlefan, Billboard, BMI News, Chicago Tribune, Clash, Club Sandwich, Creem, Daily Telegraph, Daytrippin' Beatles Magazine, DIY, The Face, FarOut, Gigwise, Goldmine, GQ, Guitar Player, The Guardian, The Independent, Loud and Quiet, Maclean's, The Mail on Sunday, Melody Maker, Mersey Beat, Mojo, Musician, Nashville Banner, Nashville Lifestyles, New Musical Express, New York Times, The New Yorker, Newsweek, People, Q, Record Collector, Record Mirror, Rolling Stone, Schön!, Sound On Sound, Sounds, The Sunday Times, Tallahassee Democrat, Uncut, USA Today, Wall Street Journal, The Word

Websites:

allmusic.com / beatlesbible.com / culturesonar.com / wordpress.com / mixonline.com / mygoldmusic.com / paulmccartney.com / pitchfork.com / rocksbackpages.com / sodajerker.com / songfacts.com / superdeluxeedition.com / thatwouldbesomething.com / the-paulmccarteny-project.com / theamgroup.com / thequietus.com / udiscovermusic.com / ultimateclassicrock.com

PICTURE CREDITS